INVENTING THE SAVAGE

Inventing the Savage

THE SOCIAL CONSTRUCTION OF NATIVE AMERICAN CRIMINALITY

by Luana Ross

 UNIVERSITY OF TEXAS PRESS
AUSTIN

Permission granted by the Montana Historical Society Archives, Helena, to quote from RS 111: box 11, folders 20–24, and MC 352: box 31, folder 3.

Excerpts from "A Descriptive Case Study of the Impact of Social Learning Experiences on Adult Female Inmates" (Ed.D. dissertation, Montana State University, 1995) reprinted by permission of Jerry D. McKinney.

Material previously published as "Race, Gender, and Social Control: Voices of Imprisoned Native American and White Women," *Wicazo Sa Review*, 1994, reprinted by permission of the University of Minnesota Press.

Second paperback printing, 2000

Library of Congress Cataloging-in-Publication Data

Ross, Luana.
    Inventing the savage : the social construction of Native
American criminality / by Luana Ross. — 1st ed.
      p.   cm.
    Includes bibliographical references and index.
    ISBN 0-292-77085-5 (cloth : alk. paper). —
ISBN 0-292-77084-7 (pbk. : alk. paper)
    1. Indian prisoners—Montana. 2. Criminal justice,
Administration of—Montana. 3. Women prisoners—
Montana. 4. Indian women—Montana—Social conditions.
5. Racism—Montana. I. Title.
E78.M9R67 1998
364.3'4970786—dc21   97-21014

This book is dedicated to all prisoners.

CONTENTS

ACKNOWLEDGMENTS

I am truly blessed with wonderful relatives. Heartfelt gratitude is extended to my mother, Opal Cajune, for passing on to me her philosophical reasoning and sense of social justice. I offer thanks to my husband, Daniel Hart, and children, Shane Ross and Damon Hart, for their encouragement. I appreciate and honor my sisters, Julie Cajune, Kathy Ross, Ramona Cajune, Susie Ross, Duretta Billedeaux, and Ana Rowland. They continue to offer me support in a variety of ways. I also acknowledge my close cousins Rhonda Whiting, who is constantly encouraging, and Valerie McDonald, because of her extraordinary insight into the plight of imprisoned women.

Aside from family, colleagues played a crucial role in my work. I thank Jack Forbes, who read manuscript drafts, and Grieg Bustos, Susanne Bohmer, and Steve Talbot, with whom I spent many hours discussing Native American criminality. Longtime friends who were always encouraging and helpful and who are also valued colleagues include Sharon Elise, Wendy Ng, Annette Reed Crum, Irene Vernon, Gail Small, Franke Wilmer, and Cecilia Garland. Sincere appreciation is additionally extended to Larry Culp, the first professor to enlighten me on the role of extralegal factors in the invention of "criminals."

As the project grew, it weathered the storm through several institutions. I thank Mary Romero and Linda Fuller from the University of Oregon for recognizing the topic as valuable and Rob Proudfoot for successfully decolonizing the defense of my dissertation. I acknowledge the support I received at Montana State University, particularly from Deborah Wetsit, the Women's Resource Center, and the Center for Native American Studies. At the University of California at Berkeley, the Ethnic Studies Department, especially Margarita Melville, deserves my thanks. I also extend my gratitude to the History of Consciousness Board at the University of California at Santa Cruz, especially to Angela Davis for allowing me the space and time in which to write. I am likewise thankful to all faculty and staff at the Native American Studies Department at the University of California at Davis for their support.

Gathering archival data was time-consuming and tedious. Bob Bigart from Salish Kootenai College, Elaine Way from the Powell County Prison Museum, and all staff at the Montana Historical Society were most helpful. I also acknowledge the Ford Foundation and the University of California for providing grants that afforded me the time in which to research and write.

Most important, I offer my appreciation to the prisoners and ex-prisoners who graciously and courageously shared their lives.

INVENTING THE SAVAGE

INTRODUCTION

And tears strong and deep will lift our voices in the public ear.

MONICA WALL *[Salish] (1995)*

I developed an interest in criminality, deviance, and imprisoned women because of my culture, race, gender, and experiences growing up on the Flathead Indian Reservation, home of the Sqélixʷ (Salish) and Aqlsmakni·k (Kootenai). I was raised at the Old Agency across the street from the tribal jail. This jail was a tiny one-room structure that was seldom locked. Prisoners were seen walking and visiting around the Agency; no one was alarmed that they were not secured on a twenty-four-hour basis.

When I was young my godfather was training to be a Jesuit priest when, due to the illness of his father, he returned to our reservation. He was a wonderfully brilliant man who had been imprisoned four times. How could this possibly happen to a well-educated, spiritual person? My godfather was not my only relative who was imprisoned; other relatives preceded and followed. It is common for Native people either to have been incarcerated or to have relatives who have been imprisoned. Because we are a colonized people, the experiences of imprisonment are, unfortunately, exceedingly familiar. Native Americans disappear into Euro-American institutions of confinement at alarming rates. People from my reservation simply appeared to vanish and magically return. I did not realize what a "real" prison was and did not give it any thought. I imagined that all families had relatives who went away and then returned.

Academic issues, as well as personal, influence my interest in Native criminality/deviance. There is meager research on incarcerated Native Americans, although they are disproportionately imprisoned. Additionally, there is a dearth of empirical data on incarcerated women. Two topics that are especially ignored are personal experiences of incarceration and the special situation of imprisoned mothers, although most imprisoned women are mothers. Similarly neglected in the literature are imprisoned women of color, who represent 64 percent of the total population of women incarcerated in state prisons (Snell and Morton 1994). There is scant recognition of the special problems women of color may face while incarcerated. An underlying assumption is that all women are equally afflicted; thus, the majority of studies on imprisoned women refer to women as a homogeneous group and ignore the interaction of race/ethnicity, gender, and class.[1] Although insufficient attention is given to imprisoned women of color, the subject of imprisoned Native American women is virtually an unexplored area. Imprisoned Native women are invisible, and, as put forth by Patricia Hill Collins (1991), invisibility allows structural arrangements of inequality to exist.

I conducted the first study of imprisoned Native American women in 1990–1992. The purpose of the research was to give voice to these women by describing and defining their experiences as prisoners. I listened to the voices of the women, to their perceptions of their experiences as prisoners. While the state of Montana defines these women as "criminal" and "dangerous," I find their lives complex—bound up in race/ethnicity, gender, and class oppression. It is exhausting to recount the narratives of imprisoned women—they were troublesome to hear. It is distressing to describe and name their pain. In the words of bell hooks (1992, 2), "The more painful the issues we confront the greater our inarticulateness."

This is a book about the racialized and gendered experiences of incarceration, with a focus on Native American women and the loss of sovereignty as it is implicitly tied to Native criminality in complex, historical ways. This is also a book about the complexity of racism, as it evolved and took root in Montana, and the importance of race/ethnicity in Euro-American society.

Michael Omi and Howard Winant (1994) suggest that race is a socially constructed category that changes over time. The authors separate the shifting of race and racism into three chronological stages. In the first period, during the colonization of this country, race was discussed in biological terms complete with notions of the biological inferiority of people of color. In the second period, the early part of the twentieth century, ethnicity was substituted for race as differences between groups were defined and categorized. During this time, culture was added to the understanding of racial/ethnic relations and assimilationist paradigms were developed. The third period, emerging in a time of turmoil—the late 1960s and early 1970s—witnessed radical and nationalist movements, such as the Red Power and Black Power groups. The focus was on the differences between white Euro-America and people of color. The structure of society was used as a significant explanatory factor in the obvious inequality. Accordingly, race and racism were explained in terms of class- and nation-based theories. Ruth Frankenberg (1993), using the framework of Omi and Winant, asserts that all three movements and accompanying attitudes are found in contemporary Euro-America. Agreeing with Frankenberg, I term this *convoluted racism* or, as it relates specifically to Native Americans, *neocolonial racism*. The social control of indigenous people is reflected in this complicated racism.

The history of Native-white relations in Montana that I present, albeit simplistically, reveals that racialized attitudes and ideology of long ago thrive in Montana today. If we are to move toward a place of racial/ethnic understanding we must first recognize the unfortunate history of Montana's indigenous people and the dynamics of racism.

Additionally, we must acknowledge the concept of Native American sovereignty. Sovereignty is a fragile concept whose meaning is shaped and reshaped by legislation and court decisions. At the same time, sovereignty is inherent; it comes from within a people and their culture. Some would argue sovereignty cannot be given to one group by another because ultimately it comes from spiritual sources. Whatever the case, sovereignty cannot be separated from a people or their culture. As expressed by Jolene Rickard (1995, 51), "Sovereignty is the border that shifts indigenous experience from a victimized stance to a strategic one. The recognition of this puts brains in our heads, and muscle on our bones."

The history of the colonization of America's indigenous people is a tragic one. From the time of European contact to the present day, these people have been imprisoned in a variety of ways. They were confined in forts, boarding schools, orphanages, jails and prisons and on reservations. Historically, Native people formed free, sovereign nations with distinct cultures and social and political institutions reflecting their philosophies. Today, Native people are not free; they are a colonized people seeking to decolonize themselves.

Important components of colonialism, according to Robert Blauner (1972), are the restriction of the movements of colonized people and the undermining and transforming of their culture. Blauner submits that the colonizer attempts to destroy the culture of the colonized; in this way, culture itself becomes a method of control. Accordingly, the colonized can, in turn, use culture as a powerful weapon against oppression. Colonialism as control and denial of culture is clearly evidenced by the number of incarcerated Native Americans and by their experiences in prison.

METHODOLOGY

The major part of this study was designed to focus on women from two different races/ethnicities—Native American and white—who were incarcerated in a small, rural, state prison: the Women's Correctional Center (WCC) in Montana. Comparing these groups allowed me to examine the specific effects of race/ethnicity. The findings were based on tape-recorded in-depth interviews with twenty-seven imprisoned women (fourteen of the seventeen Native prisoners and thirteen of the forty-eight white prisoners) and similar interviews with prison staff and a state employee. Prisoners were questioned regarding the prison's social environment, their concerns as imprisoned mothers, and the institutional support offered to them as imprisoned mothers. Interviews with prison staff and the state employee focused on programs offered to imprisoned mothers and how the mothers' relationships with their children were facilitated.[2]

The interviews were supplemented with nonparticipant observation, informal conversations with prisoners and staff, reports from the State Department of Institutions, reports and letters from the American Civil Liberties Union (ACLU), reports from the WCC, reports from the Confederated Salish and Kootenai Tribes, prisoners' legal records, prisoners' journals, and my personal correspondence with prisoners. Archival data was gathered from the Montana Historical Society, the Montana Territorial Prison Museum, Montana State University, and the D'Arcy McNickle Library at Salish Kootenai College.

By comparing the experiences of Native American and white women, we gain insight into the operation of social institutions. I am interested not only in personal biographies but in how they are tied to the larger social structure. Stratification by race, gender, and class leads to different life experiences. Because I was interested in how racism and sexism functioned inside prison and affected imprisoned women, I concentrated on the women's subjective experiences of prison. Some critics of my work and of other qualitative research argue that prisoners do not tell "the truth." But I believe there are many truths; I present the truths of imprisoned women in Montana. Unlike statistical research on the prison system, my book reveals the amazing diversity of women prisoners and makes the experience of imprisonment exceedingly personal rather than reducing the women to numbers as the penal system does.

In an attempt to highlight prisoners' voices, I use lengthy quotations. The identities of the women are disguised; I altered details that would threaten their anonymity. Race/ethnicity is identified but not, in the case of Natives, specific tribal affiliation. For readability, and in an effort to humanize the prisoners dehumanized by prisonization, I gave them fictitious names.

OUTLINE

Proposing that Native American criminality is tied, in a complex and historical way, to the loss of sovereignty, I begin the book with important historical information on the disruptive formal and informal federal and state policies that chipped away at the sovereign status of Native people. Through various procedures, state and federal governments defined Native Americans as "deviant" and "criminal." The historical background uncovers how the "savage" was created, invented in Montana. Native people, however, were not passive in the process of colonization but resilient and adaptive. They responded to the policies and accompanying racialized attitudes in ways ranging from warfare to cultural adaptation efforts. An overview of policy illustrates the process of colonizing and criminalizing Native Americans, as well as the evolution of colonial and neocolonial racism. As such, the historical background provides a foundation and context for the second part of the book, which focuses on imprisoned women and the criminalization process.

Chapter 3 offers demographic, social, and personal information on women incarcerated in Montana from 1878 through the early 1990s.

This history exposes important differences between Native women. Significantly, reservation status emerges as crucial in the criminalization of Native women: nonreservation Natives are jeopardized by their status as Landless Indians.[3]

Chapter 4 demonstrates how extralegal factors contribute to the criminalizing of various behaviors and the subsequent incarceration of women. Because of systematic oppression, women are vulnerable to various types of violence, and their individual experiences disclose the violence that permeates many social institutions. For instance, most imprisoned women were trapped by chaotic lives of poverty and abusive husbands. This chapter examines the types of abuse imprisoned women endured prior to incarceration, their respective reactions to the violence, and how their responses affected their eventual criminalization and prisonization. Racial/ethnic differences and gender dynamics are illuminated by exploring the relationship between individual lives and the structure of society, which is characterized by racist and patriarchal relations.

Chapters 5, 6, and 7 analyze imprisoned women's experiences, which vary according to the race/ethnicity, location of confinement, and sexual preference of the women. While prison officials often speak about the concept "rehabilitation," the primary function of the prison is strict control of prisoners' behavior. Although all prisoners are critical of the prison's rehabilitation attempts, Native prisoners additionally perceive these efforts as culture-bound and racist.

Prison policy is gendered and racialized. As such, it is based on distorted stereotypes that affect experiences in prison. Moreover, the violence experienced by women prior to incarceration continues inside the prison in a variety of forms including sexual intimidation, the overuse of mind-altering drugs, lengthy stays in lockup, and the denial of culture for Native Americans. In practice, prisoners' experiences with rehabilitation are less salient than their experiences with control. Depictions of relationships among prisoners and between prisoners and staff, as well as of prisoners' responses to punishment and control, offer additional understanding into prisonization experiences.

Chapters 8, 9, and 10 investigate the concerns of imprisoned mothers, the prison's parenting program, and institutional support offered to maintain family stability. Whereas race/ethnicity is a significant factor in the overall experience of prisonization, reservation status again emerges as prominent in an analysis of mothering behind bars. For example, reservation status has an important influence on the major concerns of imprisoned mothers and on institutional support available for mothers. Furthermore, prisoner status has an effect on mothers' experiences: although women confined in the general-population building define separation from children as their major concern, women in maximum security are more immediately concerned with personal survival. Other concerns of imprisoned mothers are children's placement, behavioral adaptation, post-release problems, and contact with children. Prison support for incarcerated mothers varies by race/ethnicity, reservation status, and confinement location. While all mothers note that the prison's assistance in the maintenance of familial stability is insufficient, nonreservation Native mothers in particular determine that their needs are ignored. Additionally, Native mothers perceive the prison's rehabilitative parenting program as culture-bound.

Chapter 11 offers a glimpse into the life of a Native woman who was incarcerated at the WCC and her readjustment to life on the outside. Gloria Wells Norlin, Little Shell Chippewa (Anishinabé), was imprisoned for fifteen months for a crime she did not commit. The Montana Supreme Court agreed that she had been wrongly convicted, but only after she served hard prison time. Her righteous anger over her imprisonment is directed toward the legal system, and presently she seeks legal recourse. A well-known and accomplished artist, Gloria is now, after much struggle, reunited with her family. She owns and manages an art gallery appropriately named "Indian Uprising." Gloria's story provides an understanding of the interrelated systems of oppression that operate to confine and control Native women.

PART I   *Colonization and the Social Construction of Deviance*

The United States may not have written the book on ethnic cleansing, but it certainly provided several of its most stunning chapters—particularly in its treatment of the American Indian. . . . Americans, as de Tocqueville long ago recognized, are a future-oriented people with a short historical memory. And the accepted, widely taught versions of history are written by the victors, presented in schools as sanitized costume pageantry. This is especially true when the victory is as total as that of America's forefathers over the American Indians, who were nearly "cleansed" from an entire continent—an outcome the likes of which Bosnia's Serbs can only dream.

KENNETH DAVIS
"Ethnic Cleansing Didn't Start in Bosnia"

One

WORLDS COLLIDE

NEW WORLD, NEW INDIANS

*The more [Indians] we can kill this year the less will have
to be killed the next war, for the more I see of these Indians,
the more convinced I am that they all have to be killed or
be maintained as a species of paupers.*

GENERAL WILLIAM T. SHERMAN, *1867*
(*quoted in Sharon O'Brien,* American Indian
Tribal Governments)

Once, all Native American tribes were largely free of the impositions of external social forces. These indigenous people did not live in isolation, although each nation had separately constructed a unique world. But their meetings, even when conflictual, never followed the notion of absolute dominance by means of total war that justified European and Euro-American invasion and occupation (Jaimes and Halsey 1992).

When Europeans first came to this country, there were approximately ten to twelve million indigenous people living on the land that became the United States (Dobyns 1983). These indigenous people were divided into numerous autonomous nations, each with its own highly developed culture and history. Politically, the indigenous people were not weak, dependent groups of people but rather powerful equals whom the early colonists had to deal with as independent nations.

Over the years, Native people have been stripped of most of their resources by the aggressive "settlers" who subjected them to unilateral political and economic exploitation and cultural suppression (Talbot 1981; Weyler 1982). Although Native nations are still politically distinct from the United States, under the definition of colonial theory today's Native nations are colonies. One of the main motives of colonialism is economic exploitation, and cultural suppression almost invariably ac-

companies colonialism (Blauner 1972; Talbot 1981). Cultural suppression is a legal process that involves deculturation—eradication of the
indigenous people's original traditions—followed by indoctrination in
the ideas of the dominators so the colonized may themselves assist the
colonial project (Talbot 1981). The process, in which the colonized are
removed from their cultural context through enslavement or transplan-
tation, involves the abandonment of culture and the adoption of new
ways of speaking, behaving, and reasoning.

The destruction of indigenous cultures includes the eradication of
their judicial systems. Law has repeatedly been used in this country to
coerce racial/ethnic group deference to Euro-American power. Understanding this history of colonization is essential because Native crimi-
nality/deviancy must be seen within the context of societal race/ethnic
relations; otherwise, any account of crime is liable to be misleading.
Any explanation of Native criminality that sees individual behavior as
significant overlooks the social and historical origins of the behavior. A
thorough analysis of Native criminality must include the full context of
the criminal behavior—that is, their victimization and the criminalization of Native rights by the United States government.

NATIVE WORLDS

As with other social worlds, Native societies are the result of the world-
building activities of their members. This unending pursuit contains a
variety of aspects, some of which are included in a social phenomenon known as social control. This area, which includes the concept
of deviance and the manner and appearance of its construction, is my
concern.

There is a widely held belief that the Americas' indigenous people
were completely lawless. Nothing could be further from the truth. Although the standards of right and wrong varied widely, as did the procedures for punishing transgressors, Native groups all exercised legal
systems founded upon their own traditional philosophies.[1] The law was
a part of their larger worldview (Barsh and Henderson 1980; Deloria
and Lytle 1983, 1984; Yazzie 1994). According to Rennard Strickland,
"law" is more than statutes and balanced scales:

Law is also a Cherokee priest listening to the spirit world while holding the sacred wampums in hand and the Cheyenne soldier-society warrior draped in the skin of a wolf. In fact, a command from the spirit world can have greater force as law than the most elaborate code devised by the most learned of men. For law is organic. Law is part of a time and a place, the product of a specific time and an actual place. (1975, xiv)

As Deloria and Lytle write,

Indian tribes, as we shall see, were once primarily judicial in the sense that the council, whether it was that of a village, a league of tribes, or a simple hunting band, looked to custom and precedent in resolving novel and difficult social questions that arose. . . . The task of the council, when it had a difficult question to resolve, was to appeal to that larger sense of reality shared by the people of the community and reach a decision that the people would see as consonant with the tradition. Few new laws or customs were needed and when these occasions presented themselves the homogeneity of the community made the adoption of the innovation simple. (1983, xi)

[handwritten marginalia: "Exoticize Native American" and "make it continuous"]

We are reminded that Indian Country[2] had no prisons:

. . . as Native people, we believe in truth, and not the facts. That is why we never had to sign a receipt, because we knew we were dealing with each other in an honest way. . . . We never had locks on our tipis . . . go ahead and dig all you want to search for the history of the Americas, and you will never find evidence of prisons. (Deere 1980; quoted in Weyler 1982, 98)

Native people continue to survive and reach forth, extending, building Native worlds as best they are able. Part of these efforts concerns the recuperation of Natives whose path takes them outside the natural order or across Euro-American legal lines. It is these Natives and the manner of their contact with other Natives and Euro-Americans, especially the "official" ones, that is now our concern. The United States has the distinction of incarcerating more of its people than any other country. Natives are now locked up in great numbers, jailed in buildings constructed in line with the system of legislated law, which the United States proudly and forcefully imposes on Natives.

Prior to the coming of this law and its jails, Natives were free to follow laws seen as coming from a natural, external place instead of flowing from the pens of men. On occasion, Natives did not follow Native ways. How much this happened is difficult to ascertain, but it surely was little compared to the deviance apparent in today's society. Natives involved in these situations knew what was amiss and met together to search out a remedy. These meetings, authorized by the wise—whose age, gifts, and spirit were acknowledged—looked for a path that would compensate for the injured and recuperate the offender.

> The primary goal was simply to mediate the care to everyone's satisfaction. It was not to ascertain guilt and then bestow punishment upon the offender. Under Anglo-American notions of criminal jurisprudence, the objectives are to establish fault or guilt, and then to punish. . . . Under the traditional Indian system the major objective was more to ensure restitution and compensation than retribution. (Deloria and Lytle 1983, 111)

Precontact Native criminal justice was primarily a system of restitution—a system of mediation between families, of compensation, of recuperation. But this system of justice was changed into a shadow of itself. Attempts were made to make Natives like white people, first by means of war and, when the gunsmoke cleared, by means of laws—Native people instead became "criminals." *Criminal* meant to be other than Euro-American. We will see that Euro-Americans sought to delegitimize Native worlds and attacked their constructs, including Native justice systems, which were systematically torn down, eroded, and replaced.

One damaging effect of colonization has been its influence on the structure of Native governments. The expansion of Euro-American legality contributed greatly to the further decline of tribal systems, already rocked by foreign invasion. For instance, except in a few early treaties, in regulating Native-white relations, Euro-Americans insisted that disagreements and crimes be disposed of in Euro-American fashion.[3] Consequently, political discretion, generally handled in Native societies by a council of elders and the clans, came to be assumed by Euro-Americans, greatly weakening the traditional councils.

FENCING INDIAN COUNTRY:
DISRUPTIVE POLICY AND LEGISLATION

By the end of the eighteenth century the newly independent United States had cleared the eastern seaboard of most of its original inhabitants (Josephy 1984). At the turn of the century, the most intense wave of westward migration began in earnest, driven by land speculation. Speculators, often backed by New England and European banks, cheaply purchased large tracts of land from the federal government, who had procured it (often forcibly) from Native nations. The land was sold in smaller tracts, at considerable profit, to white settlers (Johansen and Maestas 1979).

Colonialism, thus, did not end with the Declaration of Independence. The United States continued colonizing after its revolutionary war. All the characteristics of colonialism—unilateral political control, economic exploitation, and cultural oppression—were present in Euro-American expansionism in the nineteenth century. Colonialism remained, albeit manifested more subtly.

Racialized oppression, then as now, was not a discrete phenomenon independent of larger political and economic tendencies. Nineteenth-century laws and their enforcement can readily be seen as instruments for maintaining social and economic stratification created in the centuries before. In a greedy, expanding young nation building law and custom on the ownership of property, crime control was part of the maintenance of that sacred foundation. Law-enforcement officials were not simply bystanders in this history; they participated in and encouraged lawlessness in the interests of suppressing minorities. As remaining Native lands were seized and resisting tribes massacred, federal officials often looked the other way or were actively involved (Brown 1970). Genocide against Native people was never seen as murder. Indeed, in the Old West the murder of Natives was not even a crime (Heizer 1974; Hurtado 1988; Schwartz and Disch 1970). Native men and women, their humanity cast aside, were commonly referred to as "bucks" and "squaws." Those not exterminated faced dire circumstances. For instance, the state of California enacted "The Act for the Government and Protection of Indians" in 1850, amended in 1860. Despite the title of the act, it allowed white people to simply take Native children, those orphaned or supposedly with parental consent, as indentured slaves (Hurtado 1988). The law also "virtually compelled

Indians to work because any Indian found 'loitering or strolling about' was subject to arrest on the complaint of any white citizen, whereupon the court was required within twenty-four hours to hire out arrestees to the highest bidder for up to four months" (Hurtado 1988, 130).

During early contact with Europeans, tribes retained exclusive jurisdiction over such issues as law and order. This right followed the assumption that tribes possessed complete sovereign powers over their members and lands. Tribal sovereignty, as defined by Euro-American law, was upheld in two early major U.S. Supreme Court cases: *The Cherokee Nation v. Georgia* (1831) and *Worcester v. Georgia* (1832). Tribes did not intend to give up their culture, social organization, or self-government; therefore, according to treaties, tribes were to retain their system of criminal justice (Ortiz 1977).

Native legal and political status changed, however. One factor in this transformation was the view Europeans and Euro-Americans historically had, and continue to have, of Natives. Indigenous people's land and other resources were desired by ethnocentric Europeans and later Euro-Americans, who expressed their cultural superiority as the justification for the expropriation of Native lands. Natives were regarded as "savages," legitimizing the removal of Natives from the westward path of civilization's progress (Berkhofer 1978). The ideology of Native inferiority was used to justify both genocide and attempts to supposedly assimilate Natives into the dominant society. Whatever the intent, the common denominator was the assertion that Native societies were lower on the evolutionary scale. Accordingly, the stereotype of the "savage, inferior" Native was carefully developed, and Natives were seen and treated as deviant. In this manner, the ground was prepared for the entry of "modern, rational" Euro-American law into Indian Country.

One product of colonialism is, thus, the controlling of indigenous people through law. The values that ordered Native worlds were naturally in conflict with Euro-American legal codes. Many traditional tribal codes instantly became criminal when the United States imposed their laws and culture on Native people. New laws were created that defined many usual, everyday behaviors of Natives as "offenses." The continuous clashing of worlds over the power to control Native land and resources constantly brought Native people in conflict with the legal and judicial system of the United States, which demonstrates the political intent and utility of Euro-American laws.

Crucial to understanding Native criminality is knowledge of the disruptive events brought about by assimilationist, racist policy and prohibitive legislation mandated by federal, state, and municipal governments. These policies and accompanying criminal statutes were concerned with cultural genocide and control as the tenacious Euro-Americans, seeking to replace tribal law and order with their own definitions of criminality and due process, increasingly restricted the power of Native nations.

The Euro-American surge to gain legal and judicial control over tribes included the creation of the Bureau of Indian Affairs (BIA). To relieve the military while retaining control of tribes, the federal government created the BIA within the War Department in 1824. In 1849 the BIA was transferred to the Department of the Interior. Additionally, the early part of that same century saw the federal government's first attempts to impose federal criminal laws on nonconsenting tribes. The effort to facilitate Euro-American encroachment on Native lands was led by the U.S. Congress, which awarded itself federal jurisdiction over Natives by passing the General Crimes Act in 1817. The tribes retained exclusive jurisdiction only over offenses in which both the offender and the victim were Native (Barsh 1980). In all other cases, tribes now held concurrent jurisdiction with the federal government.

Another intrusion by the federal government into Native affairs was launched in 1825, when Congress passed the Assimilative Crimes Act. This act expanded the number of crimes that could be tried by federal courts when offenses were committed on Native land. The act is limited to interracial crimes and is not applicable when crimes are committed between Natives on reservations (Deloria and Lytle 1983).

From the mid– to late nineteenth century, the overriding task of the federal government was, in theory, the "civilizing" or "Americanizing" of tribes (Prucha 1973). In practice, the goal seems to have been to obtain Native land and resources. This era featured the "Friends of the Indians," a group of Euro-Americans that worked in common to "save" Natives from their "primitive" ways. This well-placed group, which can be likened to Howard Becker's (1963) moral crusaders, applied considerable political pressure in an effort to get their reforms enacted. The reformers, solidly agreeing that the Americanization of Indians required that they be brought under the protection and restraints of Euro-American law, worked to bring a special set of courts and procedures to the reservations. These procedures were to hasten their illusive assimilation.

The influential reformers pressured the Department of the Interior to take action against the "savage and barbarous" practices of the Natives (Prucha 1973). The vehicle chosen to accomplish this task was the Court of Indian Offenses. These courts were composed of Native judges, handpicked by BIA Indian agents, who satisfied the agents, not tribal communities (Deloria and Lytle 1983). The judges were supposed to be men with high moral integrity who "engage in civilized pursuits"; the requirements stated also that "no person shall be eligible to such appointment who is a polygamist" (Morgan 1882; quoted in Prucha 1973, 301).[4] Preference was given to those who read and wrote English. The judges were to bring Natives "under the civilizing influence of law" (Teller 1883; quoted in Prucha 1973, 299). Indirect rule, along the British colonial model, was thus established with the formation of Indian police and judges in the latter part of the nineteenth century (for a full description, see Hagan 1966). These men were employed to police other Natives according to Euro-American law in another attempt to Americanize indigenous people.

The regulations for the Court of Indian Offenses were drawn up in 1883 by Thomas Morgan, then Commissioner of Indian Affairs. Morgan listed offenses and the appropriate punishments. The following constituted offenses: plural or polygamous marriages; immorality; intoxication; destroying property of other Natives (this speaks to mourning practices: destroying the property of the deceased was customary in many tribes); any Native dance "intended and calculated to stimulate the warlike passions of the young warriors of the tribes" (Teller 1883; quoted in Prucha 1973, 296); and the practices of medicine people, which were seen as "anti-progressive," because medicine people used their power in "preventing the attendance of the children at the public schools, using their conjurers' arts to prevent the people from abandoning their heathenish rites and customs" (Teller 1883; quoted in Prucha 1973, 297–298). In some tribes spiritual leaders had assumed broader roles after the slaying or arrests of war leaders, so by criminalizing their practices the courts seized the authority of traditional tribal leaders.

Misdemeanor offenses generally covered Native neglect to engage in what Euro-Americans defined as "work." The Protestant work ethic was upheld to Natives, and failure "to adopt habits of industry, or to engage in civilized pursuits or employments," brought swift punishment (Morgan 1892; quoted in Prucha 1973, 304). Clearly these courts were used to suppress Native worlds, which were made criminal, and especially to attack their religion. This repression of religion forged ahead at full steam until 1934, when the Indian Reorganization Act somewhat lessened the court's powers. The ban on alcohol, which came in the early nineteenth century, was not lifted until 1953.

In 1881 an important event occurred in Indian Country. A Lakota named Crow Dog killed another Lakota by the name of Spotted Tail (Harring 1994). As their tribal custom decreed, the matter was remedied by Crow Dog's family paying restitution to the victim's family. Under Lakota law Crow Dog would not be further punished, let alone executed. White people, however, were enraged over the much-publicized case and demanded that the United States seize jurisdiction over the tribes and punish Crow Dog "properly." *Ex parte Crow Dog* (1883) opined that the United States did not have the jurisdiction to prosecute a Native when the crime was against another Native. Euro-American reformers thought that to allow such a "primitive" form of justice to prevail was lawless (Deloria and Lytle 1983). Their furor led to the passage of the Major Crimes Act of 1885, whereby Congress unilaterally gave federal courts jurisdiction in Indian Country (when the offenders were Native) over seven major crimes. The act was later amended to include fourteen felonies.[5]

This delineation of certain crimes in Indian Country to be federal offenses outside tribal jurisdiction established a pattern that has held to the present. By taking jurisdiction over crimes, the federal government also assumed the power to punish. Significantly, the act applies only when the offender is Native, although the victim may be Native or non-Native, and the offense must be committed within the legal definition of Indian Country (Deloria and Lytle 1983).

Some of the daily operations of this act are seen by Dumars (1968), who contends that Native Americans charged with major crimes on an Indian reservation receive harsher treatment than non-Natives charged with the same crimes on a reservation. Using the example of assault with a deadly weapon, Dumars demonstrates that Natives convicted of this crime receive from federal judges penalties twice as harsh as those given non-Natives committing the same crime but falling under state jurisdiction. Hence, in their lurch to possess Indian Country, Euro-Americans in Congress defined crime differently for Natives than for themselves, with the Native definition requiring less proof for conviction in Euro-American courts (Deloria and Lytle 1983).

In 1887 another direct violation of treaties came with the passage of the General Allotment Act. This policy, again backed by Euro-American reformers, was aimed at the destruction of Native worlds by making their reproduction impossible. Reformers determined that the individualization of property in Indian Country would spark Native initiative. The "civilizing" design was intended to break up the alleged communistic notion of holding land in common and, most important, to open up Native land for Euro-American takeover (Prucha 1973). The president was awarded absolute authority to allot Native reservation lands to individual Natives and turn over the "surplus" to white people. As a result, Native lands were reduced from 138 million acres in 1887 to 48 million acres by 1934, and the reservations subjected to allotment are now checkerboards of white and Native land. The General Allotment Act left a tangled legacy of land ownership and jurisdictional patterns, persisting even today, that pushed Natives further into poverty.

The degree of Native acceptance into white communities, a supposed goal of the Friends of the Indians, demonstrates the treatment of Natives by the Euro-American legal framework. One way to test an ethnic group's acceptability is their eligibility for citizenship. In colonial times, for example, Natives were never considered citizens; accordingly, they did not hold voting rights, nor could they participate in colonial politics (Kawashima 1986). In 1871 voting rights were denied in Montana Territory to those living at Indian agencies, on reservations, or in Indian Country. Furthermore, the Montana Enabling Act, passed in 1889 (the year Montana secured statehood), again prevented Natives from voting in their homeland (Svingen 1987).[6]

The troublesome legal status of people of color in the United States during the nineteenth century is well documented in a series of court decisions. For example, in *People v. Hall* the California Supreme Court decided in 1854 that a California statute excluding Natives and African Americans from testifying in court cases involving whites additionally applied to Chinese Americans (Cushman and Cushman 1958). Forbidden from testifying against whites, people of color were deprived of the usual means of legal protection. For example, in 1851 in California a white man was released for the murder of a Native man because the only witness was a Native, and the law did not permit his testimony (Heizer 1974). In 1866 Congress, overriding President Johnson's veto, gave equal rights to all persons born in the United States—except Natives (Brown 1970). In 1884, in *Elk v. Wilkins*, a Native man was denied the right to vote in Nebraska on the grounds that he was not a citizen of the United States, although he was living off the reservation (Barsh and Henderson 1980). This decision explicitly ruled that Native people did not have the right to citizenship (Hoxie 1984).

The technological world of the nineteenth century was represented by the philosophy and accomplishments of Francis Amasa Walker, Commissioner of Indian Affairs during the 1870s. Using a scientific management theory, Walker proposed that the federal government impose on Natives "a rigid reformatory discipline" (Takaki 1979, 186). According to historian Ronald Takaki,

> The crucial term is *reformatory*. The "discovery of the asylum" in white society had its counterpart in the invention of the reservation for Indian society. Based on "the principle of separation and seclusion," the reservation would do more than merely maintain Indians: It would train and reform them. (1979, 186; emphasis in original)

Walker viewed Natives as biologically inferior beings with "strong animal appetites and no intellectual tastes or aspirations to hold those appetites in check" (quoted in Takaki 1979, 187). Once confined on reservations, Natives would be obligated to work as part of the Americanizing project.

As the nineteenth century closed, Native people were confined, imprisoned on reservations. Those who resisted had been forcibly removed from their homelands, with many massacred in the process. One outrageous example is the 1890 Wounded Knee massacre, in which the U.S. Army murdered over two hundred unarmed Natives, including many women and children. The Army later opposed compensation to the survivors on the grounds that the "battle" (massacre) had been essential in the dissolution of the Lakota Ghost Dance religion (Johansen and Maestas 1979). Cultural oppression of Natives remained blatant, and Native opposition—whether militaristic, legal, or spiritual—would not be tolerated by the federal government.

In the obstructive policies of the nineteenth century, which caused intense jurisdictional conflicts and unequal justice, the social construction of deviance becomes obvious. Euro-American interest groups' involvement in the development of new laws for Natives created a situation in which, as put forth by Austin Turk (1969), the interests of the more powerful groups were legitimate while those of the less powerful were made illegal.

The pervasive political, economic, and cultural control of Native nations by the federal government continued into the present century. For all its brutality and intensity, this colonial control has not terminated Native sovereignty. It has, however, suppressed its exercise. Cultural oppression facilitates economic exploitation, and twentieth-century federal policy toward Natives follows this pattern. Aside from laws, the federal government has actively pursued policies, rules, and regulations designed to suppress the Native worlds. For instance, in 1901 all agents and superintendents were notified to enforce the "short hair" order. To the federal government, long hair signified a primitive culture. All Native men who refused to cut their hair were refused rations, and those working for the government were released from their duties (Prucha 1984). During the 1920s the BIA strictly limited Native dancing, and those under age fifty were prohibited from participating in their traditional dances (Price 1973). A BIA document issued in 1924 noted that "there are large numbers of Indians who believe that their native religious life and Indian culture is frowned upon by the government, if not actually banned" (Price 1973, 207).

The BIA saw its powers enhanced with the passage of the Indian Reorganization Act (IRA) in 1934. This act was ostensibly intended to strengthen tribal authority and legal systems by letting tribes establish their own governing organizations—the elected tribal councils of today. However, it smacks heavily of indirect rule, again along the British colonial model, as the United States recognizes only the leadership of the councils. Natives were empowered to rule other Natives, incredibly complicating reservation life when traditional tribal leaders were usurped by elected tribal councils.

The IRA also converted Courts of Indian Offenses into tribal courts, and the modern tribal court system was born. Tribal codes enacted after 1934 followed the BIA model. Tribal courts and codes are subject to the approval of the BIA and are limited in their power to the handling of misdemeanors. Although this policy gave the appearance of maintaining the status quo, Deloria and Lytle (1983) offer that the new tribal courts did promise to resurrect the traditional customs of Native people. The balancing act for tribal courts today is to recuperate and retain tribal traditions of justice despite being immersed in contemporary Euro-American jurisprudence. Tribes work to retain their ways and are reluctant to follow Euro-American legal procedures exclusively. On Indian reservations,

> The desired resolution of an intratribal dispute is one that benefits the whole Indian community (family) and not one designed to chastise an individual offender. Non-Indian critics may not understand such a concept of justice, but within Indian traditions it is an accepted and expected norm. (Deloria and Lytle 1983, 120)

Issues of sovereignty are vital to Native people and the tribal court system, no matter what the cost. Tim Giago, editor of *Indian Country Today*, contends that tribal courts on Indian reservations must acknowledge their sovereign status. Discussing the case of Peter Mac-Donald, a former Navajo tribal chair who is serving a fourteen-year sentence for conspiracy and bribery in tribal and federal courts, Giago expresses:

> [I]f the Navajo Nation really believed in sovereignty it would have tried Mr. MacDonald within the borders of their Nation instead of allowing federal officials to take him off the reservation and try him before an all-white jury in Prescott, Arizona. This was hardly a jury of his peers and few, if any, of the jury members understood anything about the Navajo Nation, its laws, customs, or traditions. (1995, 2)

THE COMPLICATED EFFECTS OF PUBLIC LAW 280

Plunder normally characterizes only the early stage of colonialism, although it is possible to find subtle forms of plunder by the United States in the twentieth century. For example, beginning in the late 1940s and lasting into the 1960s, the federal government shifted toward a policy of termination, another violation of treaties. Rather than struggling to dominate tribal land, the government started to do away with Native nations themselves, making their lands "open" lands. A simple resolution of the House of Representatives in 1953, House Concurrent Resolution 108, terminated the sovereignty of one hundred Native nations.

Another element in the process was the transfer to certain states of federal jurisdiction over reservation areas. The authority for this transfer was Public Law 280, passed by Congress in 1954—one of the most bold and discriminating actions against Natives in the legal and judicial system. Moving without tribal consent, PL 280 initially handed five states jurisdiction over offenses committed by or against Natives on reservations; eventually, nine other states assumed limited jurisdiction. Upon the expansion of their legal domain over Natives, states mistakenly hoped to increase their revenue by taxing Native land and by receiving federal assistance to improve enforcement, corrections, and judicial agencies.

The timeworn argument was that reservations were "lawless." In 1952 Representative D'Ewart of Montana said that there was a "complete breakdown of law and order on many of the Indian reservations" and that the law was driven by "[t]he desire of all law abiding citizens living on or near Indian reservations for law and order" (quoted in Barsh and Henderson 1980, 128–129). The principal concern of Congress was, therefore, the reaction of white people to the perceived lawlessness (U.S. Commission on Civil Rights 1981). White communities that had settled on or near reservations, their growth partially a result of the allotment policy, were concerned about law and order outside their direct control and held the belief that Native law was irresponsible and federal law distant. PL 280 provided for their interests by endowing to various states criminal and civil jurisdiction on reservations. Witness the language used in a 1963 report titled "A Study of the Problems Arising from the Transfer of Law and Order Jurisdiction on Indian Reservations to the State of Montana":

> Indian people hesitate to give up this powerful position which they hold in the United States society. They do not fully realize however, their responsibility when they seek to protect this powerful position. They must maintain a standard of society which is acceptable. This probably is the greatest weakness in the Indian position on law and order. The trend in modern society requires that Indian people conform to reasonable acceptable community standards of law and

order. . . . Any time that there is segregation in an area like law and order the attitude of segregation spreads into other areas. Segregation always sows the seeds of discrimination and racial problems. (Montana Office of the State Coordinator of Indian Affairs 1963)

Natives are depicted as irresponsible and "backward," as though they have not yet been civilized—all couched in terms of the fear of segregation. But segregation existed prior to 1963 and exists today in Montana.

Many Montana Native people were in opposition to PL 280 (known in Montana as House Bill 55). The chief proponent was state representative Jean Turnage, an enrolled member of the Confederated Salish and Kootenai Tribes (from Lake County on the Flathead Reservation) and a member of the Inter-Tribal Policy Board. Opponent Bill Youpee, chairman of the Fort Peck Tribal Council, expressed that the Inter-Tribal Policy Board was "influenced by outside interests" (*Great Falls Tribune*, 10 February 1963). The Flathead Tribal Council, under the direction of Walter McDonald, supported the transfer of jurisdiction to the state, although not all tribal members were in agreement. Moreover, all other tribes in Montana opposed such action, principally because PL 280 violated rights reserved in treaties and likewise violated the self-determination of sovereign nations. Another major issue was that PL 280 was a step toward the dreaded termination of all Indian reservations, as evidenced by House Resolution 108. PL 280 was passed by Congress in 1953, and in 1965, with the endorsement of the tribal council of the Confederated Salish and Kootenai Tribes, House Bill 55 (that is, PL 280) was implemented on the Flathead Reservation.

Many Natives perceive the imposition of state laws on reservations without tribal consent as blatant discrimination (U.S. Commission on Civil Rights 1981). Although the Indian Civil Rights Act of 1968 amended PL 280 to require tribal consent, this act also limits the penalties in tribal courts to imprisonment for six months and/or a fine of five hundred dollars, thereby effectively confining action in tribal courts to misdemeanors. Furthermore, the amendment authorizes states to retrocede jurisdiction already assumed—that is, relinquish it if burdensome. Tribes, however, are not empowered to demand retrocession (Barsh 1980).

PL 280 denies Native nations the right to govern themselves. There is also concern that under PL 280 state police and courts are treating

Natives and whites differently. Refusal to cross-deputize Native law enforcement personnel creates an imbalance whereby Euro-American police steadily send Natives to Euro-American courts and jails, while tribal police can only stand by and observe white criminal behavior. The result is a continuous and increasing supply of Native American "criminals." According to noted attorney Russel Barsh, "Arrests of Indians reportedly increase when per capitas or lease monies are [due to be] paid, to generate fines. Tribes contend that sentences are 'light and ineffective' for crimes against Indians, 'harsh and unjust' for crimes against non-Indians" (1980, 10).

PL 280 is curious in its uneven application. Not all states chose to apply its measures, and some selected only certain reservations within their boundaries. For instance, Montana has seven Indian reservations, but only on the Flathead Reservation is Euro-American jurisdiction extended through PL 280. Not surprisingly, Flathead includes a large white population due to various acts of Congress, including allotment and homesteading implemented at the turn of the century. A challenge would be to determine the proportion of Salish and Kootenai—the tribes of Flathead—among the Montana Natives involved in the state's criminal justice system. One would expect to find more Salish and Kootenai pass through the legal system than members of other tribes, with the exception of Landless Native Americans.[7]

Non-Natives are now immune from tribal prosecution, in both criminal and civil matters, due to a 1978 U.S. Supreme Court ruling in *Oliphant v. Suquamish*. In states where cross-deputization has not been worked out, many non-Natives who violate state law on reservations go unapprehended. This has been, and continues to be, a national Native American concern as tribal leaders fear white people will see the reservations as areas to "do anything they please without fear of arrest or judicial reprisal" (Wachtel 1980, 13). Moreover, in 1981 in *Montana v. United States*, the U.S. Supreme Court ruled that white people who own land on the Crow Reservation are not under the authority of Crow hunting and fishing laws on or near the Big Horn River. This decision violates the Crow treaty of 1868. Additionally, this case takes the ruling in *Oliphant* one step further toward the dissolution of tribal sovereignty (Churchill and Morris 1992).

Five statutory enactments of the U.S. Congress—the General Crimes Act, Major Crimes Act, Assimilative Crimes Act, PL 280, and the Indian Civil Rights Act—in addition to the court cases cited, all infringe upon tribal powers to tackle crime issues on reservations (Deloria and Lytle 1983). These statutes have forged a legal sword that slashes at tribal sovereignty, and the cuts are not clean as continual redefinition by these statutes creates the problem of determining which among multiple authorities may handle alleged Native criminals. The road to legal jurisdiction on reservations travels through mazes. It is not a product of logic other than that of sporadic legislative responses to the demand for Euro-American hegemony over Indian Country. Meanwhile, a major handicap for reservation Natives today is the multiplicity of jurisdiction, wherein

> The accused ordinarily confronts two jurisdictional "layers," general federal criminal laws applicable everywhere in the United States and concurrent state criminal law defining both related and separate offenses. On an Indian reservation the accused confronts as many as six jurisdictional layers, with as many as four possible forum-law outcomes: federal-federal, federal-state, state-state, and tribal-tribal. This does not mean that reservations are safer, only that it is harder for reservation residents to know fully their rights and liabilities, and easier for jurisdictional conflicts to arise. (Barsh 1980, 3)

The fundamental question, according to Deloria and Lytle (1983), is which level of government assumes jurisdiction over criminal offenses on reservations. Part of the answer requires determining the race of all involved to the extent of investigating past generations, the precise location within overlapping political boundaries where the alleged crime all or in part occurred, the appropriate statute of competing codes under which the violator can be prosecuted, and who has the political initiative at the moment. Indian reservations are the only places in the United States where the criminality of an act relies exclusively on the race of the offender and victim (Barsh 1980).[8]

PUBLIC LAW 280 AND RETROCESSION

Since 1968, some tribes have been successful in their efforts to retrocede state jurisdiction to federal control (O'Brien 1989). Other tribes, however, encounter stereotypic expectations that Native Americans cannot behave responsibly enough to exercise effective law enforcement, thereby threatening the safety of non-Natives (Barsh 1980). This is the attitude that the Confederated Salish and Kootenai Tribes face in their pursuit of retrocession. Opponents to retrocession cite that white people do not want to be subjected to a justice system they fear will discriminate against them because they are white. What they do not understand is that the withdrawal of PL 280 will not result in the confinement of white people in Flathead's tribal jail because prior court cases have opined that tribes do not have jurisdiction over non-Natives.

In the 1990s the Confederated Salish and Kootenai Tribes seek to withdraw from PL 280 jurisdiction for two basic reasons: to further self-determination and promote tribal sovereignty, and to develop a justice system that is culturally appropriate (Confederated Salish and Kootenai Tribes 1991). The tribes argue that they have made economic progress—after all, this has been the goal of federal policy—since they consented in 1965 to the implementation of PL 280. They offer as evidence a tribal budget of over $70 million and twelve hundred tribal employees in the 1990s, compared to the eleven employees and budget of less than $250,000 in 1963. When PL 280 was first proposed in 1963, the tribes were not financially able to provide law enforcement for people on the reservation, but this is no longer the case. Moreover, the tribes cite that the notion of justice predates European contact and that judges and courts have always existed in the social and political structure of the tribes. Subsequently, they have integrated traditional justice frameworks with Euro-American jurisprudence.

The Major Crimes Act of 1885 postulated that tribes did not have tribal institutions sufficient to maintain law and order (Barsh 1980). This was not true in the nineteenth century and it is not true today. The Confederated Salish and Kootenai Tribes boast a competent justice system, a system more capable than some counties in Montana (Confederated Salish and Kootenai Tribes 1991). The current tribal justice system on Flathead includes a tribal court system with three divisions (a trial court, a youth court, and an appellate court), a law and order department, fish and game enforcement, advocate program, and social service programs.

In 1989 54 percent of all arrests in Lake County, the primary county on Flathead, were Native American (Confederated Salish and Kootenai Tribes 1991). The Confederated Salish and Kootenai Tribes recognize that most arrests on the reservation are alcohol- or drug-related. Responding to this issue, the tribes developed an extensive substance abuse program. They argue that withdrawal from PL 280 will enable them to rehabilitate those arrested for misdemeanors (felonies would fall under federal jurisdiction). In fact, the tribes have more substance abuse counselors than Lake County (nine compared to one) and are, therefore, better equipped to handle substance abuse problems than the county.

RECUPERATING NATIVE WORLDS

Policies governing Native American affairs are legally bound to protect Native resources and treaty rights, but these policies have been perverted by Euro-American economic interests. The product is a system that imposes on indigenous populations cradle-to-grave control designed to obliterate worldview, political independence, and economic control. To resist is to be criminal, risking the wrath of multiple state law enforcement agencies. In the Americas, this exploitation has been the backbone of a colonial relationship now hundreds of years old yet still vigorous.

The Euro-American legal system, based on English common law and Euro-American statute law oriented to Euro-American values and philosophy, has never been able to accommodate within its bounds the different culture and aberrant status of the indigenous people. The goal of justice ostensibly sought by the legal system often results in the opposite when Natives are involved. The mechanisms of Euro-American law either are incapable of recognizing the cultural and legal separateness of Natives or are deliberately designed to destroy that independence (Washburn 1971).

Even when Native nations agreed to acculturate, they not only were thwarted but suffered additional castigation. There is probably no better documented case study of the cultural adaptation of a traditional legal system than that of the Cherokee Nation. *Fire and the Spirits* (1975), written by Rennard Strickland, examines the development of Cherokee legal institutions and the Cherokee Nation's attempt to acculturate. The Cherokee applied Euro-American laws that fit their needs and rejected those that did not. Their legal experience illustrates that it is in fact possible to create Native versions of Euro-American ways. The outcome was not what Euro-Americans expected, as the Cherokee became deserving Native opponents, insisting that their customs should be honored. Yet the ways of Euro-Americans had been learned too well: Strickland concludes that in the end the Cherokee Nation would be obliterated. Damned if you do, damned if you don't; while assimilation is theoretically offered, equality is not a part of the bargain.

Although the Confederated Salish and Kootenai Tribes present another case of cultural adaptation with the blending of their traditional legal system and Euro-American jurisprudence, their fate may prove similar to the Cherokees'. The retrocession of PL 280 for the people of the Flathead Indian Reservation may never happen. Montana Senate Bill 368, which would give tribal police and courts additional criminal jurisdiction on reservations, died in 1993.

The Northern Cheyenne Tribe, a non–PL 280 reservation, presently struggles to reclaim their traditional system of law and order, one in which the Warrior Societies play a major role.[9] Evidently in agreement with the Cheyenne Tribal Court, the Warrior Societies recently employed traditional Cheyenne justice and banished two nonmembers from the reservation for a period of one hundred years (Crisp 1995). This action has not met with agreement from all tribal members, however, and the Northern Cheyenne remain divided over the actions of the Warrior Societies. A significant aspect of this case is that the Northern Cheyenne's justice system, as they are recreating it, demonstrates that modern tribal court systems and traditional systems can work together.

Chief Justice Robert Yazzie (1994) of the Navajo Tribal Court describes the Euro-American system of justice as one of hierarchies and power—a vertical system of justice. The Navajo word for "law," brought to them by the Holy People, is *beehaz-aanii*, which means "fundamental, absolute." Yazzie conveys that law is the source of a meaningful life, precisely because life emerges from it. In the Navajo system of law, one of horizontal justice, all parties are allowed to explain their views, and there is no one authority that ascertains the "truth." This is a system of restorative justice based on equality and participation, with a notion of justice that involves recuperating both the offender and victim.

The concept of solidarity is important to Navajo healing and justice. Although difficult to translate, Yazzie expresses that solidarity

> carries connotations that help the individual to reconcile self with family, community, nature, and the cosmos—all reality. That

feeling of oneness with one's surroundings, and the reconciliation of the individual with everyone and everything else, is what allows an alternative to vertical justice to work. It rejects the process of convicting a person and throwing the keys away in favor of methods that use solidarity to restore good relations among people. Most importantly, it restores good relations with self. (1994, 30)

The healing process, called *peacemaking* in English, is a complex system of relationships where there is no coercion or control because there is no need for such power. Additionally, there are no plaintiffs or defendants, and no one is right or wrong. The Navajo have a different concept of equality. The focus is not on equal treatment *before* the law; people are envisioned as equal *in* the law. For example, the vertical system of justice—the Euro-American system—requires of the defendant a plea of innocence or guilt. In the Navajo language there is no word for *guilty*—a word that assumes fault and thus punishment. Yazzie advises that the word *guilty* is a nonsense word in Navajo, because the Navajo focus on healing and reintegration with the goal of feeding and preserving healthy, ongoing relationships.

Navajo law is also based on distributive justice. According to Yazzie, Navajo Court decisions emphasize aiding the victim, not finding fault. The victim's wishes of compensation and the offender's financial ability are taken into account. The offender and his or her family are responsible to the victim and must pay compensation. The focus of distributive justice is the well-being of everyone in the community. Taking the notion of responsibility further, Yazzie conveys:

If I see a hungry person, it does not matter whether I am responsible for the hunger. If someone is injured, it is irrelevant that I did not hurt that person. I have a responsibility, as a Navajo, to treat everyone as if that person was my relative. Everyone is part of a community, and the resources of the community must be shared with all. (1994, 30)

The contemporary Navajo Peacemaker Court is founded upon the traditional principles of distributive justice and restoration over punishment. The Navajo operated under a vertical system of justice from 1892 to 1959 under the Court of Indian Offenses and from 1959 to the present day under the Courts of the Navajo Nation (Yazzie 1994). Intensely weary of the vertical system, in 1982 they created the Navajo

Peacemaker Court. The court selects a peacemaker, or *naat' aanii*—a person known for wisdom, integrity, and respect. His or her job is to ensure a decision in which everyone benefits. The court attempts to reclaim the original philosophical reasoning of traditional Navajo rather than simply blend cultures and philosophies.

The variance between Euro-American and Native worlds is apparent in how they work to maintain the social order. In Indian Country collective ways were developed to right an offensive activity with the larger harmony, recuperate the offender, and thereby protect the people. On the other hand, the Euro-American system of institutionalized justice featuring legislated law, aggressive enforcers, and punitive judges acts beyond controlling activity within the Euro-American world; it is also instrumental in fulfilling the Manifest Destiny of the Euro-American world—its own expansion. Intrusion into Indian Country was spearheaded by Euro-American law and the territory secured in the same manner. The federal government has embraced conflicting policies regarding Native people, shifting from genocide to expulsion, exclusion, and confinement, and later to supposed assimilation—the rhetoric was integration, the reality was confinement and domination. Amid the roller coaster of federal policy, one thing is crystal clear: at every stage of colonialism, Native people have been disempowered.

Some Euro-American criminologists agree that the Euro-American justice system represents the interests of the powerful and is inherently oppressive (Hartjen 1978; Quinney 1970; Turk 1976). The recognition that law and its administration is biased against certain categories of people is crucial to understanding Native American criminality. Nevertheless, one must first distinguish between Euro-American and Native worlds to grasp the role of Euro-American law in their collision.

To mechanically explain Native Americans by means of production, skin color, cultural practices, and so on is to peer through a tunnel—a tunnel engineered straight, perhaps, but a tunnel nonetheless. Absolutely, race/ethnicity, gender, class, and lifestyle are important concerns to Natives who feel the weight of their consequences both within Indian Country and in relations with Euro-Americans, but care must be taken not to let those issues obscure the broader battle between worlds and the emergence of neocolonial racism.

History tells us that Native "criminals" were not lawless "savages" but rather were living in the turbulent wake of a cataclysmic clash wherein

Native legal systems, along with everything else, collided with a most different world. Native worlds have been devastated by their relationship with Euro-Americans and their laws. The number of jailed Natives is a disheartening indication—a reminder that because deviance is a social construct, official crime statistics reveal discretion in defining and apprehending criminals. The behavior of reservation Natives, from both PL 280 and non–PL 280 reservations, is clearly subject to greater scrutiny, especially considering the number of criminal jurisdictions they fall under, and there is a greater presumption of guilt than for Euro-Americans. This assumption is based on the prevalence of Native Americans in the official crime statistics and the composition of prison populations. But the battle for jurisdiction in the remainder of Indian Country, where various Euro-American legal entities led by the federal government compete for primacy over tribes, is a telling example of the continuing struggle for sovereignty.

Two

RACIALIZING MONTANA

THE CREATION

OF "BAD INDIANS"

CONTINUES

*Cultural domination, because it is total and tends to
oversimplify, very soon manages to disrupt in spectacular
fashion the cultural life of a conquered people. This cultural
obliteration is made possible by the negation of national
reality, by new legal relations introduced by the occupying
power, by the banishment of the natives and their customs
to outlying districts by colonial society, by expropriation,
and by the systematic enslaving of men and women.*

FRANTZ FANON, The Wretched of the Earth

The racializing of Montana can be easily divided into the theft of Native resources, the creation of Native deviance, Native resistance to Euro-American policies and laws, and social interaction between Natives and whites.[1] The process and evolution of colonial racism appear to begin simply: directly intrusive actions in conjunction with blatant racism. Over time, this gives way to a more complicated neocolonial racism and accompanying intricate strategies of survival by Native people.

By the middle of the nineteenth century the valued resources gold, silver, and copper were discovered in what became known as Montana, bringing a flood of white people to a land owned by indigenous people. By 1899 61 percent of all copper in the United States (23 percent of all copper in the world) was produced in Montana. Montana's white population grew more during the late 1880s than during any other period, with a 265 percent increase from 39,000 in 1880 to 143,000 by 1890

(Toole 1972). While the white population exploded, the Native population declined sharply. Between 1880 and 1890 the Native population was reduced through warfare, disease, and starvation from 21,650 to 10,765 (Belue 1990). Native Americans would not see a substantial population increase until the 1930s (Office of the Coordinator of Indian Affairs 1987). Euro-Americans continued to garner Native resources and amass millions, while Montana's indigenous people faced abject poverty. During the early 1890s Butte boasted many millionaires, and by 1894 Helena had more millionaires per capita than any other place in the United States (Toole 1972).

Native land that was not obtained illegally by gold seekers and homesteaders was stolen by cattle barons. In 1866 Nelson Story, one of Montana's "founding fathers," trespassed on Crow land as he drove the first cattle to Montana from Texas (Belue 1990). The cattlemen discovered that they required a considerable amount of land to support their great herds.

Cattle barons not only needed land; they also felt a need to protect their herds from the indigenous people. By 1880–1881 the buffalo was nearly extinct due to mass slaughters occurring during the 1870s (Toole 1959). White ranchers in northern Montana saw the resultant hunger and desperation of Native people as a threat (Overholser 1932). In a letter dated 18 April 1881, another one of Montana's "founding fathers," Granville Stuart, petitioned the secretary of the interior:

> for we have no time to lose; for if something is not done, these cursed Indians will all be back among our cattle by September 1st. and we don't want any more of that if we can avoid it. Those damned Blackfeet and Cree are now back somewhere between Box Elder and Musselshell and don't intend to go north at all, but we will see that they do, by some means. (quoted in Overholser 1932, 68)

Natives did eat cattle owned by whites, but subsistence, rather than resistance, was a primary motive.

Although the direct threat to their herds was a concern, cattle barons who poured into Montana primarily perceived Native people as barriers to white progress in two ways: Natives owned the land, and they possessed numerous horses that seemingly depleted the range. One solution to this supposed problem was to empty Montana of "Indian ponies." In 1885 Granville Stuart proposed to do away with horses owned by Natives because they ate the prized grass presumably reserved for cattle owned by white men. To this end, thousands of horses owned by Natives, including thirty thousand Crow horses, were destroyed (Belue 1989a).

The other approach, naturally, was to first expropriate Native lands and then rid them of "Indian ponies." In that spirit, a former Indian agent at Flathead, W. H. Smead, wrote,

> Were it not for the large number of ponies of an inferior grade ranging upon the reservation, it would be an ideal stock country. These little ponies are very destructive to ranges, and considering their numbers they have during the past few years been a heavy tax upon the ranges. With the opening of the reservation these herds of Indian ponies will necessarily be disposed of. (1905, 67)

Preparing the way for the theft of Native lands, Smead wrote that his employment on Flathead afforded him an "exceptional opportunity." His position as Indian agent provided him with information for white people "who may contemplate obtaining a home or a business location in Montana upon the beautiful and fertile land of the Flatheads" (Smead 1905, n.p.).

The attitudes of whites toward Natives ran the gamut from subtle to blatant racism. Their racialized ideology justified the ill treatment of Natives and the theft of resources. Smead's views of Natives were as evident as they were commonplace when he wrote, "Indians are slow to take up the ways of the white man. His vices they soon adopt but his virtues they are slow to accept. . . . He needs the guiding hand of one in authority" (1905, 62–63). Smead advocated the opening of Native lands for more civil folk: "for thousands of settlers, where by labor, industry and thrift, happy and prosperous homes will be builded" (70). A shrewd Smead continued, "The ruthless progress of white civilization has finally demanded its surrender, and the land of the Indian will soon be the land of the white man" (71).

The indigenous landbase in Montana was reduced sharply through federal policy, including the Allotment Act of 1887 and various Homestead Acts that were implemented from the late 1800s to the early 1900s. Advertisements offering Native lands in Montana to white "settlers" were common. For instance, one such advertisement appeared in a publication out of Missoula, *The Western Homeseeker*, in 1905. The Flathead Reservation Information Agency, not surprisingly operated by W. H. Smead, urged white people to obtain land before the best, richest soil was allotted to Natives. The next year, predicting the "opening" of the Flathead Reservation and urging white people to exercise their homestead "right," another advertisement in *The Western Homeseeker*, titled "Are You Prepared? We Are," promised:

> We are prepared to prepare you for the opening of the Flathead Indian Reservation that is soon to occur. We are prepared to guide you, every step, toward the acquiring, by you, of one of these immensely rich homesteads. If you have not exercised your home-stead right, you cannot afford to neglect the opportunity of doing so at the time the Flathead Indian Reservation is opened. Think of it! An Inland Empire of virgin soil, rich as any in the United States! No hardships of any kind. (Flathead Reservation Information Agency 1906, 30)

Business deals of this sort enabled white people to gain much Native land, not only in Montana but additionally in other states. The Flathead Reservation was opened to homestead entry in 1911. In 1910 the Native people of Flathead owned 1,250,000 acres; this figure was systematically reduced to 750,000 in 1930, with the best land obtained by white people (Toole 1959). Today, as a direct result of this policy, Natives on Flat-head are a numerical minority on their own reservation. White people, chasing dreams and looking for "free" land, were enticed in a variety of ways to relocate to Montana. By 1909, the year the Enlarged Home-stead Act was passed, white people owned more than 1,000,000 acres of indigenous land in Montana. The next year another 5,000,000 acres were taken by these newcomers, and between 1910 and 1922 they secured over 40 percent of the entire state, or approximately 93,000,000 acres (Toole 1959). By 1978 Native people held only 2.4 percent of the total land in Montana (Office of the Coordinator of Indian Affairs 1987).

Native people were controlled in other ways besides theft of their re-sources and resultant starvation. Their behaviors, grounded in Native philosophies, were regulated legally as the creation of Native devi-ance continued. Aside from laws, special regulations to control Native people, such as the pass system, were created in the nineteenth century.[2]

Once segregated on reservations, under the pass system Natives were not allowed to leave unless they obtained legal permission. According to Francis Amasa Walker, commissioner of Indian Affairs during the 1870s, this system was a way to prevent Natives from violating white settlements (Takaki 1979). The pass system, thus, was developed and effectively operated to imprison Natives on their respective reservations. For those Natives in Montana who did not comply, laws of vagrancy were implemented, and officials were notified

> to arrest all buck Indians belonging to his [the Flathead Indian agent's] agency, found in Butte, and prosecute them for vagrancy. The agent thinks that if this be done the squaws will return to the agency and the bucks will be taught a lesson which will keep them at home. (*Weekly Missoulian*, 27 June 1894, 2)

In addition to their freedom and material resources, Native people in Montana and elsewhere in Euro-America were denied their culture as well. Federal policy had outlawed Native spiritual practices, and in the region of the Northern Plains it was the Sun Dance ceremony that was to be destroyed. Natives, especially seeking solace in their culture during this time, were puzzled and resisted such efforts. A Blackfeet Native, illustrating the importance of the sacred to Native people and the confusion about white religion, articulated the following regarding the ban on the Sun Dance:

> We know that there is nothing injurious to our people in the Sun-dance. On the other hand, we have seen much that is bad at the dances of the white people. . . . I do not understand why the white men desire to put an end to our religious ceremonials. What harm can they do to our people? If they deprive us of our religion, we will have nothing left, for we know of no other that can take its place. . . . We do not understand the white man's religion. The Black Robes (Catholic Priests) teach us one thing and the Men-with-white-neckties (Protestant Missionaries) teach us another; so we are confused. (Anonymous; quoted in Nabokov 1992, 225)

Native people fought the enforcement of the ban on Native spirituality. On 13 June 1894, the *Weekly Missoulian* reported that "renegade

Cree Indians" were preparing for a most solemn and important ceremony—the Sun Dance. The article stated that the governor had issued
a proclamation against the ritual, and it cited the governor as declaring the Sun Dance "inhuman and brutalizing, unnatural and indecent,
therefore abhorrent to Christian civilization." The ban on the Sun
Dance was reaffirmed in 1921 by an order from the Office of Indian Affairs in Circular 1665. Regulations against gambling give-aways and restrictions on dances were reaffirmed in 1923 in a supplement to Circular 1665 (Price 1973).[3] These prohibitions, whether laws or simply
federal orders and regulations, were not lifted until 1934. This favor-
able ruling was strengthened in 1978 with the passage of the American
Indian Religious Freedom Act.

Policy makers, as well as local whites, often lamented the lack of
"civilization" among the Natives. Illustrating the attitude that Natives
were "immoral" and their "evil" religion should be suppressed, in 1901
the commissioner of Indian Affairs proposed that

> Indian dances and so-called Indian feasts should be prohibited.
> In many cases these dances and feasts are simply subterfuges to
> cover degrading acts and to disguise immoral purposes. You are di-
> rected to use your best efforts in the suppression of these evils.
> (quoted in O'Brien 1989, 6)

Another report to federal officials expressed the concern that "deficient" Native cultures hindered progress and assimilation into a supposedly superior way of life.[4] Also, this particular superintendent, addressing the social conditions at Flathead, specifically targeted Native
women, who "cling" to their culture more than Native men.

> The dances of the Indians held on the reservation by the older Indi-
> ans are a hindrance to progress in that they induce idleness and take
> the Indians away from farm work. . . . Effort is constantly made by
> the field employees to get better sanitary conditions about the homes
> of the Indians. This is one of the features of the work that does
> not progress as rapidly as we would like. Home conditions almost
> always depend upon the attitude of the women of the homes and
> the Indian women, as a rule, are much more conservative and cling
> more to the old practices of their ancestors than the men. (*Superin-
> tendent's Annual Narrative and Statistical Reports, 1910–1923*)

The superintendent's 1919 report on Native dancing stated that although the dances were being held and Natives continued to be "immoral," the most important issue was time, in the spirit of the Protestant work ethic:

> The Indians indulge in the old tribal dances to a considerable
> extent. . . . An objection to the dances of the Indians is the time
> at which they often are held and the length of the period in which
> they indulge in them. They will leave their homes and spend days
> at a dance when they should be on their farms attending to their
> crops or irrigating their fields. There often are attendant feature
> of gambling at dances of the Indians, and some disregard of proper
> relations of the sexes. Education is the only solution that occurs
> to this office. Arbitrary prohibition is not practicable to eliminate
> dances. (*Superintendent's Annual Narrative and Statistical Reports,*
> *1910–1923*)

In the 1920 superintendent's report, in addition to the concern about time, the waste of money on seemingly unimportant items was portrayed as problematic: "Another practice [that] causes considerable loss of time and expenditure of funds is the feasts given after the death of an Indian. These feasts last one or two days and cost the relatives of the deceased from $75.00 to $150.00" (*Superintendent's Annual Narrative and Statistical Reports, 1910–1923*).

The superintendents' annual reports from the late 1880s to the late 1930s disclose that the majority of crimes on the Flathead Reservation were gambling, adultery, and liquor violations. For instance, the 1925 data (which do not include alcohol-related violations) reveal that adultery accounted for 41 percent and gambling offenses 26 percent of all arrests. Both were seen as "serious evils." This pattern, carried over from previous times, remained year after year (*Superintendent's Annual Narrative and Statistical Reports, 1907–1938*). Statistics from 1927 divulge a significant number of arrests for liquor violations, while other "crimes" included resisting an officer, vagrancy, failure to attend school, failure to send children to school, and desertion from a nonreservation school (*Superintendent's Annual Narrative and Statistical Reports, 1907–1938*).

Punishments for the above-mentioned crimes were lengthy and severe. Between 1898 and 1908, the charge of drunk and disorderly could result in ninety days of hard labor, fifty lashes, or a fifty-dollar fine.

Likewise, gambling could bring eighty days in jail, a five-dollar fine, or fifteen lashes. The destruction of a school landed two people in jail for twenty-five days and an additional forty-five lashes. An adulterer could spend as long as one hundred days in jail or receive thirty lashes, and the serious transgression of insulting a priest resulted in a fifteen-dollar fine and ninety days in jail (O'Neal 1968).

Native customs were slow to die, and the subjective idea of morality continued to be a significant issue for Indian agents and missionaries, who were particularly concerned with traditional Native marriage and divorce laws. A report from the agency superintendent proposed that prosecution had resulted in lower arrest rates for the "primitive" Natives:

> Some of these Indians have very primitive ideas as to the marriage relation, and a number of cases of adultery are known to exist. Cohabitation is very frequent, and is not looked upon as being wrong by the greater part of the tribe. However, in this respect, I think they are improving, probably on account of the prosecution of adultery cases both in Federal Court, and in the Court of Indian Offences. (*Superintendent's Annual Narrative and Statistical Reports, 1910–1923*)

The prosecution for adultery had the effect of criminalizing Native people and their culture. As late as 1931, a superintendent's report regarding "deviant" Natives read, "Moral conditions are not satisfactory among the Flathead Indians. There seems to be no particular odium attached to adultery and Indians desert their legal spouses and live with another partner quite frequently" (*Superintendent's Annual Narrative and Statistical Reports, 1907–1938*).

RESISTANT AND RESILIENT NATIVES

Early "crimes" of resistance by the indigenous people in Montana came in the forms of warfare, the protection of homelands, and the continuation of sacred practices. Montana's indigenous people fiercely resisted colonization. For example, in 1872 the Salish were forced to relocate from the Bitterroot Valley, which was opened to white settlement. Many resisted, and it was not until 1891 that the remaining impoverished

A resident of the Flathead Indian Reservation, this prisoner was stripped of his identity when his long hair was cut and he was given a prisoner uniform. He is simply described in the prison register as "an Indian." He was convicted of stealing horses and imprisoned at the Montana State Prison in 1905. Courtesy of the Powell County Museum and Arts Foundation, Deer Lodge, Montana.

Salish were forcibly removed from their traditional homeland. In 1874 William Belknap requested five hundred soldiers to protect "endangered" and "annoyed" white settlers against Natives in western Montana, particularly those on Flathead, and vowed to stop Natives from using their traditional route to buffalo hunting grounds (Belknap 1874). In 1876 proud resisters of encroachment, the Lakota, Cheyenne, and Arapaho, proved formidable opponents for the U.S. Army at the Battle of the Little Big Horn. After the defeat of General George Armstrong Custer, Native people in Montana were punished severely. While forts were erected to protect white citizens, Natives were imprisoned in forts and on reservations. Life as Native people knew it would never be the same.

Although the massacre at Wounded Knee in 1890 has been called the symbolic end of freedom for Native people (Brown 1970), as the

This fifteen-year-old boy from the Flathead Indian Reservation had his long hair shaved off. His humanity removed, he was described by the prison register as "an Indian" with "squaw" features. He was convicted of stealing horses and imprisoned at the Montana State Prison in 1905. Courtesy of the Powell County Museum and Arts Foundation, Deer Lodge, Montana.

century drew to a close Native people continued to seek their freedom by opposing white intrusion. In 1889 a harried telegram from the mayor of Missoula, located just off the Flathead Reservation, to General Ruger of the Commanding Department of Dakota in St. Paul, Minnesota, demanded that weapons be given to citizens because of the "Indians on Flathead Reservation in arms and in conflict with Sheriff's posse, one Indian killed" (Sloan 1889). Another letter regarding the same incident from R. V. Belt, acting commissioner to the secretary of the interior, communicated to the secretary of war that he had just received a telegram from the Indian agent at Flathead stating that the "Sheriff has killed one Indian. Shall I call for troops if prospect of an uprising" (Belt 1889).

Crimes of resistance by impoverished yet courageous Natives are noticeable in the number imprisoned during the late 1800s for vagrancy and the early 1900s for stealing horses and cattle (grand larceny) from

This Native from the Flathead Indian Reservation was arrested for burning down a reservation jail and confined at Montana State Prison in 1906. Courtesy of the Montana Historical Society, Helena.

white men, burning jails (arson), and neglecting to send children to school. Although the treaty specified that Natives could hunt, fish, and pick berries off the reservation boundaries, new settlers of indigenous land did not adhere to the treaty. Legally, Natives did not need a state hunting license; nevertheless, many Natives were arrested while hunting off the reservation during this period. On 15 September 1905, the *Daily Missoulian*, using common racist language of the day and citing that some Natives had passes to leave the reservation, reported,

> Big Mouth Charley, a Flathead brave, is now enjoying the hospitality of his "Great White Father" in the Ravalli county jail as a penalty for having . . . killed a total of 48 deer without a license. . . . He was sentenced to pay a fine of $25 or serve 21 days in the county jail. He had no money and is obliged to serve out his fine. He considers his sentence a holiday, however, and when taken to his cell said that it was just the place he was looking for. "Heap fire, heap grub, heap

blankets and nothing to do," said he. Several other bands of Flat-heads were encountered and held up for investigation. They all were able to show their licenses, however, and also their permits to leave the reservation.

Perhaps the insurgent "Big Mouth Charley" was simply playing the "dumb Indian" in an effort to further his resistance and regain his humanity.

During this period, many Natives, on the verge of starvation, were reduced to relying on government handouts or to leaving their reservations "illegally." In 1914 Natives at the Blackfeet Reservation, particularly those at Heart Butte, were starving to death. As late as 1928, the Atsina and Assiniboine at Fort Belknap, as well as the Blackfeet, were reported to be seriously malnourished (Bryan 1985). In a 1920 report presented to the U.S. Board of Indian Commissioners, Walter Camp argued that the problem with Indians ("savages") was that they were not capable of being self-sufficient (Hoxie 1984); their widespread poverty was seen as an internal deficiency. But the problem was not internal: Natives were no longer permitted to hunt and fish in their usual and accustomed places. Many transgressors were jailed, as "Big Mouth Charley" was.

ARREST THIS MAN WHEREVER FOUND

Wanted for Cattle Stealing.

Peter Little Plume wanted for cattle stealing on the Blackfeet Indian Reservation. He is a full blood Blackfeet or Piegan Indian, age 23 years. Height, 5 ft. 10¼ in.; weight, 140 pounds; slender build; brown complexion; black hair, smooth shaven; maroon eyes; nose rectilinear. El; M; M; M; shoes prison color from confinement. Wore black suit and light shirt. Tatooed flesh pierced with dagger 4¼ inches above left wrist front; small oval scar 1½ inches above right index finger, rear; scar 1½ inches horizontal just above larynx. Out angle of eyes elevated.

Bertillon measurements: 78.5—82.0—90.5—19.1—15.5—14.6—6.6—24.9 —11.2—8.9—48.6.

Peter Little Plume was released from the U. S. Penitentiary at Leavenworth, Kansas, Oct. 14th, 1916, was arrested shortly after his release along with Ed LaRue, William Boy Chief and Bob Albertson for cattle stealing. These men broke jail at Browning, Montana—LaRue, Boy Chief and Albertson have been recaptured. Little Plume is still at large and wanted. Arrest, hold and wire either

SUPT. C. L. ELLIS, Blackfeet Agency, Browning, Mont.
A. R. SELLARS, Stock Inspector, Havre, Mont.
FRANK C. LAVIGNE, Chief Stock Inspector, Helena, Mont.
Helena, Mont., Jan. 15th, 1917.

PETER LITTLE PLUME—ESCAPED PRISONER.

Frank Lavigne, Chief Stock Detective, issued a wanted poster in 1917 for twenty-three-year-old Peter Little Plume (Blackfeet) for stealing cattle. Courtesy of the Montana Historical Society, Helena.

MONTANA'S LANDLESS NATIVES:
A STORY OF DEFIANCE

In a time when we are all reminded of America's homeless population, we forget that the first homeless were indigenous people. Montana has a relatively large number of Landless Natives, descendants of indigenous people who were disenfranchised by the federal government: the Cree, Pembina Chippewa (Anishinabé) or Little Shell, and the Métis or Mitchif (mixed-blood). (According to Little Shell tribal member Bob Van Guten, "Most Little Shell, if not all, are Metis, and we don't really work at making a distinction" [Bryan 1985, 98].) Those Cree, Chippewa, and Métis without a reservation in Montana are known collectively as Landless.

The Métis initially came to Montana from the Red River country in Canada and the Assiniboine River country of North Dakota (Bryan 1985). The Pembina Chippewa came to Montana with some Métis and Cree from Turtle Mountain, North Dakota, and many settled at what came to be called Lewistown (Dusenberry 1958). While their relatives were barely surviving in oppressive accommodations at Turtle Mountain, by the 1880s the Montana Métis were nestled into the Judith Basin, which was rich with game. Many mixed-bloods who were followers of the famous Gabriel Dumont and Louis Riel, able mixed-blood resisters of colonization, fled to North Dakota and Montana after the Riel Rebellion of 1870 in Canada. Another Métis rebellion was staged in 1885, an outgrowth of provincial land policy in Canada, and Riel, at the solicitation of Dumont, led the revolt. Riel was eventually captured by the British and killed for treason, and Dumont returned to Lewistown (Dusenberry 1958). Some of the mixed-bloods, mainly Canadian Cree from the Red River country and Pembina Chippewa of North Dakota, were integrated on existing reservations in Montana, while other exiled Natives continued to wander the territory in search of food and shelter.

In 1882 the commissioner of Indian Affairs gave over nine million acres of Pembina land in North Dakota to white homesteaders. The Natives reserved for themselves a small landbase consisting of two townships. Turtle Mountain became an official reservation to thirty-one Chippewa and twelve hundred Métis (Dusenberry 1958). The extermination of a major food supply, the buffalo, propelled these Natives, like others in Montana, into "illegal" activity to survive. Indian agent John Cramsie warned of the consequences of starvation when he wrote of these Natives and their appalling conditions:

> If poverty and ignorance in abject form is to be found in this world, I know of no better place to seek it than among the half breeds of the Turtle Mountains. With but few exceptions, the half breeds have lived on the buffalo all their lives, and now that their means of subsistence have all disappeared, I cannot tell how they are to make a living without assistance. Fifty thousand dollars worth of stock and farming implements would hardly supply their wants, and without it they will starve or be compelled to steal. Unless generous aid and instruction are furnished these people, the near future will see our jails and penitentiaries filled to overflowing with their prolific rising generation. (Cramsie 1884; quoted in Dusenberry 1958, 33)

While Turtle Mountain Natives were reduced to stealing for their survival, another important element entered the picture: deciding who was truly Native and therefore entitled to be a resident at the Turtle Mountain Reservation. In 1890 the president of the United States designated a three-man commission to bargain with Turtle Mountain Natives for the termination of rights and removal to an approved settlement. The commission was also to ascertain the number of Chippewa and mixed-bloods qualified to receive government considerations (Dusenberry 1958). By this time, recognized traditional leader Little Shell and his followers were in Montana. In August of 1891 Little Shell proposed to the commissioner of Indian Affairs that they exchange Turtle Mountain for more prosperous land *near* the Fort Peck Indian Reservation in Montana (Dusenberry 1958). The offer was denied and the commissioner of Indian Affairs replied that there was sufficient land *on* the Fort Peck Indian Reservation in Montana for Little Shell and his band, if they desired to relocate.

Also in August of 1891, and perhaps not coincidentally, the Indian agent at Turtle Mountain selected thirty-two men, sixteen full-blood Chippewa and sixteen Métis, to represent the welfare of the Turtle Mountain Natives in their negotiations with the federal government. Additionally, in another example of indirect rule, the Indian agent handpicked five members of the committee, both Chippewa and Métis, to expunge names of individuals who were not qualified to participate. This resulted in 525 Native people taken off the rolls (Dusenberry 1958).

The presidential commission arrived at Turtle Mountain in 1892, two years after its inception. Little Shell objected to the easy erasure of so many people from the rolls and made a plea for those who had been in Montana searching for food and subsequently deleted from the register. Nevertheless, the presidential commission stated that only the committee selected by the Indian agent would be received and duly heard. The commission published the list of enrolled Natives and was to give a copy to Little Shell's attorney, a Métis, but elected simply to post it on the church doors. Furthermore, Little Shell's attorney received a letter from the Indian agent announcing that he, the attorney, was not recognized as an authority, and all Natives not on the list were instructed to leave the reservation immediately (Dusenberry 1958). Little Shell was astonished at the agreement and immediately issued a protest to federal officials. He heard nothing for six years. In the end, the enrolled Turtle Mountain Chippewa and Métis agreed to withdraw their claim to the 9,500,000 acres at Turtle Mountain. In return, the federal government offered to pay them one million dollars; hence, the transaction became known as the "ten-cent treaty."

As Little Shell fought for the rights of his people, exclusionary laws—also active in other regions of the United States—were implemented against indigenous people in Montana. White people in Montana, as well as the governor of the newly created state, pressured Congress to deport all of Montana's Landless Native population to Canada. In 1896 U.S. troops swept up 537 Landless Natives and sent them, some in cattlelike fashion in railroad boxcars and others on foot for 258 miles, to a supposed secure landbase in Canada (Bryan 1985). Once across the imaginary border into Canada, Cree leader Little Bear was promptly arrested for participating in the Riel Rebellion. Little Bear was ultimately released, and, recognizing that the pledged reserve was a ploy, he and the expelled Natives returned to Montana.

Remembering his people and their fight against the federal government, Little Shell sent his attorney a letter in 1898 reaffirming that he would never sign the ten-cent treaty. A worn-out yet persistent Little Shell wrote,

> The chief, Little Shell here speaks: We are tired, fatigue since so long waiting for the settlement of our claims. Even though we are

fatigue, we keep strong—firm—to stay by you and your efforts in our cause. . . . In regard to the affairs and doings of the three commissioners—the ten-cent treaty commissioners—we are very much troubled in here about it; but I repeat to you here again . . . that I would never sign their affairs, the ten-cent treaty; I am all the same yet and now. My greatest fatigue is to see my people so poor and going hungry. (quoted in Dusenberry 1958, 36)

Years rolled by as the Turtle Mountain Natives waited for the settlement from the federal government. Twelve years after the presidential commission submitted its report in 1904, Congress finally ratified the treaty.[5] Still, the question of where to put the Turtle Mountain Natives loomed, because they had ceded the majority of their land to the federal government. Written into the treaty was a provision that they would receive land that was "vacant" or could homestead on "public domain" (Dusenberry 1958). In 1906 549 people filed for settlements on public land in Montana and North Dakota. Nevertheless, the next year the commissioner of Indian Affairs reported that there were over 1,300 Natives without land and, displaying Euro-American economics, that "protests have been made against their taking so much of the public domain in these states, because the lands will remain untaxable as long as they are held in trust by the government" (Leupp 1907; quoted in Dusenberry 1958, 37).

The Montana Métis continued to encounter grim circumstances in Montana: game was scarce, the land had been taken by state and federal governments and white homesteaders, and their existing homes had been burned (Dusenberry 1958). Some settled on established reservations in Montana, but most suffered as the poorest of the poor and were greatly discriminated against by whites and other Natives.

Reservations were created in Montana in the mid- to late 1800s, although the Chippewa and Cree were not assigned a landbase until 1916. This tiny reservation, Rocky Boy's, was designed to take only a small number of applicants; consequently, some Natives were still homeless. Those deemed ineligible for enrollment were mainly Little Shell Chippewa and Métis, who became known as "garbage can Indians" because they roamed the state in search of cast-off food and clothing (Bryan 1985, 99). Many Cree who allied with the Canadian Métis were eventually granted amnesty and placed on Rocky Boy's Reservation (Dusenberry 1958).

Residents at existing reservations were reluctant to share their land-base with the Landless Natives, and unquestionably white communities did not want them. In 1927, in an effort to gain federal recognition, Joseph Dussome organized a group called "The Abandoned Band of Chippewa Indians" (Dusenberry 1958), later renamed "The Landless Indians of Montana." During the Depression years of the 1930s, the government promised to secure 37,000 acres near Box Elder for the Landless. The government, however, did not live up to the agreement and resolved that the land in question belonged to the Rocky Boy's Reservation. Also during the 1930s, the government considered land near Great Falls as a possible home for the Landless. The white citizens of Great Falls, however, greatly protested, and the dream of an uncontested landbase again eluded the despondent Natives. During the early 1940s, a government resettlement plan emerged (Dusenberry 1958). In this scheme the government pledged to buy land in Phillips County for the Landless, yet when World War II erupted the arrangement was forsaken for more "serious" efforts. By the mid-1950s, citizens of Great Falls initiated efforts to give land to these Natives. Nevertheless, the federal government refused their noble efforts, citing plans to terminate Indian reservations and stating that the project of donating land was inconsistent with their own of the dissolution of tribally owned land (Bryan 1985).

Although all Natives in Montana were in dire need, the Landless were extraordinarily distressed. Without a landbase and accompanying authority, the destitution was as relentless as it was overpowering. For instance, in 1941 five children starved to death at Hill 57 (Bryan 1985), the dismal community near Great Falls where many had settled. On 11 February 1957, the *Great Falls Tribune* reported that the poverty of the Landless was so severe that state citizens sent Senator James E. Murray a petition to aid them. The newspaper reported that previous efforts in 1955 by Senator Mike Mansfield had been defeated because the federal government claimed that the Landless Natives were not their responsibility.

In the 1990s, as in the past, Landless Native Americans—the non-reservation indigenous of Montana—seek the federal recognition they are denied, although they are commonly accepted by the state of Montana and have always been acknowledged by other tribes. The thirty-seven hundred enrolled Landless Natives in Montana have a formal tribal government and continue to pursue federal recognition, which would give them access to government services and grants that other tribes enjoy.[6] They likewise continue their quest of securing a landbase, an Indian reservation, in Montana.

CONTEMPORARY RACIALIZED MONTANA

The land represents a profound symbol, as well as a reality, to Native people. The importance of a landbase is interwoven with the feelings Natives have regarding tribal sovereignty: to be sovereign is to have authority, responsibility for the land. Winona LaDuke and Ward Churchill remind us that land has always been central to North American economics and politics: "Those who control the land are those who control the resources. . . . Some hold that if fraud were removed from land dealings, Indians would still legally own America" (1985, 107–108). The indigenous economy was destroyed through policy, particularly the reservation system, and Natives were reduced to paupers relying on the federal government for survival (Ortiz 1980). Most Natives, whether acculturated or traditional, whether reservation, urban, or Landless, are concerned with tribal sovereignty. Sovereignty is a fragile concept as well as a shaky reality, and it is continually redefined by Natives working with each other in their struggles to maintain Native American nations.

Social Darwinism, Manifest Destiny, the white man's burden, survival of the fittest—all assumptions of white superiority were used to justify the ill treatment and outright robbery of Native people. Albeit some may argue that these notions are not blatantly racist, the attitude behind them clearly illustrates a racialized assumption that was transmitted in federal, state, and local policy toward Native people. Most significantly, these kinds of racism, essentialist and colonial, became complex as times changed and surfaced with zeal in twentieth-century attitudes toward Native people.

Colonialism emphasizes differential power that encompasses social, cultural, political, and economic realms. Unequal distribution and control were initially established by force, as evidenced in the historical overview, but now, in the twentieth century, they are institutionalized. Under both the old and new colonialism, Native people are forced to subsist in impossible conditions, and many are homeless in their own country. In Montana, as elsewhere, Native people remain socially, culturally, politically, and economically oppressed.

Couched in assimilationist rhetoric, racialized events—including treaties, reservations and pass systems, land allotments, boarding schools, and bans on Native religions—influence who Native people are today. An understanding of the dynamics between Natives and whites is important if one is to truly grasp the experiences of Native Americans in the Euro-American criminal justice system. Most whites in Montana view Native people as profane. The social distance is immense between these ethnic groups in all parts, although it is more observable at the Flathead Reservation (because of the large white population and PL 280) and among the Landless, who typically live off Indian reservations. Everyday interactions involve rules of propriety that effectively regulate the degree of social distance. For instance, on the Flathead Reservation there are separate bars, schools, museums, newspapers, churches, and so forth for Natives and whites. The segregation, although invisible to outsiders, is glaring in its oppressiveness. History describes the evolution of colonial and neocolonial racism in Montana, made structurally complex by federal and state policy and further complicated by individual attitudes. This complexity is made clearer as we journey through the dynamics of Native-white interaction.

Albert Memmi (1965) explains that one consequence of a colonizer/colonized relationship is "colonial racism." Colonial racism is built from cultural differences, in conjunction with exploitation, and is dependent upon racism because it is the basic relationship that ties the colonizer to the colonized. The differences between the groups are used as standards of absolute fact, with the culture of the colonizer upheld as the ideal. The result is a systematic devaluation of the colonized, which entails the objectification of a people and the perpetuation of stereotypes. Indeed, Natives have been reduced to a dichotomous image: the good Indian and the bad Indian. Good Indians, the silent ones, know their place; bad Indians are shiftless, savage, drunk, immoral, dumb, criminal.

White people attempt to project and defend images of themselves as competent and unblemished, often implicitly (and sometimes explicitly) at the expense of Native Americans. Natives, therefore, continually face condemnation from their white neighbors in nearly all spheres. For instance, many whites in Montana hold the belief that many Natives are lazy and unreliable. Stigmatizing produces racialized interaction. Some

Natives attempt to hide their supposed failings and, as Erving Goffman proposes (1963), cope with the stigma of being Native by covering their Nativeness. Part of the purpose of this process is to win the acceptance of white people by acculturating, as best they can, into the Euro-American world where they will be transformed into "good Indians." Furthermore, because some Native people have internalized whites' impression of them, they frequently feel ambivalent about themselves and other Natives.

Many of those perceived as profane continually labor toward acceptance. We all know some Natives who work exceedingly hard at becoming especially good white people, unwittingly playing to racist attitudes. Some Natives react so powerfully to the Indian of the white imagination that they become more "white" than whites actually are (Lopez n.d.). Memmi (1965) refers to this, in the context of colonialism, as the colonized imitating their oppressors. He suggests that some place themselves in a superior position to other members of their racial/ethnic group and are fooled into accepting the inequalities of their social position. While assimilationists (for example, Gordon 1964) term this "identificational assimilation," Memmi is clear in his meaning and intent when he labels the same behavior "colonized mentality." The oppressed imitate their oppressors to escape persecution, to escape the label of Other.

Internalized oppression is incessant in Native communities, which suffer every social ill possible, with high rates of substance abuse, homicide, domestic violence, and poverty, to name a few. The etiology of the anger, frustration, and violence behind these problems is debatable. Some Native scholars (for example, Allen 1986, Holm 1992, Jaimes and Halsey 1992) believe that the internalized brutality, the warring against members of our own communities rather than the "real" enemy, is an unfortunate byproduct of colonialism. Because of institutionalized racism, the "real" enemy is, by now, invisible.

Another avenue open to Native people in their struggle to manage racialized attitudes is to withdraw and seek self-definition within their Native communities. According to Cooley: "Mortification, resentment, jealousy, the fear of disgrace and failure . . . are exhausting passions; and it is after a severe experience of them that retirement seems most healing and desirable" (1964, 250). This withdrawal from the Euro-American world is distinctly different from Goffman's notion of covering (discussed above) because it does not involve acknowledgment of Euro-

American values. That is, covering of Native ways happens because of the possibility for embarrassment; withdrawal involves the admission that what is perceived as Native is preferable over what is viewed as white (Braroe 1975).

Native people sometimes respond to discrimination with great resiliency and adopt a variety of strategies to combat oppression. The reactions to being defined as profane are as varied as Native individuals are. For instance, one response to being defined as morally inferior is an act of subtle, invisible resistance. One can display what appears to whites, but not necessarily to Natives, as laziness and irresponsibility. This is an age-old strategy that has been employed by people of all racial/ethnic backgrounds when they are viewed as the Other. Natives will represent themselves to whites as the sort of person whites expect them to be, and will present themselves to other Natives as something quite different— much as "Big Mouth Charley" might have been toying with the police in Missoula. This process is similar to African Americans who don the Sambo mask. The "real" African American or Native is invisible. As described by Ralph Ellison,

> I am an invisible man. . . . That visibility to which I refer occurs because of a peculiar disposition of the eyes of those with whom I come in contact. A matter of the construction of their inner eyes, those eyes with which they look through their physical eyes upon reality. I am not complaining, nor am I protesting either. It is sometimes advantageous to be unseen. . . . I remember that I am invisible and walk softly so as not to waken the sleeping ones. . . . I learned in time, though, that it is possible to carry on a fight against them without their realizing it. (1953, 7–9)

In Goffman's terms, backstage, Natives "drop the front" and "the impression fostered by the performance is knowingly contradicted as a matter of course" (1959, 112). According to Braroe (1975), Native people use much humor, and whites are teasingly depicted as naive and gullible. In their effort to get along, Natives capably perform "the dumb Indian." In this way, by conning whites, Natives can maintain their integrity and save face with other Natives.

Negative images, hideous stereotypes, run rampant in Montana, influencing how Natives are perceived and treated by whites and other Natives. The stereotype of the drunken Indian, fueled by anthropological and sociological research (for example, see May 1977), abounds in the United States and is alive and well in Montana.[7] As in the nineteenth century, Natives are still viewed as irresponsible, childlike, "drunken Injuns." Note the following letter from Robert McConkey, dated 27 March 1974, and addressed to the attorney general:

> I read all the articles on "Bloody 93" [Highway 93]. . . . I have never seen the biggest cause of accidents on "93" publicied at any time. As you well know the "Bloody 93" is right through the Flathead Indian Res. The cause of a big percentage of the fatal accidents [is] "Drunk Injuns." I would like to have the actual percentage that are caused by drunks but I know it is big. I would also like to know the percentage of Indians killed on all of our highways in Montana. I am sure it is a much higher percentage than whites per capita. (McConkey 1974)

Another example is illustrative of neocolonial racism in Montana. In 1969 a Blackfeet woman requested a loan to purchase cattle. The following letter was written by Barney Reagan, from the Montana Legal Services Association, to attorney Don Marble. The letter addressed the proposed loan, the operation of repayment, cattle programs on the Blackfeet Reservation, and the perceived irresponsibility of "drunken Indians":

> The only comment that I have Don is, and I believe that it strikes at the heart of the problem, the stupidity of some of the loan boards in giving these loans originally. As I have observed the situation many of these loans are given to people that have no more ability to take care of a bunch of cattle than I do in flying to the moon. . . . As a practical matter the first things that one of these young people do is go out and but [sic] a pick-up, a big hat, and a pair of boots, a horse and a silver mounted saddle. The horse and the silver mounted saddle are never used and the big hat and the pair of boots are just used to separate one end of the individual from the other while they run the imaginary cattle up and down the local bar. The pick-up is parked outside. This is my impression of what a majority of these loans are used for. . . . I feel, and it is my impression on the Blackfeet Indian Reservation that you have to [sic] many cowboys. . . . I have taken the liberty of copying your letter to me and am going

to attach a copy of this letter to it and am sending it to the Credit Office of the Bureau of Indian Affairs at the Blackfeet Indian Agency. I would appreciate it if they would give me some sort of a comment on this. (Reagan 1969)

A response Reagan wanted and a response was issued; however, I doubt it was the one he expected to receive. The reply strikes at the heart of the disrespect shown toward the Blackfeet; that, indeed, Reagan did not view their council as a "serious" authority or governing body invested with intellect and power. In a lengthy and poignantly worded letter, Tom Cobell, member of the Blackfeet Credit Committee, wrote to Reagan and reminded him that Montana Natives would no longer tolerate the "dumb Indian" image:

> . . . I consider this a personal attack upon my judgement as a member of this Committee, other members who have and are now serving on the committee, the Tribal Councils who have appointed these members, and an indication of the ability of these credit committees and council members as well as an indication of your regard for the ability of many of our loan clients. . . . But again let me repeat, I feel a letter of the kind you wrote to Mr. Marble . . . is an indication of your lack of familiarity with the Government of the Blackfeet Tribe and an indication of the low-esteem—bordering on ridicule—you have for duly constituted Tribal programs of the Tribe in general. . . . Perhaps in spite of your low regard for our intelligence, we may be able to further the best interests of the Blackfeet Tribe. . . . No attempt is made to correct the typographical errors or misspelled words in the attached letters copied from the Xerox copies you sent to the Credit Office at the Blackfeet Agency. . . . (Cobell 1969)

NATIVES EXERCISE SOVEREIGNTY, WHITES REACT

During the 1960s Native people nationwide began publicly to assert their political clout, bolstered by various congressional acts and court decisions, and white people generally responded disapprovingly. So, too, in Montana we witnessed a movement of insurgency, as Native people redefined who they were. Although people in power do not respond to people out of power any more than necessary, events were changing the landscape of Native-white relations. Many white people on Montana reservations were overwhelmed with the degree of authority tribes were politically expressing. Natives were no longer "good Indians" confined to their reservations, and local whites responded with racialized hatred as Native people resisted colonialism and exerted their rights of sovereignty.

It was a wonderfully liberating time for many, but not for whites who were afraid of the power Native people were amassing. In their search for sovereignty, one of the initial steps the Confederated Salish and Kootenai took was to require a small yearly fee from those recreating on tribal lands. Racialized outrage was the response, mainly expressed by white locals. Note the language and attitudes expressed in the following letter, where Natives are viewed as children irresponsibly squandering government money. Written by Wesley Leishman in 1969 and addressed to Montana's attorney general, the letter additionally communicated that the silent, "good Indian" was gone:

> For the past few months, we have heard nothing but the cries of the Indians on the Flathead Indian Reservation. Poverty, discrimination, their rights denied, to name a few. We feel it is time to tell the other side of the story. We, as non-Indians, on this reservations, pay extremely high property taxes. We have never discriminated when hiring help on our farm. Our only requirement is that they will stay with us and finish the job, and put out the same effort any freshman in high school can. The problem we have had with the Indians we have hired is that they don't come back if they have any money to spend. We are getting a little tired of our federal tax money being poured in here through O.E.O. [Office of Economic Opportunity] and other programs, and being administered and mis-used by the Indians. Now, they are asking us to pay $5 a person to "set foot on their land".... There are 2,400 people who claim to be Indians, some have no Indian blood, living on this reservation. In the last 3 or 4 years, there has been approximately $9 million pumped in here through various federal programs, and administered by the Tribal Council or the B.I.A. Over and above this, they have the commod-

ity program, with much of this food being either thrown or traded away. This reservation was ready for termination 20 years ago, long before all these federal funds were being pumped in here, and has been going down hill steadily since. There are only 8 full blood Indians left, and they deserve to be taken care of for the rest of their lives. . . . After being born and raised on this reservation, for the first time in our lives we are being pitted against people we have been friends with. By this I mean that until now we were not Indian and non-Indian. Now this is fast becoming the case, and it is getting worse all the time. . . . (Leishman 1969)

Letters of the same ilk, complete with the how-dare-they-after-all-we've-done-for-them attitude, can be found in the archives. These "irresponsible" Natives were and are frequently asked to work the fields or tend livestock, and for very little money, for local white landowners. Although history tells us the land rightfully belongs to the Natives, Natives are now the laborers rather than the proprietors, thanks to the punishing policies of the nineteenth century. Perhaps General Sherman was right after all when he declared in 1867: "[Indians] all have to be killed or be maintained as a species of paupers" (quoted in O'Brien 1989, 63). In fact, unemployment on Montana's reservations ranges from 27 percent at Flathead to 79 percent at Fort Belknap (Office of the Coordinator of Indian Affairs 1987). Nationally, unemployment rates on reservations range from 50 percent to 90 percent (Bachman 1992). The gendering of unemployment is revealed in the fact that since 1959, Native women continue to earn half of the salary of white males (Sandefur 1991).

The new racism is demonstrated in white property owners' demand for "equal" rights, a situation that illustrates white resentment of Native economic and political clout. In this type of equal rights, whites benefit financially and Natives are pushed farther into poverty. White people in Indian Country typically present themselves as innocent victims when tribal governments assert their sovereign powers (Limerick 1987). Behold the following quarter-page advertisement, paid for by a group known as The Lake County Coin Operators Association (apparently feeling victimized by the Confederated Salish and Kootenai Tribes). The alarmist ad, which appeared in the *Missoulian* on 16 June 1993 (C3), brazenly borrowed from both a slogan of the Revolutionary War and the statement about Nazi Germany attributed to Pastor Martin Niemoeller. It claimed to speak for reservation residents but was obviously directed at non-Natives only.

> ATTENTION: FLATHEAD RESERVATION RESIDENTS
> WHO WILL BE LEFT TO STAND UP FOR YOU?
> First, the tribe came for our docks. Nobody stood up to fight and now we all pay taxes for our docks. Then, they came for the recreationalists. Nobody stood up to fight and now we have to pay taxes to hunt, fish, and recreate on our own lands. Next, they came for the farmers and irrigators. Now they're fighting an uphill battle. Now, they are coming for 60% of the gaming operators' revenue. If you don't stand up and fight now, who is going to be left to fight when they come for your income? Are you next, Mr. Retailer or Ms. Homeowner?
> NO TAXATION WITHOUT REPRESENTATION
> SAY NO TO THE SALISH AND KOOTENAI TRIBES
> Please write your congressman and your local government officials (including Tribal Council) and let them know how you feel about the minority rule that is being imposed upon us.

Other letters from 1969 evinced that local whites had already formally organized against the notion of tribal sovereignty. The following letter, written by Lewis Palmer in 1969 to the attorney general, addressed the fee charged by the tribes for recreational purposes and the Ranger Program in charge of collecting the fees:

> We as F.R.E.E. members are taking action by writing letters regarding the policies and activities of the Reservation Ranger Program under the supervision of Tom Swaney. . . . Listed briefly are suggested points to be made. . . . Our tax dollars are being used to promote poor race relations. . . . Ownership by the Tribe has never been established. . . . 82% of the reservation population is non-Indian. 18% of the reservation population is Indian. The rates being charged are exorbitant. The tourist trade is offended when asked to pay the fee and resents being overcharged. Our economy is being hurt, a grievance we cannot control nor stop. The authority of the Rangers is not justified as a law enforcement agency. . . . (Palmer 1969)

Sensing that not enough was being done to keep Natives in their place, and clearly unaware of the Natives' legal and social status, Josephine White sent the following letter to the Attorney General in 1973. The letter was accompanied by 1,162 signatures and signed by the secretary of a group of Montanans called Citizens Against Discrimination.

We enclose a copy of a petition and signers for your consideration in hopes you will be sufficiently interested in justice and equality among American Citizens to take some definite action. On the eve of another "so called" Independence Day, we are saddened by the fact that in less than 200 years the independence our forefathers fought and died to establish has been "sold down the drain" by many of the men and women we helped to elect. By continuing to subsidize the Indians they have became a group of out and out free loaders wanting their handouts and all the privileges of American Citizens and none of the responsibilities. The situation is now crucial. We can no longer afford to keep still but will be forced to vote against any man or woman who votes for continued handouts for the Indians. We will also be forced to take any other action deemed necessary to remain free citizens. We are, too, from many proud races—English, Irish, Scotch, French, German, etc. We, too, are proud of our heritages, but we have learned to keep our dead buried and live today and not yesterday. May we have a personal answer? (White 1973)

Citizens Against Discrimination evidently resolved that the push for tribal sovereignty infringed upon their rights, and they call Native people "free loaders." The group issued a strong warning to all elected officials, possibly affecting state policies toward Natives, who were a numerical minority in the state and not a strong political bloc.

Another letter, referring specifically to *Moe v. The Confederated Salish and Kootenai Tribes* (1976), was sent by Earl Johnston to the attorney general's office in 1976. Although quite lengthy and riddled with errors, it deserves to be read in its entirety because it offers an excellent example of the racialized malice Native people faced on Flathead. Natives are not seen as "real," and a manufactured image of the hardworking, tax-paying white citizen is contrasted with the image of the lazy Indian, continually dependent upon the government dole. The author, reminiscent of the nineteenth century, ends on a frightening proposal calling for violence. In his letter, he issues a call for "a full scale war":

To say the least I was greatly appauled at the decession of the Supreme court last week. I was not aware until then that these people in the United States who were souverin and warrented being considered a special case or situation, or aggangement by the Federal Government. In case you have forgotten the Federal Government is us, the people, tax payers who pay your wages. . . . When most of the Indians on the Flathead Reservation are so light complected you can't tell them from the non Indians, how in the Hell will the vendors of tax free materials (cigaretts, gasoline, and liquor, yess this is in the plan also, know weather he is selling to Indian or white men? If an Indian don't pay tax on his care, fine: give him, or better yet let the tribe issue an Indian head plate that is leagal on the reservation but not off of it. I am a tax payer and I want to let the rest of the people know who is paying the bill and who is not. There is discrimination in other areas also. These Indians sell you a tribal permitt, and then post signs on the roads which white taxes built that say CLOSED TO MOTORCYCLES AND SNOWMOBILS of non tribal members only. Bleve me this is hurting out tourist trade, our sale of realstate in the area. I am not a member of Mod [Montanans Opposed to Discrimination] yet, but Friday May 7 at the annial meeting I plan to try to start a petetion to call for a tax strike on the reservation to commence immediately. . . . We are all getting sick of having half of our wages taken away every payday for tax, and then pay out the rest at the end of the year for taxes on personal property, while the Indian across the road refuses to take a jobe even because he is living so well on commodities I pay for. Also I prepose a law suit against the Federal Government, which again is us, but more of us all over the land, for the largest amout that can be put in figures for miss representing this reservation land to us when they opened it to settlers with the promis the reservation would be disbanded, and then turning around and giving it ot a bunch of 2 droppers. If the above fails I then will call for a full scale war against every Indian whoes name appears on the tribal rolls or even claims to be an Indian and every white who sleeps with one. (Johnston 1976)

The above letter also commented on the official, supposedly legal opening of the reservation during the early part of the twentieth century, in addition to a court case that exempted tribal members from paying state taxes on cigarettes (*Moe v. The Confederated Salish and Kootenai Tribes*). The attorney general, agreeing with many non-Natives' position on taxes, responded to the above letter with a call for additional legislative action against tribes:

> As you know my office worked long and hard on this law suit. I used every legal argument possible in my attempt to have the judiciary hold that reservation Indians are legally and morally obligated to pay taxes for personal property purchased and used on the reservation. The courts held contra to my position. I believe that the only recourse the state and its citizens have now is to urge Congress to enact new legislation that would cure these alleged inequities. I urge you to contact our congressional delegation. (Woodahl 1976)

Montanans Opposed to Discrimination (MOD) sprang up on Flathead during the early 1970s. Steadfastly opposed to tribal rights and sovereignty, they continued their age-old battle of controlling Native land into the succeeding decades and recently changed their name to All Citizens Equal (ACE). This group and other similar ones are numerous in Montana and continue into the 1990s in opposition to Native nations and their battle for indigenous rights.[8]

Another letter raised the issue of Natives' waste of government money and the notion that Native right to landownership on reservations had never been resolved. Moreover, the author of the letter, similar to others, questioned the authority of tribal law enforcement at the Fort Belknap Reservation—a common misperception among local whites. The following, written to Montana's attorney general in 1974 by a justice of the peace, claimed that tribal police were not "real" police officers:

> A situation has recently arisen in the Fort Belknap–Harlem area that is causing me some concern. The Fort Belknap Tribal Police have taken it upon themselves to enforce traffic laws on the reservation against non-Indians by issuing violators a form of the Uniform Traffic Ticket and Complaint. . . . The tribal police expect me to handle such tickets in the same manner as those issued by the Sher-

iffs Department or the Highway Patrol. It is my feeling that the tribal police are not "peace officers" within the meaning of R.C.M. 95–210 and therefore not authorized to accept bond or to issue notices to appear. (Miller 1974)

Colonial domination disempowers Native people, and systems of control are clearly visible in policy and law. In the time of the popular *Bell Curve* (Herrnstein and Murray 1994) controversy and the proposed relationship between race, class, and intelligence, we are reminded that it was decades ago when Frantz Fanon (1963) argued that those colonized are imaged as biologically inferior and their culture deficient. Nevertheless, the process of colonialism prompts the colonized to assert themselves in their struggle for dignity. Built into colonialism is the dialectic between oppression and resistance. Although Fanon viewed the struggle as a violent one because colonialism itself was founded and maintained on violence, Native people in the twentieth century typically did not engage in violent acts.

Combating white oppression and racism, racial/ethnic groups in the United States began to mobilize in the 1960s and 1970s. One such effort was the American Indian Movement (AIM). Although I agree with Gerald Vizenor that many AIM leaders can be defined as "kitschymen of tribal manners" (1994, 42),[9] this Pan-Indian political movement did mobilize and energize many Native Americans. No longer were Natives "dumb little Indians"; now they were decolonizing, redefining, renaming who they were as individuals and as a collective.

The early 1970s in Montana offered an opportunity for political Pan-Indianism, as the Red Power groups emerged throughout the United States. Although Montana was slow to feel the effects, a few Natives from Montana were involved in the American Indian Movement. As with other recuperative actions on behalf of Natives, white locals initially reacted with astonishment and then fear. Consider the following letter written by Lake County Attorney Richard Heinz in 1973 and sent to Governor Thomas Judge. Heinz expressed his concern over PL 280 and suggested that perhaps the practice of incarcerating numerous Natives in Montana institutions would provoke the dreaded American Indian Movement to organize in Montana:

Sheriff William A. (Bill) Phillips and I share a concern over reports we have received recently which suggest that members of the American Indian Movement (A.I.M.) may be contemplating a demonstration in Lake County similar to those being staged in South Dakota. The reports we have received are unsubstantiated, but they come from responsible and reliable sources including Federal officers. We understand that two of the local Federal officers, Mr. Vance Curtiss and Mr. Vern Erickson, Juvenile Probation Officers of the Bureau of Indian Affairs have been briefed at Billings recently concerning the affairs at Custer and Rapid City, South Dakota. These men are not alarmist. As you know, most of our County is included within the Flathead Indian Reservation and we are the only County in our State which has been given jurisdiction over Indians in criminal and certain civil matters including juvenile delinquency and dependent and neglected children matters. As a consequence, we have a relatively high number of commitments of Tribal members to Montana State Prison and to State agencies handling juveniles such as the Montana Children's Center at Twin Bridges [orphanage], the Pine Hills School for Boys [reform school] and the Mountain View School for Girls [reform school]. The availability of these rehabilitative facilities has been of tremendous benefit to the Confederated Salish and Kootenai Tribes, and I believe that a majority of the members of the Tribal Council are grateful that such facilities are available to Indian use. On the other hand, Mr. Vance Curtiss has been unduly criticized for the number of children and youth who have been placed in these State agencies; he believes that this is at least one of the factors which could lead the A.I.M group to focus attention on the Flathead Indian Reservation. . . . It is reported to us that the A.I.M. group proposes to enlist enrollees of the Kicking Horse Center [Indian job corps] in their proposed activities here on the Flathead Reservation. I trust and believe that the supervisory personnel of the Center are alert to this possibility and that they will take such reasonable measures as are possible to forestall an organized demonstration or take-over of the camp by the A.I.M. group. Sheriff Phillips and I are informed that one of the defendants in our pending criminal calendar . . . is himself a member of the A.I.M. group. He is charged with Attempted Robbery and Sheriff Phillips feels that his trial may be made into an occasion for a militant demonstration against our State authority. . . . At this time we would like to establish a line of communication with your office and with the office of the Attorney General as head of the Highway Patrol in order to effectively mobilize the assistance which the Sheriff of Lake County would need in the event that serious disturbances do occur here on the Flathead Reservation. . . . We believe that some organized response to Sheriff Phillip's request should be planned immediately. . . . Should matters become more serious, we would approach your office for the assistance of the Montana National Guard. . . . We assure you that it is our intention to do our best to keep the peace here and protect the persons and property of the residents of this County from violance [*sic*], should it occur. . . . (Heinz 1973)

The above letter is reminiscent of the telegram to General Ruger in 1889 that demanded the arming of white citizens because of the supposedly imminent Native revolt, and of the letter from the acting commissioner to the secretary of the interior asking, "Shall I call for troops if prospect of an uprising." The letter from Heinz was reactionary and alarmist, and his worries proved to be unfounded. Although there were a few peaceful protest marches, there was no violent uprising. No "savages" on the warpath here; rather, Natives were fighting their battles in courtrooms and classrooms.

Other counties were equally reactionary in their response to the anticipated Indian uprising of Montana Natives under AIM guidance. Four months later, written after Heinz's letter regarding Flathead, a letter from Glacier County Attorney John P. Moore (1973) was sent to the U.S. district attorney and the Federal Bureau of Investigation regarding an expected "insurrection" on the Blackfeet Reservation. The letter conveyed that there were "indications" that a "planned insurrection by the AIM group" would take place in the Browning and on the Blackfeet Indian Reservation around their annual social gathering in July. Again, resources were requested to "put down any trouble that comes up."

Responding to exceedingly high push-out rates,[10] another way for Native people to combat the psychological consequences of neocolonial racism was to focus on educational needs. What was needed was a self-esteem-building formula: a decolonized education for Native people. As early as 1968, Native people in Montana were observant of the educational system and its impact on Native children. In the March bulletin of the State of Montana's Department of Indian Affairs, tribal leaders reported that "the white man's school system, by trying to impose an alien culture on their children, was driving the children to alcoholism and suicide. They [tribal leaders] wanted a voice in running the schools to teach Indian culture, not just a lot of unattainable white middleclass values" (1968, 1).

The state was slow to respond; nevertheless, in 1977, in a reply to an increasingly tense climate between Natives and whites, Montana nobly passed a law (Revised Codes of Montana, 1947) that required public school teachers on or near Indian reservations to expand their knowledge of Native cultures by taking a mere six hours of Native American studies by July 1979. Although the law was quickly wiped from the books, [11] it prompted a fury of criticism from white schoolteachers, as evidenced by the following letter. Written by Ron Wall and Monty Cranston in 1977, the letter was addressed to Senator John Melcher:

> We believe this law is in violation of our rights both as Montana
> residents and as United States citizens. First, in the total of 12 years
> of teaching here, we have had about 3 children who you could call
> full-blooded Indians (or even half). . . . The present white guilt
> complex concerning Indians is no more edifying than the past
> "dirty savage" stereotype of the 19th century. An appreciation
> for Indian culture *should not, nor cannot* be legislated. Why stop at
> Indian Studies? How about Mexican Studies? (Many more of that
> race reside in Billings). The State of Montana justifies this law on
> grounds that these local school districts are eligible for federal funds.
> We submit that the federal trusteeship (or continued dependency)
> of Indians on the federal government is *not* justification for a state
> policy. We all know too well the terrible inadequacies of continued
> federal dependency. The culture of Indians now on reservations is
> hardly pure Indian Culture as would be required for us to teach.
> The current Indian life style has been destroyed by, among other
> things, the B.I.A. and other federal government agencies. Tying
> our education up to long misguided notions of guilt-ridden legis-
> lation is foolish . . . and will never *really* help the Indian gain the
> respect, self worth, and independence he seeks (and deserves). . . .
> Problems arising because Montana Indians feel their culture is
> being slighted are not in keeping with the 14th amendment and
> clearly take away our rights if we are forced to learn about them to

keep our jobs. In the long run, feeling will be against the Indian, not with them. . . . (Wall and Cranston 1977; emphasis in original)

In the above letter, the authors state that their rights were violated because of the law, although they did not mention the rights of Native Americans. Moreover, according to these schoolteachers, the violation of white rights would only intensify racism. The teachers also charged that "real" Natives were nonexistent and, therefore, Native students would not recognize the "real Indian culture" they were to teach. Again, as always, the issue of Native dependency upon the government surfaced.

Braroe (1975) suggests that many whites criticize Natives for not being sufficiently Native, and this holds true in Montana today. In this vein, many whites regard Natives as culturally impoverished because they fail to maintain their traditions. The assumption, based on white superiority, is that whites know what Native traditions are and Natives do not. At the same time, whites criticize Natives for not being adequately white. Natives are many times placed in these no-win situations, and whites, accordingly, are free to assert their own moral superiority over Natives and thereby justify their behavior and attitudes. Many whites do not understand Native cultures and ensuing behaviors; therefore, stereotypes and misinterpretation are rampant.

Natives continue to use education to decolonize, and their efforts continue to be thwarted. In present-day Montana, some white parents at the Flathead Reservation removed their children from a class on Native Americans, charging that an "unAmerican" curriculum was offered (Julie Cajune, personal communication 1995). A cultural diversity and substance abuse conference, planned by Crow students at Hardin and coordinated by the Native American students and the Crow Tribal Housing Authority, was easily transposed into ugly neocolonial racism when no white students attended: 150 white students reportedly received permission from their parents not to attend the event (McCracken 1995). A week later, seemingly in an effort to escalate already existing racialized tension, Ku Klux Klan literature was left in various places around Hardin.[12]

Alvin Josephy Jr. (1984) proposes that racialized stereotypes found in the past continue to affect whites' treatment of Native people. Present-day Montana offers an abundance of such racialized treatment firmly based upon the history of Native-white relations. For example, the Confederated Salish and Kootenai Tribes recently proposed to the federal government that they manage the National Bison Range, which is located within reservation boundaries. A public meeting was held at the Lake County courthouse to discuss the proposed plans. As Bernard Azure reports, the unruly crowd of approximately one hundred people contributed this: "Shooting wildly from the lip [local white people] fired ignorant stereotypical epithets with scattergun imprecision at any and all Indians and their perceived shortcomings" (1995, 4). Furthermore, and incredibly as though transported back one hundred years, "according to Angie Read of Ronan, Indians are lazy, and it would take 10 non-Indians to make sure an Indian did the job right." Another opponent, Lisa Morris of Moiese, articulated that she was "not interested in cultural and spirituality at the Bison Range" and that she had a "problem with people losing their jobs and revisionist history" (Azure 1995, 4).

As noted by journalist Woody Kipp, it is curious that at one time white people killed buffalo for sport or to clear the land for cattle, and now they want to manage the buffalo. With good humor couched in realism, Kipp remarks:

> I am not sure what the fascination is for white people concerning the buffalo. They have skin like a cow, horns like a cow, hooves like a cow. Why can't they just go look at a herd of herefords, their own cattle, and be satisfied? I guess it goes back to the description the Lakota have for the white man: wasichu, which translates into "fat taker," meaning one who wants everything. . . . To the whites, the bison remains an anomaly, something upon which to attempt to perpetuate the frontier mentality. Sorry folks, it's over. You who have been here for three or four generations will soon be (if you aren't already) getting a taste of what the native felt a century ago as your wealthier white kinfolk move in and buy up the land that your children are not going to be able to afford. Your stories of the bison are of the great slaughter. . . . The native stories are of the great medicines brought by the buffalo people. . . . That's the difference between your world and ours. That's why the Flathead tribes have the right to manage the range. One white woman had the utter gall to say, "Why don't they get their own bison range?" Sit-

ting on stolen land in the middle of the Flathead reservation she had the gall to say that. That's the difference. (1995, 2)

Some argue that one way to combat a racialized criminal justice system is to hire people of color as police officers. However, because of institutionalized racism and powerful gate-keepers, that is not always possible. The story of Bill Wilkinson Jr. provides such an example. In November of 1994, Wilkinson, an enrolled member of the Hidatsa tribe, was awarded financial compensation for the racial discrimination he experienced at the hands of Hill County in northern Montana (Fenner 1994; *Without Reservations* 1995). Wilkinson alleged that the Hill County sheriff's office, specifically county sheriff Tim Solomon, violated his civil rights by repeatedly denying him a promotion because of his race. At a hearing conducted in 1994, Hill County deputy sheriff Gordon Inabnit testified that during a conversation he had with Sheriff Soloman, Soloman remarked: "Howard [Taylor, former Hill County sheriff] got rid of the nigger and I guess I got to get rid of the Indian" (Fenner 1994, A10). This statement was in reference to former sheriff Howard's firing of an African American employee, and "the Indian" referred to is Wilkinson. At the hearing, Solomon testified that he did not remember the conversation, although he admitted to having used the word *nigger*. Also at the hearing, the sheriff's office dispatcher testified that she had received a call requesting assistance for a suicide at the Rocky Boy's Reservation, and that, in the context of the suicide, Sheriff Soloman had laughed and made a remark about there being "one more good Indian." Additionally, it was reported that during the investigation of the suicide Sheriff Soloman had mocked the speech pattern of the Cree and Chippewa from the Rocky's Boy Reservation. Solomon, with his the-only-good-Indian-is-a-dead-Indian attitude, was re-elected without opposition in 1994 as Hill County sheriff.

As evidenced by the sheriff's comments regarding the former African American employee, Native people are not the only victims of discrimination in Montana. It was recently reported that three minority police officers filed a discrimination lawsuit against the city of Billings on the basis that they were denied promotion and faced harsher working conditions than white police officers (Ehli 1995c). Moreover, former police officer Pedro Hernández, who is now a justice of the peace, declared that when he was a police officer in Billings he was repeatedly referred to as a "spic" or "wetback." Hernández reportedly left the police department because he knew his chances for promotion were minimal. In another report (Ehli 1995a), a Billings man filed a complaint against the city police department because the department secretary made a racialized comment regarding him. The man had telephoned the police department to report a dispute. The secretary thought that she had put him on hold as she conversed with others about the case, during which time she allegedly referred to him as "another Mexican Hernández" (Ehli 1995a, A1). The complainant expressed that he thought the comment was in reference to Judge Pedro Hernández's recent publicized statements about racism in the police department.

Another example of neocolonial racism, Montana style, proves enlightening. On 10 February 1995, Julie Cajune was to represent the Confederated Salish and Kootenai Tribes regarding the passage of a language bill, House Bill 376 (Cajune, personal communication). The man who introduced the bill withdrew it, so Cajune and other Native people in Montana did not attend the proposed session. Without sufficient warning to Native communities, the bill was reintroduced the next week. There was, consequently, no cohesive group of Native Americans in attendance. While we are not in the days where Natives are not allowed to speak their language, the message is the same: with the passage of House Bill 376, proposed by state representative Dick Simpkins, English is now the official state language, although there are seven Indian reservations and a large Landless Native population. The law offers nothing practical; it is an obvious affront to Natives living in Montana. If we are really serious about English as the only valid language, we should heed Harold Gray's advice: "Lawmakers will have to remove from all state records the word 'Montana' since that is a Spanish word for mountains" (Anez 1995).

As seen decades earlier, the new colonialism continues, and the racialized experiences of Native people in Montana persevere. Montana newspapers teem with articles on hate-group activity and neocolonial racism—for example, reservations fight with the state of Montana over gaming issues,[13] and the mayor of Polson, a small town on Flathead, suggests that either the reservation be abolished or non-Native-owned land be removed from the reservation boundary. Tribally controlled newspapers regularly receive letters from concerned tribal members about the prejudice they encounter in their everyday lives:

When I go to Missoula or Kalispell, I can expect the less-than-white treatment that I sometimes receive. However, it's so obvious in Lake County grocery lines, looks that you receive and transactions that it's all I can do to keep from verbally expressing my feelings towards these rude employees. I've personally encountered this in our Post Office, local hospitals, grocery and retail stores. (Michel 1995)

This Native woman's plea demonstrates the segregation that is in full swing on her own reservation. It discloses what happens when she frequents "white" places—places where "good Indians" do not go. Native people have been stereotyped and proscribed "appropriate" roles complete with "appropriate" activities. Natives who step out-of-bounds are punished, as this woman is in her daily encounter with white people in her own homeland. These acts of hatred carry the message that indigenous people are trespassers.

Another form of precise, direct racism surfaces in the case of Senator Conrad Burns, who, when asked by a white rancher how it was living with "niggers" in Washington, D.C., replied, "It's a hell of a challenge." The Confederated Salish and Kootenai Tribal Chair, Mickey Pablo, countered, "It's a challenge to Montana's Indian community to fight racism when one of our state's highest elected officials makes statements like this" (*Bozeman Daily Chronicle*, 26 October 1994, A2).

In 1990 another high-ranking official denied the existence of racism in Montana. Montana governor Stan Stephens, reacting to a statement by Corky Bush, Affirmative Action Officer at Montana State University, on racism and sexism in Montana, said he was "really disturbed" by her statement. Stephens added, "We have some social science gadflies that, quite frankly, are out of touch with what is going on" (*Billings Gazette*, 24 September 1990, A5). And, according to Governor Stephens, "There isn't racism and sexism in Montana" (*Billings Gazette*, 24 September 1990, A5).

Not many people today, at the close of the twentieth century, dispute the racialized environment found in Montana, although many fall under the spell of what historian Patricia Nelson Limerick (1987) terms "selective amnesia." Conclusively, by anyone's standards, many different forms of discrimination are active in Montana; the neocolonial racism is direct and indirect, long ago institutionalized. Although neocolonial racism permeates social interaction between whites and Natives and is woven into the fabric of all institutions in the United States, one of the most punishing institutions is the criminal justice system. Indeed, its job is to penalize and confine the criminal, the deviant. As in the past, today Native people encounter overwhelming odds at every stage of the Euro-American criminal justice system.

PART II

Creating Dangerous Women

NARRATIVES OF IMPRISONED

NATIVE AMERICAN

AND WHITE WOMEN

CELLS

Cell, brick, cement, bars, walls, hard,
tv's soaps, stories, tears, no visitors
allowed, lawyers, liars, guards, big,
touch guns, mean fingers, small bed,
green cloth, disinfectant, toilet, sink,
bars, no window, no door, no knob to turn,
no air, no wind, cold, nightmares, screams,
no touch, no touching.

  I want to touch someone. I want to hold
  that woman who cries every goddamn night.

  I WANT TO TOUCH SOMEONE.

IMPRISONED NATIVE WOMAN
(*quoted in Beth Brant*, A Gathering of Spirit)

Three

PRISONER PROFILE

PAST AND PRESENT

The only apparent advantage women have over men in America's penal system is that fewer of them are exposed to it.

KATHRYN W. BURKHART, Women in Prison

Incarcerated women are only a small fraction of the entire prison population, accounting for 6.1 percent of both state and federal prisoners (Beck and Gilliard 1995). Of all women incarcerated in state prisons, 36 percent are white whereas 64 percent are women of color, with African Americans in the majority (Snell and Morton 1994). Just over 16 percent are between the ages of 18 and 24, while 50 percent fall into the age range of 25–34, and 25.5 percent are between the ages of 35 and 44. Forty-six percent report that they have some high school education, yet 16 percent have less than an eighth-grade education. Twenty-three percent are high-school graduates and just over 15 percent have some college education (Snell and Morton 1994). Given the low educational level and the fact that women of color are overrepresented in prison, it is not startling that 53 percent of the women were not employed prior to their incarceration (Snell and Morton 1994). Most women who were working before their incarceration were predominately in service jobs or other poorly paid positions (Rafter 1990).

Reasons for conviction have remained relatively constant since the early 1960s, with the exception of an increase in drug offenses. Thirty-three percent of all women in state prisons are incarcerated for drug offenses, and nearly 50 percent were under the influence of drugs or alcohol when they committed the crime of which they were convicted (Snell and Morton 1994). The significant number of drug- and alcohol-related convictions illustrates the severe addictions women encounter prior to incarceration, as well as the conceivable connection of drug and alcohol use to involvement in criminal activity (Merlo 1995).

Of the total women's state prison population, 60 percent were sentenced for nonviolent crimes (Snell and Morton 1994). Just over 32 percent are incarcerated for violent offenses, and 50 percent of those incarcerated for violent crimes were convicted of homicide or manslaughter. It is important to note that 32 percent of women imprisoned for homicide committed a violent act against a relative or intimate partner, and the victim was most likely male. In contrast, incarcerated men are more likely than incarcerated women to victimize a stranger. Furthermore, approximately 43 percent of imprisoned women report that they were at one time victims of sexual or physical abuse, and abused women were more likely to commit crimes of violence—generally against a relative or intimate partner (Snell and Morton 1994). Data also show that those who were abused are more likely to be in prison for a violent crime (Snell and Morton 1994). Fifty percent of women incarcerated for a violent crime, and who were abused prior to incarceration, were convicted for homicide (Snell and Morton 1994).

Official data show that whereas violent crimes are rare for white women, they occur with greater frequency among African American women (Lewis 1981; Naffine 1987). The average sentence for women convicted of a violent crime is twice as long as that for women who commit either a property or drug offense. Women convicted of murder, which includes non-negligent manslaughter, receive the longest sentences, with the average just over sixteen and a half years (Greenfeld and Minor-Harper 1991).

In an attempt to explain why African American women are disproportionately represented in the criminal justice system, several scholars (Lewis 1981; Rafter 1990; Rice 1990) advise us not to rely on monocausal explanations but to examine the interrelationship of racism, sexism, and classism. Diane Lewis (1981) proposes that there may be a significant relationship between income level, employment opportunities, high rates of unemployment that plague African American women, and crime. Citing an earlier study by Glick and Neto, Lewis suggests that African American women were more than twice as likely as white women to have been on welfare when they were arrested, and more likely than white women to come from impoverished backgrounds. The Glick and Neto study (1977) also revealed that imprisoned African American women were more likely than white women to be living with their children prior to incarceration and more likely to be the primary financial caretaker. Causes of crime, therefore, need to be located within the context of structural characteristics that involve race, gender, and class.

Lewis contends that African American women are more severely sanctioned than African American men by the criminal justice system. Lewis cites French (1977), who disclosed that in North Carolina in 1977, African Americans comprised 66 percent of all imprisoned females, compared to 55 percent of all imprisoned males. Referring to the Department of Justice statistics from 1977, Lewis informs that in that year 56 percent of all women in federal prisons were African American, whereas African American men comprised 38 percent of all males in federal prisons. She argues further that although racism is an important variable and aids in the explanation of why African American women are overrepresented in arrest and incarceration rates, "their significantly higher relative rates as *women*, reflect the extent to which sexism exacerbates existing disadvantages of racism" (Lewis 1981, 100; emphasis in original).

Lewis suggests that the overrepresentation of African American women in the criminal justice system lies in official reactions to them. Citing studies on arrest rates, parole violations, length of sentences, and parole eligibility, Lewis maintains that African Americans are perceived by the system as more criminal than whites, and that both African American men and women are introduced to racism in many stages of the criminal justice system. The relationship between gender and race is shown by Foley and Rasche (1979), who conclude that the treatment of women in the criminal justice system varies by race. For example, their study found that although white women convicted of murder receive longer sentences than African American women, African American women convicted of murder actually *serve* longer sentences than white women convicted of the same offense (26.7 months versus 23.0 months).

Looking specifically at gender issues, Lewis submits that official reactions contain elements of sexism. She suggests that lower overall rates of incarceration for females can be explained by leniency shown to white women but not to women of color. This leniency is reserved for women who follow the dominant society's gender-role expectations, and often African American women do not meet these expectations. Chesney-Lind and Smart (cited in Lewis 1981) argue that women are punished as much for gender-role violations as for illegal behavior. When leniency is applied, it is reserved for "those who are married, charged with nonviolent offenses, and who display a feminine demeanor" (Lewis 1981, 101). Thus, the interaction between race and gender is perceived as a major factor controlling incarceration decisions.

African American women are more likely than white women to be single, and are more likely than white women to be heads of households (Rice 1990). Bernstein, Cardascia, and Rose (1979) found that marriage is an important in-court variable in determining whether or not a convicted woman will be incarcerated. Their study further concludes that women are dealt with more harshly by the courts when they commit a crime against a person instead of a property crime. Person crimes are perceived as less acceptable for women to commit (Datesman and Scarpitti 1980). A study by Lois DeFleur (1975) reveals that police officers are inclined to free female suspects who behave in stereotypic ways (e.g., passively). In contrast, women violating gender expectations are treated more severely by the criminal justice system (Hepburn 1978; Visher 1983).

Several scholars (Lewis 1981; Rafter 1990; Rice 1990) suggest that African American women are socialized to be assertive and, subsequently, are seen as less feminine than white women. Lewis argues that

> Black women, then, display gender role behavior, a social status and a crime pattern, all of which contradict acceptable feminine behavior, as defined by the dominant society. They tend to be assertive, function as unmarried heads of household and be convicted for violent person crimes. In short, they epitomize the type of deviant women the criminal justice system is committed to punish. (1981, 102)

Definitions of crime, in conjunction with the criminal justice system, operate as systems of social control, and bias in the criminal justice system based on race/ethnicity, gender, and class functions to imprison more women of color. Although no data exist specifically on Native American women, several qualitative and quantitative studies well document that Native Americans—similar to African Americans—are more frequently arrested and processed than whites, and that they are discriminated against at all levels of the criminal justice system. Discrimination against Native Americans is described as existing in arrest situations (Bachman 1992; Chadwick et al. 1976; Cross 1982; LaFree 1995; Lundman 1974; Mann 1993; Minnis 1963; Snyder-Joy 1995), in the courts (Bynum and Paternoster 1984; Hall and Simkus 1975; Randall and Randall 1978; Snyder-Joy 1995), and in parole decisions (Bynum and Paternoster 1984).

Native Canadians, similar to Native Americans, encounter discrimination in all stages of the criminal justice system (LaPrairie 1984). Illustrating a gender bias, Native Canadian women are more likely than Native men to be overrepresented. Faith (1993b) cites a study by Karen Masson on women imprisoned in Canada, which discloses a correlation between race and severity of sentence, indicating a racialized criminal justice system. Native Canadian women are more likely to receive a custodial sentence than white women, who are more likely to receive probation or a fine.

In sum, Native women face overwhelming odds at every stage of the criminal justice system. Rafter (1990) suggests that extralegal factors, such as race and gender, influence not only incarceration rates but treatment of prisoners while incarcerated. Racism and sexism clearly affect the treatment of women and people of color when they encounter the criminal justice system in Montana. A summary of Montana's early women prisoners offers insight into the interrelated systems of oppression and contemporary prisonization experiences.

MONTANA'S FIRST WOMEN PRISONERS

The Montana Territorial Prison was established in 1871 in Deer Lodge. Between 1878 and 1889, only two women were incarcerated in Montana's prison, and they were located on the third floor in the same building as the men.[1] Felicité Sánchez, a twenty-year-old Mexican national, was convicted of manslaughter and began serving her sentence on 3 December 1878. She was given a three-year sentence and was pardoned by the governor two years later. On 22 November 1878 the *Weekly Missoulian* reported that Sánchez had killed a white man who was "given to liquor, a reputed tramp, and was suspected of being in the illicit traffic of the ardent to the natives." Sánchez was described in the same newspaper as "a Mexican, a drunkard, an adept on other occasions with the knife and pistol. . . . Her reputation is essentially bad, and her standing for a regard of human life is quoted greatly below par." On 23 November 1878 another newspaper, the *New North-West*, added that

although Sánchez had killed the man in self-defense, she "is very depraved and will probably be better off in the penitentiary than any-
where else." The same newspaper, on 18 December 1878, described a
flamboyant Sánchez as she arrived at the Montana Penitentiary: "Being
taken by the officer, she put her feet on the stove and proceeded to roll
a cigarette, which she fabricated with great skill and smoked with manifest enjoyment." This, of course, occurred at a time when "ladies" did
not smoke. Sánchez was portrayed as "masculine," as criminal.

In 1879 Mary Angeline Droullard became the second woman incarcerated at Montana's prison. This twenty-four-year-old white woman
killed her husband, the sheriff of Missoula County. Droullard received a
fifteen-year sentence for murder and was pardoned by the governor in
1882. She was incarcerated at the Missoula County jail for one year
prior to her transfer to prison and was impregnated while in jail. (It is
easy to speculate that she was raped in jail.) The baby was born inside
the prison in June of 1880 and sent to an adoptive family. While imprisoned, a despondent Droullard tried to commit suicide.

The state's third woman prisoner, received on 26 April 1889, was an
African American, Jessie Stuart. The nineteen-year-old, with no previous convictions, served ten months of a four-year sentence for assault.
The prison listed her occupation as "demi-monde" (prostitute). The
next month, the prison received its fourth woman prisoner, Rose Bennett, a twenty-one-year-old white woman whose occupation was noted
also as demi-monde. She served five years of a twelve-year sentence
for second-degree murder. Between 1889 and 1897 twenty-one women
were imprisoned. Most were described as prostitutes, and the majority
were convicted of grand larceny.

Ella St. Clair, an African American described as a "dusky cyprian,"
was accused of murdering a white man (*Daily Missoulian*, 16 August
1894) and became the state's fifteenth woman prisoner. She was eventually convicted of grand larceny, although no hard evidence existed that
she either murdered the man or stole his money. St. Clair was sentenced
to twelve years in prison and ordered to pay the costs of prosecution.

The first Native woman imprisoned in Montana was Madeline Trottier, a Cree originally from Canada's Red River country. She was incarcerated in 1897 for rape and was described by the prison as a "halfbreed
Indian," twenty-seven years old. She had no previous convictions and
served four years and three months of a six-year sentence. An article in

the *River Press*, 10 February 1897, reported that R. Trottier, Madeline's husband, was in jail for the rape of a "half-breed girl" and was accompanied by "a female prisoner, who is charged with being an accessory to the crime." Madeline's "crime" was being at the crime scene when her husband committed the rape. On 10 March 1897 the same newspaper reported that the district court went into the evening hours to dispose of the Trottier case. Madeline Trottier and her husband were both convicted of rape, and while he received a thirty-year sentence, Madeline Trottier, who pled guilty, was handed a six-year sentence.

On 10 November 1899 Warden Frank Conley sent a letter to the governor regarding the prison's only female prisoners at the time: Madeline Trottier, who had been imprisoned nearly three years, and Ella St. Clair, who had served five years and was described by the warden as suicidal. The warden, aware that Trottier did not commit a crime, begged the governor to release these women. He asked for a pardon "on grounds of humanity" because Trottier and St. Clair were the only women imprisoned with 325 men. When the women were taken outside for fresh air, the men had to be locked in their cells, and the inconvenience made it nearly impossible to ensure that the women exercised daily. Referring to Trottier as "an ignorant Indian," and arguing that prison was more difficult for women than for men, the warden implored:

> One year in the women's quarters is certainly worse than five years to the men. Ella St. Clair has become very much discouraged and we have had hard work to keep her from suicide. Madeline Trottier is an Indian woman and can only speak a few words of English and for that reason the two women are not even company for each other. To be perfectly frank about it the situation of these two women is nothing short of horrible and we are powerless to alleviate their position. It certainly seems to us that the five years and more than Ella St. Clair has been here is more than sufficient. The Trottier woman, if she be guilty of the crime for which she is imprisoned, is entitled to some leniency from the fact that she is an ignorant Indian and at the best is not expected to have the highest ideas of morals. . . . We hope that we can prevail upon you to pardon these people and if you consent to do so, why not do it to become effective say on Thanksgiving Day? (Conley 1899)

In a politically charged reply, the governor succinctly denied the pardon. His response to the warden read, "When a pardon is granted to a prisoner from northern Montana, the people there pretend to be indignant, and while I would like to do some thing in these cases, I do not feel that I can at the present time" (Smith 1889). The governor could not release Trottier and St. Clair because the white people (the voters) in northern Montana would become "indignant." These documents testify to racism, prison conditions, and Native-white inter-actions—particularly in northern Montana, where indigenous people were fiercely resisting colonialism.

From 1878 to 1910 a total of sixty-two women were imprisoned. Forty percent were described as demi-mondes or street-walkers, and 50 percent were convicted of grand larceny. There were relatively few Native women incarcerated during this period—they were virtually imprisoned on six Indian reservations in Montana, due to formal and informal federal and state policy. African American women, on the other hand, were disproportionately imprisoned. With relatively few African American citizens, and especially African American women, in the state, from 1878 to 1910 African American women represented 37 percent of the female prisoners.

The African American population in Montana grew from 183 in 1870 to 1,834 in 1910 (Riley 1988).[2] African American women accounted for 28 percent of the total African American population in Montana in 1870, increasing to 42 percent by 1910. African American women moved to Montana for a variety of reasons, including to escape the vile racism in other parts of the United States and to seek employment. Although discrimination prevented many from obtaining anything but servile employment, a few African American women operated cafés or boardinghouses. Others were housewives, as in the case of Sarah Ir-vin, the wife of the first African American policemen in Helena (Riley 1988). Important historical work by Ann Butler, however, reasons that for imprisoned African American women, "The West appears to have of-fered an uncertain freedom and little justice. Rather, these black women found that, in the West, a forge of racism shaped the chains of slavery into the bars of a penitentiary" (1988, 35).

Butler reveals that most African American women imprisoned in the West (including Montana) from the 1860s to the early 1900s were young, uneducated, and with limited resources. Commenting on the vicious racism these women experienced in the criminal justice system, Butler charges that

> When apprehended by the law, black women found a series of injustices set into motion: their crimes were often minor or nonexistent, serious charges materialized around the most questionable or circumstantial evidence, the issue of guilt or innocence became unimportant, a prison sentence tended to exceed the seriousness of the crime, parole and pardon procedures favored white female prisoners, and treatment inside the prison emphasized brutality. (1988, 34)

From 1911 to 1943, 136 women were incarcerated, and African American women represented 21 percent of the total female prisoner population. Grand larceny accounted for 25 percent of the crimes, while 19 percent were violent crimes. The combined offenses of drug possession and selling accounted for 23 percent of the convictions. From the early 1900s until the 1930s, most women prisoners were described by the prison as prostitutes and narcotic addicts. After that period, most prisoners were classified as housewives.

On 2 July 1927 the Montana State Prison received its second Native woman prisoner. This twenty-four-year-old, born in Canada, was a Landless Cree convicted of stealing beadwork. She pled not guilty; nevertheless, she was found guilty and sentenced to one to two years for grand larceny. Her three brothers were convicted of the same crime; two were sentenced to prison terms, one for five to ten years and the other for one to two years, while the younger brother was sent to reform school (*Flathead Courier*, 16 June 1927). A male friend, who used a Salish interpreter at the trial, was also convicted of this crime and received one to three years in prison.

This Landless Cree was also the first woman in Lake County to be charged with first-degree murder. She denied knowing the man, whose remains were found two years after his death in 1940, let alone killing him (*Flathead Courier*, 23 and 30 April 1942).[3] Although she pled not guilty, a white jury found her guilty of manslaughter. Deliberating more than twelve hours, the jury clearly had their doubts regarding her guilt (*Flathead Courier*, 30 April 1942). In 1942 she was sentenced to ten years in prison; she served just over four years of that sentence.

During the Depression, in the 1930s, forty women were sent to prison in Montana. As described by Paula Petrik, most were "middle-aged, impoverished, illiterate, retarded, or mentally or physically ill" (1985, 6). A majority of the women received no correspondence from family or friends. According to Petrik, it was their economic status that resulted in incarceration rather than being placed in another institution. Economics clearly played a role in their criminalization: women were imprisoned for such "crimes" as forging a ten-dollar check, falsely obtaining five gallons of gasoline, or stealing four dresses, table linen, or food. Other women were imprisoned for violent crimes, which were typically against their husbands.

On 13 February 1930 the *Great Falls Tribune* reported that a mixed-blood Native woman, tried by a white jury, was sentenced to prison for eleven years for the murder of Joe Monroe from the Blackfeet Reservation. The Montana State Prison thus received its third Native woman prisoner on 24 February 1930. Her brother allegedly shot Monroe and was found guilty of second-degree murder. According to the newspaper, this woman "asked and advised" her brother to kill Monroe and then watched the shooting through a window. Her brother pled self-defense and was sentenced to ten years at the state prison. According to Petrik, the sentence differential between the woman and her brother was explained by her "boastful, masculine behavior" (1985, 7).

Testimony during her brother's trial, heard also by an all-white jury, revealed that Monroe had hit her, knocking her against the wall and causing her mouth to bleed. A doctor testified that Monroe's "disposition to disobey hospital orders, his habits as a drinking man of dissipated life and the symptoms of a venereal disease might have been conditions that hastened if they did not actually cause his death" (*Cut Bank Pioneer Press*, 31 January 1930, 1).

According to Petrik (1985), it was a case of animosity between mixed-bloods and full-bloods, in combination with medical evidence that Monroe's wound would not have proven fatal had he followed medical advice, that ultimately put this mixed-blood woman behind bars. Testimony by full-blood Native women at the trial was damaging to the defendant, while testimony by mixed-blood women favored her. The convicted mixed-blood's mother wrote, "It was such a dirty frame-up amongst those breed and Indian girls. They were jealous of her popularity. Why punish her for what some(one) else done, she didn't tell them to do it" (Petrik 1985, 7).

Animosity between Natives was a reality in the past and continues today. I suggest that the antagonism Petrik refers to was created by the federal government, because during this period the mixed-bloods held power via tribal councils on reservations. These early councils were an extension of the Bureau of Indian Affairs and essentially puppet governments displaying indirect colonial rule. Full-bloods, and many mixed-bloods, had a great distaste for this type of governing body. Complicating issues was the Euro-American lust for Native land. Natives with a landbase were afraid they would lose what little land they had to Landless Natives. Mixed blood was associated with landlessness; thus, all mixed-bloods were questionable.

From 1948 to 1977 the number of imprisoned African American women decreased dramatically: between 1948 and 1977 only five were imprisoned. The first three convictions were for grand larceny (stealing $250), selling liquor without a license, and taking linen worth $100. In 1967 an African American woman with no prior convictions pled guilty to the murder of her husband; she received a five-year sentence, of which she served just over eight months. One African American woman was imprisoned three times between 1969 and 1977. Initially, she was convicted of selling $3 worth of marijuana. The second conviction was for possession of cocaine, and a third conviction for "bad checks" and forgery resulted in a ten-year sentence.

The lower incarceration rates reflect a reduction in the total African American population of the state. While other racial/ethnic populations were increasing, African Americans in the state from 1960 to 1970 numbered only one thousand—0.15 percent of the total population in Montana. African Americans were leaving Montana for other regions of the United States, most likely fleeing the racial hostility.

From 1911 to 1943 Native women accounted for 7 percent of the total female prisoner population. Between 1944 and 1966, during a period of racialized assimilationist federal and state policy, the number of imprisoned Native women skyrocketed to a startling 25 percent, while Native Americans comprised between 3 and 4 percent of the state's overall population. This high incarceration rate for Native women is also indicative of relaxed policy regarding the confinement of Natives to their respective reservations: without the pass system effectively jailing Natives on reservations, the incarceration rates increased in the state prison.

From 1967 to 1977, in an era of supposed self-determination for Native Americans and during a time when an astounding number of Native women were involuntarily sterilized by the federal government,[4] Native women were again disproportionately represented and accounted for 30 percent of the total female prisoner population. An overwhelming majority of imprisoned Native women from 1897 to 1977 were Montana's Landless Natives, who were generally convicted of crimes of property. Because they had no reservation to confine them, Landless Natives had never been subject to the pass system; hence, their high incarceration rates may well reflect their more direct exposure to discrimination.

Race/ethnicity, gender, and class play critical roles in the responses of both informal and formal agents of control. The use of arrest statistics as evidence of the relative involvement of different social groups has been criticized by both labeling theorists and Marxist theorists, who argue that individuals do not come to the attention of the criminal justice system solely on the basis of their behavior. The definition of behavior as "criminal," in addition to the course of action taken in response to it, depends upon contextual features. Factors independent of the behavior of the "criminal" individual enter into official statistics. Responses by others to criminal behaviors are influenced by expectations regarding race/ethnicity and gender-specific behavior. In this way, the labeling of criminal behavior can be seen as a form of social control. Crime is, thus, defined as such by powerful individuals in Euro-America. This is illustrated by the composition of imprisoned women, past and present, at the WCC in Montana.

WOMEN'S CORRECTIONAL CENTER

In Montana correctional institution size is determined by the number of admissions and the average length of stay (Department of Corrections and Human Services 1992). While there was a 17 percent increase in admissions to all Montana correctional institutions from 1986 to 1991, admissions to the women's prison increased 44 percent. The male prison population's average length of stay increased 14 percent between 1986 to 1991, while that of the female population increased 71 percent.

Following national trends, during the last decade women in Montana have been receiving longer sentences. The average sentence length in 1980 was 6.2 years; by 1988 it had increased to 12.8 years (Byorth 1989b). From 1986 to 1991, women were more likely to be admitted to prison for a single conviction than men, and women had fewer total convictions than men (Department of Corrections and Human Services 1992).

There is a trend in Montana to incarcerate the female offender rather than using alternative sentencing. One report aptly stated that "the criminal justice system in Montana has increased its use of incarceration as the punishment of choice in sentencing offenders, and particularly female offenders" (Department of Corrections and Human Services 1992, 56). The consequence has been a sizable growth in the female prisoner population, presenting the illusion of an increase in female criminality.

A partial explanation for the increase in the female prison population is their incarceration for drug offenses. While men in Montana are more likely than women to be imprisoned for violent crimes, women are more likely than men to be imprisoned for drug crimes (Department of Corrections and Human Services 1992).

Another dramatic difference between men and women is that a higher proportion of women than men were sentenced directly to prison (rather than probation) until 1991, when the trend reversed (Department of Corrections and Human Services 1992). Moreover, the proportion of women imprisoned because of a revoked deferred sentence or revocation of parole is higher than that of men (Department of Corrections and Human Services 1992). The recidivism rate for women is approximately 18 percent. According to Jo Acton, the new warden, this is not because women are committing new crimes but because they fail to comply with the requirements of parole or probation (Shay 1996).

A self-report survey (Petaja 1990) reveals that 48 percent of all imprisoned women in Montana are between the ages of 26 and 35, which is slightly older than the national average. The average age at the time of admission is 29.5 years, and the average age of the prisoner population is 30.7 years. Most women have twelve years of schooling: 56 percent have general equivalency diplomas (GEDs) and 38 percent have high-school diplomas. Twenty-two percent are single, 30 percent divorced, 34 percent married, 8 percent in common-law marriages, 4 percent widowed, and 2 percent separated from their spouses. Of the total female prisoner population, 90 percent have children, and 30 percent of mothers have one child, 33 percent two children, 17 percent three children, and 20 percent four or more children. Thirty percent were on welfare prior to incarceration. Of the total, 82 percent of the women plan on supporting themselves through employment when released from prison, yet 69 percent are worried about making enough money to sustain themselves.

The preceding reports represent a different population than the one I interviewed. My sample, however, closely resembles those in the reports. The total female prisoner population during my study (1990–1992) was sixty-eight: 70 percent white (n = 48), 25 percent Native American (n = 17), and 5 percent Chicana (n = 3). The sample population for my study includes fourteen Native American and thirteen white women imprisoned at the WCC. All Native women are from Montana, and Landless Natives are disproportionately represented. The age range of the interviewees is between 18 and 45, with an average of 30.1. Of the 27 interviewees, 7 are single, 12 divorced, and 8 married. Of the 8 who are married, 4 have spouses/partners who are also imprisoned. The sample population has between 1 and 5 children, with 3 children the most frequent number reported. The educational level ranges between the fifth grade and a college degree (one woman has a college degree); the most frequently reported educational level is twelve years. It is important to note that Native American women have extremely low levels of education, with five women reporting only an eighth-grade level and one reporting a fifth-grade level. All interviewees are from lower income levels.

The following is a typical profile of an incarcerated Native female from the sample: She is thirty years old, most likely a Landless Native, single or divorced, with two children. (The number of living children would be higher, except several Native women have children who are deceased.) Prior to incarceration she experienced much violence in her life. She was not employed, and she has an eighth-grade education. Her crime is alcohol- or drug-related, and she was convicted of a "male-type" crime (murder, robbery, assault, escape, and so forth). The sentence length for Native women ranges from 5 to 60 years; the average is 19.1 years.

The following is a typical profile of an incarcerated white female from the sample: She is thirty years old, most likely divorced, with two or three children. She either completed high school or received her GED. She experienced much violence in her life prior to incarceration, and if she was employed, she held a low-level, low-paying position. Her crime is alcohol- or drug-related, and she was convicted of a "female-type" crime (e.g., bad checks). The sentence length for white women ranges from 5 to 20 years; the average is 9.0 years.

Clearly, Native women in the sample population were given longer sentences than white women. They were convicted more for "male-type" crimes than white women, which could account for longer sentence lengths. Thus, there is a qualitative difference in crime type that makes comparisons difficult. Despite this, sentence disparity warrants an immediate investigation, because when the crimes are the same, Native women receive longer sentences than white women (Native American Women Prisoners 1993).

Acknowledgment of the fact that law (a Euro-American construct) itself, and the administration of law, is biased against certain categories of people is crucial to understanding Native American criminality and the experiences of imprisoned Natives. Native worlds have been devastated by the course of their relationship with Euro-Americans and their laws. The number of jailed Natives is a chilling indication—a reminder that, because deviance is socially constructed, crime statistics exhibit discretion in defining and apprehending "criminals."

Prisons, as employed by the Euro-American system, operate to keep Native Americans in a colonial situation. Presently, indigenous people are confronted with overrepresentation in Euro-America's criminal justice system. Native people are now locked up in great numbers. Native Americans are only 0.6 percent of the total population, yet they comprise 2.9 percent of federal and state prison populations (Camp and Camp 1995). The disproportion of imprisoned Natives is more clearly seen at the state level, where they account for 33.2 percent of the total prisoner population in Alaska, 23.6 percent in South Dakota, 16.9 percent in North Dakota, and 17.3 percent in Montana compared to approximately 15 percent, 7 percent, 4 percent, and 6 percent of the overall state populations, respectively (Camp and Camp 1995). These figures are for the total number of prisoners—the percentage of imprisoned Native women is not separated from Native men. When the gender of incarcerated Native Americans is investigated, the sexism is evident. Although Native Americans in Montana comprise only about 6 percent of the total state population, Native men account for approximately 20 per-

cent of the total male prisoner population, and Native women consti-
tute approximately 25 percent of the total female prisoner population.
Nationwide, women make up only 5.2 percent of the total state prisoner
population. Thus, Native women are more likely to be imprisoned than
Native men or white women, indicating racism and sexism in Montana's
criminal justice system. Moreover, the data from my research shows
that Landless Native women are more likely to be criminalized than
women from other racial/ethnic groups or than other Native women.

As explained earlier, a factor that complicates the position of imprisoned Native women is the jurisdictional maze created by the federal
government's Public Law 280. In Montana, all Indian reservations except one are subject to federal control over criminal matters; the exception is under state control. This means that on all reservations (excluding
the one under state control), Natives sentenced to prison are incarcerated in out-of-state federal prisons; only those arrested on the state-
controlled reservation or off the reservation are sent to the state prison.
Therefore, it is safe to assume that most Native Americans in Montana's
prisons come from the one PL 280 reservation (Flathead Reservation)
or are Landless Native Americans.

Dobash, Dobash, and Gutteridge (1986) are correct in asserting that
it is imperative to research the notion of "criminality" by examining the
socioeconomic conditions in which crimes occur. Some women, Native
and non-Native, are imprisoned at the WCC for killing abusive family
members and others for writing "bad checks" to adequately care for
their children. Several women were found guilty of the same offense as
their husbands, although their husbands recognized their wives' innocence: in all cases it was the husband who assaulted foster children, but
apparently the judges assumed the wives were also responsible. Some
women are imprisoned because they pled guilty in order to spare their
spouses prison time. Other women were named by their husbands as
the guilty ones, although the women insist that their spouses committed the crimes. Being in prison it does not equate with guilt, and after
years of unjust incarceration, there is no compensation.

Chesney-Lind proposes that imprisoned women's personal lives and
crime type must be perceived within "the gendered nature of these
women's lives, options, and crimes" (1991, 64). Experiences of women,
however, are not only gendered. Clearly race/ethnicity, which includes
issues of sovereignty in the case of Native Americans, is an additional

critical factor in the lives of imprisoned women of color. Native women, as colonized people, are the least powerful in the United States, and nonreservation Natives sustain additional oppression by virtue of their landless status.

As mentioned earlier, crucial to the understanding of female "deviance" is the contextualizing of the criminalization process. The personal experiences of imprisoned women, regardless of race/ethnicity, reflect the structure of the United States in which certain subgroups are not only penalized because of their race/ethnicity (including reservation status), gender, and class but are controlled as well. This is clearly seen in the violence experienced in prisoners' lives prior to incarceration, and in their ultimate criminalization because of their supposed "deviant" behavior.

Four

LIVES DICTATED BY VIOLENCE

This is about a little girl who grew up to be a convict.
This is a story about me in many ways and I want to tell it
the only way I know how. . . . And one day soon after her
father died, her mom started drinking again and would
always beat the little girl who only loved her. And soon the
beating took a turn for the worse: this little girl was put
in a hospital time after time with broken ribs and broken
bones in different places, and as she grew older she became
to others "that crazy child." But she only wanted someone
to love her for her, and not to beat on her.

IRENE ROBERTS *[Northern Cheyenne],*
quoted in Gwenyth Mapes, The Other Side

Women are more likely than men to be violently assaulted by a supposed loved one (Bureau of Justice 1994). A study on imprisoned women in Hawaii (Chesney-Lind and Rodriguez 1983) uncovers that many women prior to incarceration were exposed to violence that began very early in their lives. Five-eighths report being sexually abused as very young children, and nearly half were raped as older children by adult males in their immediate families. These desperate circumstances resulted in many women running away from home, spending time in juvenile detention, and engaging in "female" crimes (e.g., prostitution). Chesney-Lind and Rodriguez propose that "The picture that emerges is one of young girls faced with violence and/or sexual abuse at home who became criminalized by their efforts to save themselves (by running away) from the abuse" (1983, 63).

Research on African American women (Arnold 1994) postulates that the process of criminalization begins with gender and class oppression in combination with a correctional system that operates with a blame-the-victim mentality. Arnold further argues that continued involvement in crime (from girlhood to adulthood) "is a rational coping strategy, a response to alienation and structural dislocation from the primary socializing institutions of family, education, and work" (1994, 171). The author suggests that African American women, already tagged as "deviant" in girlhood, are eventually labeled "criminal" as adults because they decline to cooperate in their own victimization.

Chesney-Lind (1991), citing national data from the American Correctional Association, reports that 57 percent of imprisoned women in the United States are young women of color, and 75 percent are mothers. One-third did not finish high school, and one-third of those quit school as a result of pregnancy. As children, approximately 50 percent ran away from home, 25 percent attempted suicide, and many had problems with drugs. Over half were victimized physically, and 36 percent were abused sexually. Chesney-Lind explains that these figures are conservative; a study by Mary Gilfus (1988) shows that when childhood abuses, physical and sexual, are combined with abuses as adults (rape and battering), 88 percent of imprisoned women have been violently victimized.

The lives of prisoners at the WCC are analogous to the national trend. Their histories are characterized by violence of every form: physical, emotional, and sexual abuse, poverty, racism, and sexism, and resulting adaptations such as substance abuse. Recent research (McKinney 1995) on social learning and educational level, conducted in Montana at the WCC, exposes that 90 percent of the imprisoned women are victims of prior abuse. McKinney reaches the same conclusions as this study: the majority of imprisoned women have been abused by immediate family members.

Some prisoners hypothesize a causal relationship between prior abuse and incarceration:

> We're all on the same path when we come to prison, on the road to self-destruction. . . . The person we punish the most, hurt the most, when we come to prison is ourselves. The only common denominator I can break it down to is the pain. Most of it, I think, comes from abuse. I do believe, in my case, that abuse had something to do with my incarceration. (McKinney 1995, 147)

Life in prison is surreal for those women who do not correlate violence and prior abuse to their eventual incarceration. Never, in their wildest dreams, did they think they would end up in prison.

For many women excessive violence began the moment they were born; for others it emerged as they matured. Sexual abuse, although predominant, is only one form of violence experienced by imprisoned women. The following statements are illustrative of the kinds of violence many endured prior to their incarceration.[1] In an effort to protect the identities of the prisoners, generally I do not specify the narrator's race/ethnicity (although these features are obvious in several narratives); additionally, such categorization is not necessary due to the similarities between Native and non-Native women regarding the violence in their lives. The quotes from McLeod (1990) are from two anonymous former prisoners at the WCC; these short autobiographies were compiled by prison staff as *Female Offender* and presented in 1990 at a state meeting for correctional officials. Narratives from McKinney's study (1995) or from a booklet of writings of women imprisoned at the WCC are so marked.[2] Those quotations not cited as either McKinney or McLeod are from my study.

Abuse by parents or other primary caretakers was rampant. For most women at the WCC it was their fathers who violated them, while for others it was their mothers. A former prisoner, sexually abused as a child by "a doctor, a youth counselor, an uncle and other people I was supposed to be able to trust," discloses this about her mother:

> I have very few memories of my early childhood. Those I have are sporadic, traumatic, laced with violence towards me. I don't even like to try and remember those young years, it hurts, and I guess I've done a pretty good job of blocking them out. I don't want to remember. . . . Bloody noses were a constant companion growing up, I got hit a lot. I flinched every time I walked by my mother, then I got hit and bloodied for flinching. (McLeod 1990)

This former prisoner, who coped with her pain by attempting suicide, describes a hateful mother:

> I felt very strongly that she hated me. This was reinforced by her telling me over the years that she did, indeed, hate me, she wished I was never born and once, that I was a wasted fuck. That particular

phrase haunts me. . . . Wasted fuck, wasted fuck, wasted fuck! How
that haunts me. . . . As I grew up my mother's anger and hatefulness
toward me progressed as well. At the age of 10 or 11, she pulled a
gun on me and my brother and would have blown us away then herself, if she could have located the bolt. . . . At about that time, my
mother cut my hair to less than 1 inch all over my head because I
had tweezed my eyebrows and she wanted to show the world what
a little whore I was. This was the second time I'd received this punishment, the first for piercing my ears. I was really feeling at the
end of my rope, my mother hated me, thought I was a whore and
wanted me dead. I went to my room with my butchered hairdo
and slit my wrists. My mom came in and found me and screamed
at me for not doing it right and punched and kicked me around.
(McLeod 1990)

As a young girl, this woman ran away from home and roamed the
streets of California. At age twelve, she began using drugs: "I liked drugs,
they took the pain away, for a while." Eventually she moved back to
Montana and became involved in an abusive relationship with an older
man. By age fifteen she had been beaten repeatedly by this man, and at
eighteen she returned to California where she secured what she termed
a "respectable" position as a secretary. She said, however, "It wasn't a
secretary he was looking for, he started to pay me for sex, sometimes
with cash or sometimes with cocaine and I developed a coke habit." Several years later, she returned to Montana severely addicted to cocaine
and took a job as a stripper. "I could make between $100.00 and $200.00
a shift and more if I wanted to turn tricks on the side, which I occasion-
ally did" (McLeod 1990).

As a young woman, she became involved with "an outlaw biker gang
and things really went downhill for me." She commented that it was impossible to get out of the gang, and she lived a life of drugs and violence:
"I also still have a hit out on me, the bikers haven't forgotten me, nor I
them. It is a feeling of pure terror." This twenty-seven-year-old woman,
given a five-year sentence for possession of cocaine, faces an uncertain
future:

Life has not been kind to me, I've come close to dying several times,
sometimes at my own hands, sometimes at the hands of others. Inside, I am a bitter, resentful, untrusting, selfish, suspicious, uncar-

ing, confused, rock hard bitch. . . . I'm not too optimistic about the future. I feel like a wasted fuck a lot of the time. I hurt all the time. Life really sucks. (McLeod 1990)

Mixed-blood Native women often have a particularly difficult time with the parent who is white. For instance, one woman's white step-father beat her when she was young because he detested Native Americans. Her white mother did not defend her; rather, she perpetuated a hideous situation. This mixed-blood woman comments:

I was never to admit that I was Indian. . . . Then when I was seven years old, my adopted father out-and-out raped me. And my mother told me, "That's what you deserve. You're an Indian—that's what you deserve." I can't forgive her for that.

This racialized violence spilled over onto her visibly Native American son:

My stepfather picked up a hammer and hit my son in the arm with it. Threw it at him and hit him with it. . . . I grabbed him by the beard and I said, "You white son-of-a-bitch, if you ever touch my kid again, I'll kill you!"

Another mixed-blood recalls verbal abuse from her Native mother and a gang-rape:

I remember what my mom used to call me when I was little. . . . She used to call me a black nigger, but that didn't really bother me because I didn't know what a black man was until I found out my father was black and I was raped by six black guys. (McKinney 1995, 108)

Not all prisoners were raised in observably dysfunctional families. A woman remembers the sexual and physical abuse doled out by her father, a minister:

I could plan on a beating probably every Sunday when I was younger because no matter what happened I was the one that was at fault. If I had to go to the restroom at church I could count on a whipping when I went home because I was not supposed to leave church. God was trying to punish me for it. It was just some of my dad's sick beliefs. I'm beginning to learn that now but at the time when the sexual abuse was committed or the incest was taking place he would tell me that if I didn't do what he wanted I was going to be evil and I was going to be punished. (McKinney 1995, 168)

Another prisoner from a superficially functional family describes her emotionally and physically abusive parents:

Mom and dad were real strict. They were like drill sergeants. Everything that they taught us to do had to be exactly the way Mom would do it. We would have a certain way to fold clothes. The hand towels had to be folded the right way and everything had to be done a specific way. If we made a mistake it was as though we did it on purpose and we got into trouble. Getting slapped and yelled at was usually what it was. It depended on the error. See, I don't think they thought it was abuse. (McKinney 1995, 171)

A former prisoner, who was adopted at age two, recalls childhood violence occurring in what appeared to be a normal ranching family. This woman, essentially raised a captive, comments:

At age four they started beating on me and I never knew what I did wrong. From age five I was numerously locked in the celler of an old house and my mom would bring me bread and water three times a day and said to me that, that's how prisoners are treated. (McLeod 1990)

Violence in her family also took the form of sexual abuse by her father. Propelled by the violence into marriage at an early age, she says:

At age ten, I was used sexually by my dad. He forced sex on me and I lived in constant fear of my parents. At age 15, I became pregnant by my father. When I found out I was pregnant I was kicked out of the home never to return. I lyed about my age in order to get a job and a place to live and also to get married to a guy so my daughter would have a different last name. (McLeod 1990)

Her parents beat her throughout her pregnancy because she would not get an abortion or give her baby up for adoption. Since the birth of her daughter, her parents continue to seek custody of the child. Fearing her father will sexually abuse her daughter, this woman refuses to give her daughter to her parents.

Some women were protected by their mothers when the abuse was at the hands of their fathers. One prisoner, sexually abused by her father, remarks: "As a result, my mom took a knife and tried to kill my dad. I can still remember him on his knees and her standing over him" (McKinney 1995, 122).

Not all women were harmed by members of their immediate family; some were abused by jailers and policemen. Such occurrences are not uncommon yet are seldom reported because of power differentials between those violated and the authoritative men committing the deviant acts. For instance, a Billings police officer was recently accused of sexually abusing women he stopped for traffic offenses (Ehli 1995b), and a jailer in Livingston admitted to fondling a young girl (*Billings Gazette*, 14 November 1995). It seems a matter of routine that women are physically or sexually abused when they encounter powerful agents of the criminal justice system.[3] A prisoner of slight build describes the beating she received in a jail in northwestern Montana:

I got beat up in the county jail. I don't even know why. I was there for a week and then [the jailer]—a big tall guy—he said, "We're going to shake your cell down; we're looking for a towel." I said, "I don't even have a towel. You guys didn't even give me one when I first got here." He told me to shut up and assume the position on the wall. So I did that, and my legs weren't spread apart far enough so he kicked me right here. And my leg went out from under me and I hit my face on one of those tables. It was all bruised up and they wouldn't let me see my father or sister because they put me in temporary lockup for two weeks. And then they brought in some other girls and my face was starting to heal. I had two hairline fractures. . . . My dad threw a big fit because he wanted to see me. He saw me when I went to court: My face was still puffy and he was mad. He wanted to know what happened and I said, "nothing." I was afraid.

Abused women use a variety of coping strategies. While some attempt or commit suicide, most prisoners at the WCC rely upon substance abuse to cope with the anguish of defilement. In fact, approximately one-third are imprisoned for drug-related offenses. One prisoner explains:

> It was my way of escaping. . . . It was my way of numbing myself. As I grew up in that family environment, I learned that I couldn't have feelings. I wasn't allowed to feel. I wasn't allowed to cry. I was just a shell of a person walking around. A shell of a small person walking around. I was beat if I cried. I was beat if I laughed. (McKinney 1995, 114)

As submitted by Arnold (1994), many women contend with abuse by not responding to their victimization. One woman offers the following examples of how she toughened up, emotionally and physically, as a way to fight off the father who was abusing her and her mother:

> You learned to toughen up because you were not allowed to cry. . . . You held everything back, and you didn't cry. Your emotions weren't important. I think I held a lot inside. I was tough on the outside, but inside I was really, really hurt. (McKinney 1995, 149)

> I lifted weights every single day for three years. I was huge, but by the time I reached my peak the abuse stopped except for when I got married. That pisses me off because I want to know why he stopped. Was it because I was at the peak of my weight lifting and that I'd had enough of his shit, or was it something else? Of course, he'll never tell me because he's in extreme and total denial. (McKinney 1995, 141)

Many women go from one depraved situation to another, and often the result is self-hate, internalized oppression. One woman, abused by her parents and husband and terrorized in reform school, voices:

> I was told I was ugly for so many years, I believe it. When my husband and I got together, I was so sick. He caught me in the bathroom one day and said, "What are you doing? I can hear things

happening in here." I was slapping myself. I'd been beating myself up in the mirror and talking to myself: "You're a dog. You're a dog."

Another prisoner's reaction to abuse was to become inconspicuous, nevertheless, filled with fear:

Being slapped on the face and body, I felt sad. I felt like, sort of incompetent. . . . By keeping quiet I didn't get slapped. If I said the wrong thing I would get slapped or yelled at. I was just jumpy and scared. I just was always afraid of things. . . . (McKinney 1995, 172)

Some women, because of prior horrific relationships with men, seek revenge as a way to survive and resist abuse. A woman who was sexually abused multiple times by men in her family and in prison for a sexual assault charge (due to her distinctive technique) describes the method she used against her son's abuser:

I beat up a guy who raped my son when he was three years old. I flipped out on this guy; I was seeing every one of the men who assaulted me in my life. . . . I was beating this guy so goddamn hard that I blacked out. And I was going to castrate him. . . . My fall-partner shoved a broomstick up his butt and told him, "That's what it felt like to a three-year-old child getting raped."

Another woman concludes that an additional way to retaliate against men is to practice prostitution. She narrates that she

was getting revenge on men thinking that every time I took their money I was getting even with them for what they had done to me. They abused me, took my dignity, so I'm taking their money. . . . I thought that, and I still do to this day because of what my stepdad did to me. I've had a grudge against men for what they did to me. (McKinney 1995, 112)

On the other hand, another prisoner reasoned that because she was sexually abused as a child, the idea of engaging in prostitution was extremely distasteful. As a drug addict, though, she had to think of a way to earn quick cash to support her habit. Calculating the range of severity for various crimes, she explains:

People used to say, "You're so pretty and you're an addict, why don't you just go out and turn tricks." I think because of my sexual abuse, I couldn't stomach to do that. I'd always say, "I play with guns, I don't play with cocks." . . . Anyway I did start turning tricks. I turned to prostitution as opposed to carrying a gun because of the severity of the penalties toward crime. Was that a conscious decision on my part? You bet! At that time I knew that I was so heavily into drugs I had to do something else. I couldn't be carrying a gun. I couldn't be sticking people up. I figured I could try prostitution. Of course I had to be high. I'd never been able to go out not high. I did turn to that for an amount of time. I did support my habit and it brought me into other things like Sugar Daddies.

Given the violence in their families, we should not be surprised when those harassed return violence, as acts of resistance and survival, to the parents who used it for many years. Imprisoned for beating her mother to death because she suspected her mother was abusing her daughter, a woman says:

When I did it, I was high and I was drunk, okay. But my daughter was in the care of my mother, and I came home and heard, you know, how like if a baby cries normally? My daughter was not crying normally. It was almost as if she [my mother] was beating the shit out of her [my daughter] 'cause she was crying so hard. I guess she was crying for too long. My mom was in the house with a bunch of people, and they were just partying away. My first thought was when I got there was she was beating her up. She was doing something physical to her like she did with me. So that's what my first thought was and I didn't care about my mom. I didn't care about anything else. I just . . . didn't want my daughter to grow up in that because I did, and it's a cycle. . . . I thought, "Well, it ain't gonna carry on anymore 'cause I'm gonna stop this." Ya know, I know how it feels, and it hurts. I do not want to have my mom do that to my own daughter 'cause I know, just know it. It's just, it's not the thing to beat up my own child like my mother did to me. I just snapped and I know I did kill my mom. It's like nothing in this world can ever hurt me again the way I hurt my ownself. (McKinney 1995, 115–116)

Another prisoner, sexually abused by her father, recalls the night she nearly killed him for assaulting her mother:

> I remember one night hearing my mom scream. I got out of bed and ran into the room where they were. I saw him choking my mom. He had her up against the wall. Her feet were off the floor, and she's screaming. I ran to the linen closet in the hallway and got my mom's gun. Then I ran back, pointed it at him and told him I was going to kill him if he didn't let her go. . . . I'm 10 years old and I have this powerful feeling like the one I later got when I was on drugs and alcohol. I never had that feeling again except the night I was doing my crime. I was seeing the man who raped me when I was 5—he's hurting my mom who loves me, and I was afraid he was going to take away from me the only one that loves me. I would have killed him if he didn't let her go. (McKinney 1995, 156)

Another prisoner describes her reaction, as a brave nine-year-old girl, toward the stepfather who continually beat her and her siblings:

> My stepfather had locked my little brother in a walk in closet. He was going to hit him with a baseball bat. I grabbed a pair of scissors near the sewing machine, and I stabbed him in the leg. That put a stop to my brothers and sisters being beat on. (McKinney 1995, 158)

It is also not surprising when violence is directed toward an abusive husband. When men murder, they typically kill other men or female spouses. Women seldom murder, yet when they do it is usually an abusive male spouse. Indeed, half of the women on death row in the United States killed their husbands (Stout 1991). From 1878 to 1977, 36 percent of the female prisoner population in Montana was comprised of women imprisoned for murdering their husbands.

Women are more likely than men to be victims of domestic violence. Married women and women who report that they were never married experience lower rates of violence by intimates than divorced or separated women. White women and women of color have equivalent rates of domestic violence; however, poor women report a much higher rate of domestic violence than women with higher family incomes (Bureau of Justice 1994).

In urban areas, 80 percent of the defendants in spousal murder cases are convicted and sentenced to prison (Bureau of Justice 1994). Contrary to popular opinion (for example, see Hale and Menniti 1995), today men typically receive harsher sentences than women when they murder their spouses, although this was not the case historically. According to Patrick Langan (1995), one of the researchers behind the Bureau of Justice's 1994 report on domestic violence, this is because many states take domestic violence into account and perceive these women as acting in self-defense. Hence, the judicial system perceives a qualitative difference regarding why women and men kill their loved ones. Nevertheless, this perception does not always affect treatment: women in rural areas, who are battered more than women in urban areas, have fewer relevant services available to them, and rural police are more reluctant than urban police officers to get involved in domestic disputes (Sword 1995).

Domestic violence has never been about love—it is about control and power over people. For one prisoner, the abuse began the moment she was married; her husband degraded her constantly. Against her husband's wishes, she secured a position as a store clerk. Describing his hostility to her new job, she explains,

> My husband was standing at the bus stop waiting for me since I was only allowed to go from home to work by the bus. . . . My husband got out of the car and accused me of not working and screwing around. He got pretty nasty. He pulled up my dress to see if I had my pants off. I was embarrassed, ashamed, and degraded. It was bad. However I was so conditioned to his humiliating me by this time that I just took it in stride. (McKinney 1995, 127)

This unstable spouse also violated their two children in a similar belittling manner:

> He was always coming up from behind them and hitting them on the back of the head. He'd just laugh about it. He'd think it was funny and if I said anything to him about hitting them, he'd do it a little more. We got so we didn't show our feelings. It was almost like we had two different lives—one when he was away from the house. We could laugh and play. When he was there everybody was

quiet. Even the kids were quiet when they were small. (McKinney 1995, 128)

Some women kill their husbands not so much to defend themselves but to protect their children. This battered woman, imprisoned for the murder of her husband, clarifies:

The last thing I remember him saying was that after he killed me he was going out and kill the kids. . . . I was just trying to get away until he said that he was going to kill the kids. . . . If he hadn't threatened the kids, I think I would have just kept going out the door. (McKinney 1995, 129)

Although the battered woman syndrome, defined by Lenore Walker (1984), has gained credibility in courts throughout the United States, it has not been a successful defense in Montana.[4] In fact, lawyers in Montana are afraid they will jeopardize their clients if they use the battered woman syndrome as a defense precisely because it is not recognized by the state. No legal code exists in Montana; correspondingly, psychologists are not allowed to discuss the syndrome in court, and any testimony regarding it is thrown out (Bloomer 1993a). One of the few women in Montana to use the battered woman syndrome as a defense was Clara Mae Hess.

The Hess case clearly illustrates the prevailing ignorance in the law and the frontier mentality (not just reserved for Native Americans) found in the state of Montana. In 1989, when Hess was sixty-five years old, she killed her husband. Her attorney, arguing that she had lived a life of fear, used the battered woman syndrome as a defense. At her sentencing, Hess asked the judge not to imprison her: "I feel that I could be of more help to battered women out there. . . . The punishment for any crime just comes from inside. There's been a lot of that. It's something I'll suffer from for the rest of my life" (quoted in the *Billings Gazette*, 27 September 1990, C2).

Battered women in many other states are given probation and counseling in lieu of prison, because they are not seen as threats to society.[5] Although the prosecutor recommended a twenty-year sentence, Hess was sentenced to thirty-five years for mitigated deliberate homicide and ordered to pay a $15,000 fine. An unsympathetic district judge, Byron

Robb, reportedly skeptical of Hess's account of the shooting, simplistically expressed that "there isn't any exception in the manslaughter statutes which allows a kindly grandmother to put two bullets in her husband's brain because he's irritable" (quoted in the *Billings Gazette*, 27 September 1990, C2). Hess's attorney, Timer Moses, immediately filed an appeal, argued in the State Supreme Court in 1992, and the judge set the bond at $50,000. Hess lost her appeal and was given a thirty-year sentence by Chief Justice Turnage (Bloomer 1993a, 6).

Another Montana case, that of Monica Wall, charged with deliberate homicide, further displays the operation of misogynist law in Montana.[6] Wall, a Native woman from the Flathead Reservation, shot her husband after fifteen years of emotional and physical abuse. Her lawyer did not use the battered woman syndrome in her defense precisely because of the ruling issued in the Hess case. It had been clearly demonstrated that the syndrome was not recognized in Montana, and any testimony would have been rejected by the court. According to Bloomer, Wall's attorney postulated that a strategy using the syndrome would have been fruitless, and "he didn't want the judge to think he was using a feminist cliché. He said he wanted to try to separate Monica's case from those of other battered women who have killed their husbands. . . . He also said he avoided the term because it's not codified in Montana" (1993a, 7).

Similar to other abusive men, Wall's husband told her that if he killed her he would also kill their children. Wall's "crime" was to defend herself and her children. Considerable evidence of the length and severity of the abuse Wall sustained at the hands of her husband was presented to the court. Psychologists hired by both the defense and the prosecution concurred that Wall suffered from "severe post-traumatic stress syndrome." More specifically, Dr. Michael Scolatti, a psychologist hired by the prosecution, concluded, "The more I dug, the more convinced I was that Monica's was the purest case of Battered Women's Syndrome I have ever seen. I tried to look at this from a criminal aspect, and I just didn't see it" (quoted in Bloomer 1993a).

District Court judge C. B. McNeil had heard more than eighteen hundred domestic abuse cases when he sentenced Wall. He reduced the charge from deliberate homicide to mitigated homicide and sentenced Wall to twenty years in prison with five suspended, *despite* an agreement with prosecutors that entailed counseling and probation and no prison time. At Wall's sentencing, McNeil communicated that she "had the alternative of separation and divorce" (quoted in Bloomer 1993a). Mc-Neil added, "You should not solve your own problem by taking it into your own hands and shooting your own abuser in the back" (quoted in Bloomer 1993b, 9). A plea to the Sentence Review Board of Montana's Supreme Court for clemency fell upon deaf ears: Judge Robert Boyd cast the only dissenting vote.

For women like Monica Wall and Clara Mae Hess, there is no legal recourse. In Montana, battered women who kill abusive husbands continue to be imprisoned as "criminals." Defending yourself against an abusive husband appears to be a crime that is not racialized in Montana when sentences are pronounced. Hess, who is white, received a thirty-year sentence, while Wall, a Native American, received twenty years.

For women between the ages of fifteen and forty-four, domestic violence is the foremost cause of injury. Men who batter will continue to do so even when presented with the most dire consequences:

> Consider John Bobbitt. His abused wife, Lorena, dismembered him—literally. We know that a child burned by a hot stove won't make that mistake again. You'd think losing a penis would be painful enough that you would recoil against repeating the behavior that got you into that fix. Yet John Bobbitt—divorced from Lorena but reattached to his penis—was charged in May with domestic battery. A police report said he threw his fiancee into a wall. Maybe the only cure would be to cut off his arms. (Newsom 1994, C2)

The narratives depict women who were criminalized because they resisted abominable conditions. Their abuse was not short-lived; it began at an early age and continued into adulthood. The relentless brutality in the lives of these women unmasks not only the societal structure but the injustices in the United States. Acts of violence against women are manifestations of patriarchy and have the power to eliminate the desire for survival. Moreover, the violence is institutionalized: these women were violated by family members, boyfriends, jailers, reform school and Indian boarding school staff, and foster and adoptive families.[7] The oppression, thus, is multifaceted; not only is it complicated, it is relentless.

There are two general reactions by women to abusive situations: to resist and step out of the place reserved for women in a patriarchal society, or to internalize the oppression and accept the image presented to them. Both reactions are replies to oppression, both are undertaken in efforts to survive, and both are perceived negatively by others. Subsequently, abused women, despite their respective reactions, are at the worst criminalized and at best seen as "deviant." Moreover, the responses are not mutually exclusive. Women do not always resist *or* internalize oppression; the response will vary depending upon the context. Nevertheless, a woman responding to violence, regardless of her reaction, is placed in a lose-lose situation. It is important to challenge the oppression all women face; I propose that there is more dignity in resistance.

Violence for these women, unfortunately, does not end when they are incarcerated; rather, it continues in a form unique to the penal system. Women imprisoned at the WCC experience violence in the form of sexual intimidation, the overuse of mind-altering drugs, lengthy stays in lockup, separation from children, and, for Native Americans, denial of culture. Other examples of brutal injustices within the context of prisonization and colonization are examined in the chapters on the experiences of imprisoned women.

Five

EXPERIENCES OF WOMEN IN PRISON

"THEY KEEP ME AT A LEVEL WHERE THEY CAN CONTROL ME"

Daily life in women's prisons is somewhat different from that found in male correctional institutions. Incarcerated women, compared to incarcerated men, generally pose less of a threat to the staff or fellow prisoners. Given this, and given that women's prisons are typically smaller than men's prisons, some scholars believe that women's prisons operate in a less rigid fashion (Bowker 1981; Giallombardo 1966; Ward and Kassebaum 1965). Nevertheless, Rafter (1990) suggests that despite the benign appearance of women's prisons there is still strict control of their behavior, and that one function of prisons is to control not only crime but also gender.

The narratives reveal that incarcerated Natives at the WCC experience prison differently from white prisoners, and that prisoners housed in the maximum-security unit, where Natives are disproportionately represented, experience prison differently from prisoners in the general-population building.[1] Lesbians are exposed to an extremely homophobic environment.

Conditions are deficient in many ways, including the physical condition of the facility, medical care, counseling and treatment programs, and other rehabilitative programs. Moreover, the social environment of the prison exemplifies control, not rehabilitation. The women's prison in Montana has a history of control. The early prisons exhibited sexist and racist policies and had trouble dealing with the problem of where to confine so few women. A summary of the history of the women's

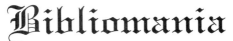

Western Montana State Prison, between 1912 and 1930. Women were confined in a facility behind the prison. Photo by Wingate Art Studio, courtesy of the Montana Historical Society, Helena.

prison provides a foundation for the atmosphere women incarcerated in Montana encounter in the 1990s.

THE EARLY PRISON

From 1878 to 1889, the two women incarcerated in Montana's prison were located on the third floor of the men's building. In 1889 a small building built was specifically for them. In 1960 the women's prison was converted to a maximum-security unit for men and the women were moved to the garage at the warden's house. In 1963 they were housed in a unit in the laundry building behind the warden's house, and in 1966 they were relocated to the basement of the guards' quarters.[2]

Following the notion that imprisoned women are in need of therapy, in 1970 some female prisoners were moved to the state mental hospital at Warm Springs. Prisoners who did not fit into the program at the state hospital were transferred to York, Nebraska (*Montana Prison News* 1970). On 22 March 1970 the *Montana Standard* reported that the prisoners at the mental hospital, who were seen as "patients," were allowed to wear their own clothes, attend school and psychotherapy, and work in the kitchen and as nurses' aides. They were under the care of a staff psychologist, who supervised their "program" (*Montana Prison News* 1970). In 1975 women were no longer sent to the state mental institution; rather, they were transferred to prisons in Nebraska and California. From 1977 to 1982 female prisoners were held at county jails while awaiting transfer to out-of-state prisons, or they were sent to the state's pre-release center as prisoners, not parolees.

Prior to 1958, the only work female prisoners were allowed to do was the guards' laundry. After that date, they were permitted to work at the offices of the Registrar of Motor Vehicles and the prison administration. Reflecting sex-role stereotypes, on 23 February 1969 the *Montana Standard* reported that female prisoners were used as the warden's housekeeper; other duties included washing and ironing the warden's clothes. They were paid twenty-five to fifty cents a day, which was quite a financial bargain for the warden because I assume the pay, albeit low, was from the state, not his personal account. The prisoners were allowed to cook their own meals. Their uniforms were blue and white striped shirt with jeans or a tan skirt with a white blouse. A dichotomized image is presented by the uniforms: jeans and striped shirt suggest prisoner status, while a skirt and blouse present a "ladylike" appearance.

Solitary confinement was described as detainment in total darkness, and many prisoners were given tranquilizers for depression (*Montana Standard* 1969). In 1969, upon their departure from prison, the women were given $25 gate-pay (the money issued when a prisoner is released) and, following the model of "true womanhood," a trip to the beauty parlor. Cosmetically sound, they embarked on reentry into society.

The imprisonment of women out-of-state from 1977 to 1982, due to the lack of a women's prison, reflected a nationwide practice. In the United States in 1973, only twenty-eight states had separate facilities for women (Chesney-Lind 1991). During 1982 women in Montana were also imprisoned at the state's alcohol treatment center and in four county jails. In 1981, recognizing the need for a women's prison, the state legislature authorized funding for forty-one women prisoners. The site selected temporarily was a vacant nurses' dormitory, known now as the

The EU (Expansion Unit) or the maximum-security building for women prisoners at the Women's Correctional Center, 1994. Photo by Shane Ross.

general-population building, located on the grounds of the state's mental institution in a remote area of Montana. On 6 May 1982, the Women's Correctional Center received its first prisoner.

THE WOMEN'S CORRECTIONAL CENTER

Previous work (Dobash, Dobash, and Gutteridge 1986; Heidensohn 1985) demonstrates that women's prisons are inferior in every way to men's prisons. The WCC follows this pattern and women are imprisoned in second-rate accommodations. In agreement with the patterns shown in earlier research (Giallombardo 1966; Rafter 1990), the geographic location of the Women's Correction Center affects prisoner-staff relations. The prison is located in a county that is mostly white. In addition, surrounding communities and towns are white.[3] The nearest Indian reservation is approximately five hours from the prison site. All staff, who are recruited locally, are white. The only exception is a Native American woman who travels from a nearby town to conduct group therapy sessions with Native prisoners.

Front view of the general-population building at the Women's Correctional Center,
1994. Photo by Shane Ross.

The prison was originally intended to confine forty women; however, there are sixty-eight prisoners. The sentencing trend in Montana results in a prison that is severely overcrowded. Some prisoners' cells in the general-population building house five women. During a period of extreme overcrowding, prisoners did not have access to legal information because the law library was transformed into a cell. When asked if the building was renovated in an effort to overcome the poor quality of the prison, prisoners respond that the changes are superficial and the building is greatly deficient in many ways.

When an evaluation group toured the prison, the visitors were so appalled at the physical condition of the prison that one woman asked a prisoner why a lawsuit was never filed by the prisoners. At the risk of a reprimand, this prisoner explained to her that one was filed but never reached its destination because that type of mail never passes through the prison administration. Prison rules specify that all incoming mail is opened with the exception of legal mail, which must be opened in front of a guard. Outgoing mail is not censored unless there is "probable cause"—for example, a letter sent to a person deemed "at risk" (e.g., addressed to a prisoner in another prison). All mail coming in from jails and prisons is read by prison staff.

This is the small yard in the back of the Women's Correctional Center. This area was reserved for the prisoners' outdoor activities. Photo by Shane Ross.

All the prisoners grumble about the water and are concerned that it causes the skin rashes that afflict many of the women. A few prisoners who have the money buy water from the canteen. The electrical wiring is unsafe, and prisoners proclaim that power surges blow up their appliances. The institutional food is prepared in the kitchen of the state mental hospital and transported several blocks to the prison. This food, which I consider unpalatable, is all many prisoners have to eat. Most prisoners fill up on bread, margarine, and Kool-Aid. Those who can afford to, purchase food from the canteen; they claim the prison food is unhealthy and makes them ill.

Although the prison is a dilapidated building, it presents an amiable appearance. There are no bars on the windows in the general-population building and no required prisoner uniforms.[4] Minimum-status prisoners can be seen walking around the grounds accompanied by the recreational director. On the periphery of the grounds is a relatively new building, known as maximum security or the EU (Expansion Unit). This unit, with its heavy doors, bars, and locked control room, houses high-risk prisoners: eleven in maximum security and four in close security in isolation cells. All doors are locked and women are imprisoned in individual cells, where they are constantly watched by prison guards.

Prisoners here, of course, do the hardest time. The smell of urine throughout the building is overwhelming. Previously the EU was the forensic ward for the state mental hospital, and guards and prisoners both say the patients urinated everywhere.

Maximum security is reserved for prisoners with "behavioral problems"—for example, they were accused of talking back to a guard or other staff, causing fights within the general-population building, or "general insubordination." These prisoners are seen as "unmanageable" women. Isolation cells are reserved for those women who cannot mix in either general population or maximum security. Prisoners in isolation exist in small cells with no windows and the sparse furniture bolted to the floor. Isolation cells are also used to house new prisoners while they are assessed by prison staff. Prisoners deemed psychotic or suicidal are sent to maximum security in the forensic ward at the state mental hospital. The length of stay at the forensic ward ranges from ten to thirty days.

ASSESSMENT

When a woman arrives at the prison she is placed on reception status in administrative segregation for seven to fourteen days, until she is medically cleared for general population. According to prison staff, prisoners are evaluated regarding educational skills, mental health needs, and other rehabilitative concerns. According to prisoners, the assessment begins with a shower and delousing and concludes with a brief visit from a psychologist, who asks the prisoners if they realize why they are in prison. This is when prisoners are supposed to demonstrate remorse for their crimes. The schoolteacher then enters and inquires about their educational needs. Assessment—conducted coldly and quickly. Prisoners allege that there is no further assessment of their needs.

Many incarcerated women experience assessment as rape, particularly the debasing cavity searches (Faith 1993b; Jose-Kampfner 1990). A Native woman at the WCC describes the intake process:

> You are taken into a bathroom and ordered to strip naked. You are searched thoroughly, which also means cavity searches which are at the discretion of the officers. And usually it depends upon how much

they have heard about you; and if they want to make it hard for you, they will do their humiliating cavity searches. Next is the shower. The shower is turned on and you are ordered into the shower with the guards watching you. You are given the solution for delousing. You are told where to wash and to wash good, or they will wash you. When the *fun* time is over, you are given a gown and put into lock-down. The room will become your life for fourteen days. It has three beds (two single beds and a wooden box used as a bed), toilet, sink, and an old dresser. The room is dark, gloomy, and always cold. The heat is shut off and there are no vents in the room. I remember it was so cold and I had been issued one small pillow, one sheet, one old army blanket. Even so, I was so thankful to have those. I had less when I was drinking around. You are later taken out and your picture is taken for identification purposes. The last process, the best of all this, is you are given your own number.

The emphasis is on the degradation and control of prisoners (see Goffman 1961 and Foucault 1979). Prisoners have already been branded, labeled as unruly; after all, they are "criminal" women. Prisoners are ritualistically dehumanized, regulated, reduced to numbers. Part of the "ceremony" of assessment is to "break a prisoner's spirit" and ready her for "rehabilitation" (Faith 1993b, 151).

MEDICAL CARE

Feinman (1986) suggests that health care in women's prisons is almost always inadequate. This prison is typical and all the prisoners complain loudly about the health care. The prison contracts with a doctor from the mental institution and retains a nurse on staff full-time (five days a week). For medical emergencies, prisoners are transported fifteen miles to a hospital. Prisoners feel that hospital visits from family will aid in their recovery; prison rules, however, state that when a prisoner is hospitalized, family members are not allowed to visit unless her condition is critical and classified as life-threatening.

The prison contracts with an obstetrician from a nearby town for pregnant prisoners. All imprisoned pregnant women are satisfied with the care provided by this doctor. They see the doctor, whom they particularly like, once a week. The prison, nevertheless, does not offer any prenatal care, and the women view this as problematic. Additionally, the prison employs one psychologist, who works at the prison five and one-half hours per week, and a psychiatrist, who is retained by the prison for three hours per week.

The prison also contracts with a dentist from a nearby town; prisoners are transported to his office for dental care. Prisoners complain about dental problems and the slow process entailed in seeing the dentist. Many women have numerous cavities when they arrive at the prison, and some are in pain months before an appointment is scheduled with the dentist.

Prior studies disclose that imprisoned women have more health problems than either women on the outside or imprisoned men (Resnik and Shaw 1980; Shaw 1982). Other research (Feinman 1986; Ross and Fabiano 1986) discloses that medical care in women's prisons does not meet the needs specific to women. At the WCC, several women with existing medical problems believe their health is in serious danger because the prison does not supply them with adequate care. For instance, one prisoner had a lump removed from her breast. She protests that her breast not only is still sore but is draining and apparently infected. The prison doctor insists there is no infection, and the prison administration refuses her an appointment with another doctor for a second opinion. One year after her surgery, an ACLU report (Crichton 1991) confirmed that her breast remained unhealed and there was a lump present.

A prisoner mentions unnecessary hysterectomies that occurred at the prison from the late 1980s to the early 1990s. When trying to talk about her experience she is overcome with tears. She was told by prison medical staff that she had uterine cancer; she later discovered that she did not. According to her, other prisoners were subjected to the same surgery, but she doubts they will divulge any information because of the subsequent emotional trauma caused by the hysterectomies. That any woman is subjected to an unneeded, unwanted hysterectomy is criminal. Moreover, for Native women it is implicative of the federal government's policy of involuntary sterilization that flourished in the 1960s and 1970s.

Prisoners briefly disclose that prison staff ordered them to clean up the asbestos at the WCC, apparently without protective equipment or proper ventilation. Several prisoners have been coughing since they completed the chore and wonder if their constitutional rights were vio-

lated. It is well documented that asbestos is dangerous—in fact lethal—
and can pose a serious medical problem. That these prisoners were not
given protective gear is cruel and unusual punishment.

A prisoner in maximum security believes the prison deliberately hu-
miliated her when she sought medical care due to gynecological problems. This woman, who suffers painful and irregular menstruation, says:

> I have something seriously wrong with my female parts. I've gone
> to the doctor three times on this. This is how disgustingly gross
> this institution is. I was in a max cell—they knew weeks before
> you're scheduled to go to the doctor—they know these things.
> I was supposed to be showered that morning; I was not showered.
> I had been on my period; had just stopped the day before. I went
> to the doctor to have my uterus cauterized, so you know they had
> to go up inside me, without a shower—this is gross. I went to that
> doctor three times. I've put in kite after kite to the nurse.[5] They
> put me on birth-control pills for three months. What the hell's that
> going to do? I need something done that's going to fix it.

In addition to being embarrassed because she was not allowed to shower
before her examination, she believes that she has serious medical problems that are not attended to by the prison. In the prisoner's view, this
neglect occurs because the state does not want to pay for her medical care.

Some prisoners convey that their illnesses are not taken seriously by
prison staff. One prisoner, who has lived a life of terror and relates her
existing physical ailments directly to her abuse, reveals:

> I have an ulcer and they took away the medicine because they said it
> wasn't serious enough. My stomach hurts all the time—all the time.
> I puked blood the beginning of this month and they don't want to
> do anything about it.

Another prisoner, who was abused prior to incarceration, explains:

> I get sharp pains in my head. My eyes get blurry. . . . I've had two
> head injuries here [in prison]. The first time I got hurt downstairs in
> the gym. I fell on my head and I was really dizzy. I vomited right

away. He [prison staff member] said, "Are you bleeding?" I said, "No," and he said, "Well, you're all right. Get up and play basketball." And two days after that, I was still dizzy and I fell on my head again. That's when they took me to the doctor. . . . One of the officers called down there and said I was faking it. I was really mad. You can't get hurt in here without them saying you're faking it.

The preceding examples of inadequate medical care not only represent medical emergencies but also illustrate the control and power wielded against women in this prison. Moreover, these examples are a violation of the Eighth Amendment: to leave prisoners medically unattended or to dole out inadequate medical care is cruel and unusual punishment (Feinman 1986).

MEDICATION AS CONTROL

Eugene Delorme (Santee Sioux), who has been incarcerated most of his adult life, discusses the overuse of Thorazine in the Washington State Penitentiary:

I'll tell you the big trick they had. They kept everybody on Thorazine, see. They give you Thorazine three, four times a day, and that was guaranteed to keep everybody quiet, in line and just kinda shuffling around like zombies, you know. I took my share of the Thorazine, then after a week or so I started hiding it because I couldn't handle it anymore. When you take Thorazine, well, you can't even think. (Cardozo-Freeman 1993, 98)

Studies in the United States indicate that incarcerated women are more heavily medicated than incarcerated men (Resnik and Shaw 1980; Sim 1991). Many women become addicted to the medication, subsequently compounding their problems—especially if they came to prison with addiction problems. Moreover, there is a sexist bias in psychiatric diagnoses in the criminal justice system (Smart 1976). The basic assumption is that women are more vulnerable to emotional disturbances and, therefore, that imprisoned females require more psychiatric treatment services, especially psychotropic drugs. In some cases, this has led to women serving longer sentences so they will have more time to "benefit" from the treatment (Haft 1980).

Interviews with women imprisoned in California (Espinosa 1993) disclose that prisoners are heavily medicated while in jail awaiting trial. The prisoners argue that the overuse of antipsychotic drugs resulted in the suppression of feelings, impairing their ability to defend themselves at their legal hearings. A study conducted on a women's prison in Great Britain (Carlen 1985) revealed that the drugs psychiatrists prescribe actually threaten a prisoner's survival. Some women experience negative side effects from the drugs, such as weight gain and a cloudy thought process—or what Carlen calls being reduced to "zombies" (1985, 160). Edwin Schur, supporting the notion that drugs are used to control women, maintains that "The prescribing of drugs is an integral part of the medicalization of women's life situations. . . . it functions very effectively to 'cool' women out, [and] to support a depoliticizing and pathologizing of their dissatisfactions" (1984, 195). Many women, therefore, are not only stigmatized because they are imprisoned; they face additional negative consequences because they are perceived as "mentally ill."

At the WCC, prescription medications and over-the-counter remedies are obtained from the nurse or guards. Prisoners allege that medication and mind-altering drugs are often given to the wrong prisoners by unqualified guards dispensing medication. When asked about health care, a Native woman communicates, "When I got sick, I couldn't get them to do anything. I didn't know what was happening. They ended up giving me somebody else's meds." When asked if the prison simply made a mistake, she replies:

No! They knew what they were doing; it was to make me numb. And, they said that they called the doctor and he told me to take them, but I don't like to take things unless I hear it from the doctor.

Although some prisoners are worried that the overuse of mind-altering drugs will compound their addiction problems, others are more concerned that, as the Carlen (1985) study indicates, medications are one way to control and "break" prisoners. Being "broken," according to prisoners at the WCC, involves processes of control used by the prison to produce compliant women or "model" prisoners. The processes include humiliation, lowering self-esteem, multiple times in lockup, and mind-altering drugs.

In February of 1995, a Klamath/Paiute woman imprisoned at the Oregon Women's Correctional Center Isolation Segregation Unit asked to see a spiritual leader from the Paiute tribe and requested cedar and sage to pray with (*GroundWork*, April 1996). Her pleas were ignored and she was given Prozac by the prison doctor. She was returned to the general population but within a short time sent back to isolation on charges of felony assault. Nash Araiza, a spiritual advisor for the Oregon Department of Corrections, maintains that the denial of spiritual support, in conjunction with the Prozac, caused this young woman's aggressive behavior and subsequent return to isolation.

Leading authorities on Native Americans and depression (see Shore and Manson 1985) warn against generalizing depressive symptoms, as defined by Western medicine, to other cultures. What may be a symptom of depression in Euro-American culture may be viewed in Native culture as a spiritual dilemma or a facet of everyday life and thus normal. Native women determine that white staff misconstrue their behavior and that this leads to the prescribing of drugs. The prison environment is alien to these women, and some respond by becoming quiet and observing how things are conducted. These women express that their behavioral reaction, one of quietness, is misinterpreted by prison counseling staff as a type of suppression of their anger and bitterness.

Agnes clearly believes that because the prison staff do not know how to relate to Native Americans, they try to control them:

> So, in order for white society to deal with the Native American, they give them a type of dependency. And, I fought with this when I first got here because they told me that they felt I should go on antidepressants. So I said—and this was a counselor talking to me—I said, "My sentencing papers say that one of the conditions are that I deal with my alcohol problem. I have an alcohol problem." And, I said, "So now I'm dealing with it. I'm going to groups and participating, but yet you people are telling me that I need antidepressants. You're going to take me off one dependent and put me on another, so when I leave here I'm going to have two dependents." I said, "That don't make sense, so this is your rehabilitation to me? This is what you're offering me?"

Fortunately, the counselor, according to Agnes, was dumbfounded when she readily delivered her opinion, and he never prescribed any medication for her.

Agnes insists that the overuse of mind-altering drugs is just another way the prison controls both Native and non-Native prisoners, and she characterizes this as "totally outrageous." Although not all prisoners are required to take these drugs, according to Agnes, many do so because they are not strong enough to refuse them, or they take them to cope with the "evil" prison environment. For instance, a Native prisoner who spent a lengthy time in maximum security initially took a drug called Haldol to cope with her experiences in lockup:

Haldol is a drug they give to people who can't cope with lockup. It makes you feel dead, paralyzed. And then I started getting side-effects from the Haldol. I wanted to fight anybody, any of the officers. I was screaming at them and telling them to get out of my face, so the doctor said, "We can't have that." And, they put me on Tranxene. I don't take pills; I never had trouble sleeping until I got here. Now I'm suppose to see [the counselor] again because of my dreams. If you got a problem, they're not going to take care of it. They're going to put you on drugs so they can control you.

Many prisoners discuss a Native woman who has been on Thorazine since her arrival. This woman is at the point of hallucinating, yet the staff continue to medicate her. She is continually shuffled between the prison, long stretches in maximum security, and the forensic ward at the state mental hospital. While this woman is described as "extremely mentally disturbed" by institutional personnel, prisoners maintain that she was broken by the prison.

Another Native prisoner, who has been in maximum security for nearly one year, insists that lengthy lockup time, in combination with drugs, broke her:

They keep me at a level here where they can control me. They think if they keep me drugged up all the time, that everything's going to go just dandy. But I've tongued my meds before and went and puked them up. I wasn't thinking straight in my head; I couldn't figure out what was going on. So much has happened. I feel like they already broke me.

Prisoners, many of whom arrive already vulnerable from prior abuse, are subjected to too much social control and, consequently, are broken.

Several prisoners mention that they are on Prozac or Tranxene, and several others are on "sleeping pills" they cannot specifically identify. Additionally, several prisoners remark that it is easier to acquire drugs legally inside prison than it is illegally on the outside.

EDUCATIONAL PROGRAMS

When discussing programs for prisoners, prison staff continually focus on the concept of rehabilitation. Nonetheless, to all prisoners, this concept is not operating. Feinman (1986) argues that rehabilitation programs for imprisoned women are fashioned so as to produce conformity to Euro-American culture. The assumption, according to Feinman, is that imprisoned women desire to be wives, mothers, and homemakers, but although most imprisoned women are mothers, relatively few are wives and homemakers. Imprisoned women are not offered the education or training necessary for their economic survival (Goetting 1985; Ross and Fabiano 1986). As in the past, training continues to reflect sex-role stereotypes, with options such as food service, clerical work, and cosmetology (Carlen 1983; Feinman 1986; Ross and Fabiano 1986). Subsequently, when women are released from prison they are prepared for low-status, low-paying, sex-segregated occupations. Again, the WCC offers no exception to these trends, and the institution considers this kind of training "rehabilitation."

The rehabilitative focus, according to prison staff, is primarily on building self-esteem. One way this is accomplished is through various educational courses. The prison offers educational classes on three levels: college courses available to all prisoners in the general population; a remedial adult education course for those in general population with high-school diplomas or GEDs but testing below a high-school level; and GED preparation classes accessible to all prisoners. Prisoners classified as Close status do not have access to any educational programs.

Prison staff determine that college courses will build self-esteem. Although the prison recently contracted with a state college to provide educational services to prisoners, the curriculum is sparse. Prisoners receive one dollar a day if they are enrolled in remedial educational classes or GED classes but receive no money if they are enrolled in college courses. Nevertheless, they get thirteen days per month of "good-time" for college courses if they maintain a C-minus average.[6] The few prisoners who are enrolled in college courses claim they are jeopardized by the existing payment system because they do not get the one dollar a day given to prisoners enrolled in other educational courses. Furthermore, prisoners not eligible for guaranteed student loans (for example, if they are not within ten years of their discharge date) are forced to finance their own schooling.

Several Native women have difficulty enrolling in college. For instance, Winona did not fill out the financial-aid forms correctly, and although she requested help, no one offered to help her. She wrote the college and asked that they telephone her. According to Winona, when the college called the prison, the staff did not call her to the telephone, and then she was reprimanded by prison staff because the college called the prison. This proved too much for Winona, who desperately wanted to go to college and was totally frustrated by the prison's hampering her progress. She recalls the reprimand with this story:

> I just wanted to pull my hair out and go, "What the hell do you want me to do?" There should be two doors here [office of prison staff]. I saw this in The Far Side [cartoon strip] the other day. A little man standing there in front of these two doors and on these doors it said, "Damned if you do" and "Damned if you don't." There's a devil back there going, "Yeah, it doesn't matter what the hell you do."

Winona managed to enroll in college courses but did not have the required textbooks for three weeks, due to similar bureaucratic mix-ups. She later found out that prison staff had extra textbooks and could have loaned them to her. Winona proposes that because she is Native and labeled a troublemaker, prison staff purposely set her up to fail. Other Native prisoners say that obtaining college classes or good in-house jobs depends upon how well they relate to the guards.

TRAINING OPPORTUNITIES

In men's prisons there are prison industries in which the men learn a marketable skill and earn money, while there are few prison industries in women's prisons (Feinman 1986). Most of the industries available to women involve sewing, which is obviously a sex-segregated occupation. Policy makers in Corrections reason that there are too few women incarcerated to expand programs and that women either will not want to work when released or will have husbands to support them (Feinman 1986). The status quo, accordingly, is maintained, and little is done to provide incarcerated women with the education or skills necessary for their survival once they are released.

The WCC has an industry program, On the Job Training (OJT) positions, and in-house jobs offered to all prisoners located in general population. The industry program employs three prisoners who are sewing camouflage nets and jackets for military personnel involved in Operation Desert Shield in Saudi Arabia. Joan has one of the three valued positions and is grateful to be making two dollars a day, instead of the one dollar a day she made when she cleaned the bathrooms. A major problem with the industry program is that when the sewing machines are operating, they interfere with the telecommunications used for educational classes. Additionally, the sewing machines are in poor condition and frequently break down.

Prisoners remark that the only jobs available until recently were several OJT positions. To obtain these, prisoners must be classified as Minimum status and must have served at least six months in prison. The OJT positions consist of secretarial/clerical work at the prison, the nearby mental institution, or the law library. There are eleven OJT positions available and a long prisoner waiting list. Although prisoners in these positions are allowed to work only four hours a day, the jobs are highly coveted because they pay $1.75 a day, which is more than in-house jobs. Whereas all positions are open to prisoners who meet the standard criteria, there are more women than positions available. With sixty-eight prisoners and fourteen prized jobs available, much tension is created among prisoners. Prisoners maintain that the positions are given at the discretion of prison staff, which perpetuates jealousy and tension among the prisoners.

A position paper issued by Native women prisoners shows that, comparable to experiences of imprisoned Native Canadian women (Faith 1993b), racism in job appointments is a major problem. Native prisoners claim that white women are given the best positions and that Native women "progress from cleaning toilet bowls to washing dishes or cleaning and mopping floors" (Native American Women Prisoners 1993, 3). After citing numerous examples of racism and the lack of training opportunities, the paper concludes, "Could it be, Indian women are somewhat viewed as inadequate and are not capable of handling such positions?" (3).

Most women enter prison poorly educated and unskilled. Prior to incarceration, many prisoners at the WCC were the sole breadwinners in their families; adequate training, accordingly, is paramount to them. These women clearly perceive the lack of training opportunities as sexism. They note that the men's prison offers a variety of training including meat cutting, furniture manufacturing, horticulture, business skills, telemarketing, motor vehicle repair, furniture refinishing and upholstery, logging, printing, plumbing, and electrical work. The women prisoners view this as unfair, while the ACLU sees it as illegal. A class-action lawsuit filed on 23 April 1993 (*Many Horses et al. v. Racicot et al.*, 1993) specifically cites "invidious" gender discrimination in educational and training opportunities available to imprisoned women in Montana.[7]

In-house positions, which are the lowest paid at one dollar a day (recently raised from fifty cents), include general maintenance, office cleaning, kitchen duty, and working in the laundry. These tasks require no skills; women know how to clean toilets, wash dishes and clothes, and peel potatoes. Clearly, this kind of work cannot be considered "training" by anyone's standards. The pay usually amounts to eighteen to twenty dollars a month, which is not enough to cover prisoners' expenses. The prisoners are responsible for buying all their personal items, such as shampoo, lotion, stamps, envelopes, and laundry soap. The state furnishes towels, sheets, and blankets. In order for the state to supply personal items (not including stamps, writing paper, and envelopes), a prisoner must be classified as "indigent," which requires that she have no more than ten dollars in her personal account. The state recently lowered the maximum from twenty dollars down to ten dollars; in the opinion of the prisoners, the state should have raised it to thirty dollars instead.

According to pregnant women, they are discriminated against regarding job assignment. Also, they are allowed to work only two days a week. Prisoners in maximum security have regular in-house duties but are not paid, and those confined to isolation cells are not assigned in-house detail.

The previously described positions train women for "women's work"; that is, for low-status and low-paying positions. In reality this type of training, which resembles the training in the early years at the women's prison, does not have the potential for "rehabilitation." Nevertheless, the work provides a small amount of money and aids in the alleviation of boredom.

Even from a cursory view of the prison, the notion of control is conspicuous. Correspondingly, issues of racism and sexism, although institutionalized, are not difficult to detect. These powerful systems of control become unmistakable in the next chapter, which examines the counseling and treatment programs, prisoners in maximum security, and the management of gay prisoners.

Six

REHABILITATION OR CONTROL

"WHAT ARE THEY TRYING TO DO? DESTROY ME?"

The WCC's rehabilitative programming is based on the notion of "therapy." The idea of therapy, as implemented in women's prisons, operates on the outdated assumption that imprisoned women are mentally deranged (see Pollak 1950). Women are seen as neurotic and in need of "treatment." Not surprisingly, the women's prison in Montana is located on the grounds of the state mental institution. Moreover, the idea of treatment is embedded in the language of prison personnel—euphemisms run amok. For instance, prison personnel refer to guards as "officers," cells as "rooms," and the prison as a "center." In pre-release, prisoners are referred to as "clients" or "residents," indicating an imagined gain in status. These euphemisms are too gentle and, subsequently, misleading in the description of the experiences of imprisoned women.

Following a nationwide pattern established in the 1960s and 1970s (Roberts 1994), the criminal justice system in Montana operates theoretically on the notion of rehabilitation. The assumption is that someone is ill or deviant in some manner, and the goal is to restore well-being through various therapeutic models and education.

The idea of rehabilitating prisoners is not new. Dobash, Dobash, and Gutteridge (1986) explain that early prisons in the United States and Great Britain attempted to create an environment conducive to moral transformation. The authors propose that from the onset imprisoned women and men were handled differently. Imprisoned women were deemed more "morally depraved and corrupt and in need of special, closer forms of control and confinement" than imprisoned men (Dobash, Dobash, and Gutteridge 1986, 1). Experiences of imprisoned women were additionally affected by the unequal treatment according to race/ethnicity. Important historical research by Nichole Hahn Rafter

(1990) informs us that women's prisons in the 1870s emerged as a bi-furcated system: white women were sent to reformatories, while African American women were housed in prisons. Although white women sent to reformatories were subjected to "therapy" based on the ideals of "true womanhood," imprisoned women of color experienced abhorrent conditions.

During the 1980s and 1990s, citizens of the United States became more fearful of crime and lost faith in the nation's criminal justice system. Consequently, according to John Hagan, many Americans are suspicious of attempts to rehabilitate prisoners, and "as a result, the American criminal justice system less often rehabilitates offenders than it perpetuates and intensifies effects of residential segregation, racial inequality, and concentrated poverty" (1994, 140). Although policy in the 1980s and 1990s may theoretically focus on rehabilitation, in practice prisoners perceive that they are controlled rather than rehabilitated. Regardless of the "truth" of the matter, prisoners' perceptions that control is the purpose of prison programs renders attempts at rehabilitation ineffective.

Rafter (1990) suggests that one function of prisons is to control not only crime but also gender and race. In addition, domination is exerted at the WCC over the prisoners not only as women but also as Native Americans. The effects of colonialism are reflected in the disproportionate number of imprisoned Native women, the general treatment of imprisoned Native women, denial of culture, and reprisal. The narratives disclose that although all women are subjected to horrendous treatment, Native women and lesbians endure additional discrimination. Moreover, those confined to the maximum-security unit encounter excessive punishment.

COUNSELING AND TREATMENT PROGRAMS

Concurring with the Glick and Neto study (1977), counseling and treatment in this prison are often left to untrained staff. The prison employs one full-time alcohol and drug counselor, a counselor for Native prisoners who comes to the prison once a week for one hour, and a full-time treatment specialist who serves as the primary counselor for a variety of group sessions. The prison contracts with a parenting-class facilitator, a psychologist for six hours per week, and a psychiatrist for five hours per week. According to prison staff, the prison offers the following classes and groups to prisoners: victims of sexual abuse, self-image, assertiveness training, codependency, healthy relationships, parenting, and a repeat-offender group. According to prisoners, these classes never meet regularly.

While it may be shocking to discover that some imprisoned women do not have access to any "therapeutic counseling" (Grobsmith 1994, 117), very few prisoners at the WCC find counseling beneficial. Prisoners do not trust prison staff, especially the guards, counselors, psychiatrist, and psychologist. Consequently, they do not engage in any real dialogue with staff, with the exception of the parenting-class facilitator and the Native counselor.

According to prison staff, all future treatment programs will be revised to concentrate on building self-esteem. A staff member asserts that the "unique" staff assist in facilitating a positive self-esteem for prisoners. What this staff member communicates directly contradicts what prisoners perceive. No prisoner discusses the boosting of her self-esteem by prison staff. In fact, prisoners express the opposite—the continual lowering of self-esteem due to disrespectful behavior shown to them by most prison personnel. In the words of one prisoner, "If you had any self-esteem when you walked in here, you can guarantee you aren't going to have any when you leave." Moreover, lesbians voice that prison staff try to force them into counseling because of their sexual preference. Conclusively, being a lesbian is perceived as "sick" behavior.

All prisoners bemoan the lack of qualified staff. Prisoners do not mention anything positive about the recently hired NA (Narcotics Anonymous) and AA (Alcoholic Anonymous) counselor. Although all prisoners proclaim that the counselor is "nice" and that they value the program, they conclude that the counselor is unqualified. He was supposedly hired after the ACLU toured the prison and heard prisoners' complaints about the lack of counseling services. According to prisoners, he was employed to pacify them. Nevertheless, some prisoners do benefit from the NA group, but only because people outside the prison are selected as guest speakers, prisoners are allowed to select topic areas, and the group consists of prisoners willing to work on their addiction problems.

Most prisoners are not satisfied with the AA counseling because they sense that others are only in it for the good-time credit; the counseling is, subsequently, superficial. Moreover, those prisoners seriously interested in receiving counseling are too fearful of other prisoners and counselors to discuss their problems openly. They are afraid that if they appear vulnerable, it will be used against them by both prisoners and prison counseling staff.

Native prisoners generally do not attend AA because they feel like outsiders and cannot relate to the group. Instead, they attend AA counseling facilitated by the Native woman counselor, whom they highly praise. They especially enjoy this group because a variety of topics are covered, including sexual abuse, codependency, substance abuse, cultural issues, and coping with prison life. The group benefits Native women because the counselor is Native, as is everyone in the group.

Another inadequacy of the counseling is apparent in the difficulty prisoners face in their attempts to be released from prison into viable substance abuse treatment programs. Many prisoners request a transfer to treatment programs as a substitute for the last part of their sentences. Prison staff select certain prisoners to go to these programs, but according to the prisoners, those who really want to attend the treatment are denied, and those who do not are selected. This is perceived by prisoners as part of the "game" played in prison. They respond by employing what they term "reverse psychology": "I tell them that I don't want to go and make a big old stink about it, and that way they'll *make* me go. And it's really bad when you have to do that."

The prison employs several counselors, including one called "Dr. Feel Good" by prisoners due to the amount of mind-altering drugs he prescribes, and another who conducts group therapy sessions and in a few cases sees prisoners for individual counseling. Most prisoners consider this counselor obscene and rude and have major complaints about his approach to counseling. Prisoners relate that he frequently calls them vile, profane names. One prisoner, for example, was accused by the counselor of having sexual relations with her parole officer simply because she has a good working relationship with him. The prisoner asked the counselor if relating well to her parole officer was all that unusual. The prisoner contends the counselor replied, "Yes," and then called her a "slut."

Another prisoner, abused as a child by members of her family, gives another example exhibiting the misuse of this word:

> [The counselor] said, "We're going to talk about your mom." I said, "What?" And, he said, "I hear that you're your grandfather's child

instead of your dad's child." I said, "So." He said, "How do you feel about that?" I said, "Well, I hate my grandfather." He said, "How do you feel about your mom?" I said, "I didn't know her long enough; she died when I was little, but I think I hate her too." And he said, "Do you think she went willingly?" And, I said, "No." And he says, "Well, what if your grandfather said the little slut just crawled into bed with him?" I said, "What? Are you calling my mom a slut?" And he said, "Yes." I jumped off the desk and he scooted the chair way back. I was going to hit him and I said, "You son-of-a-bitch! You better shut-up!" It took me a whole year to even talk to him. He'd come into my cell and I'd say, "What the hell do you want; I don't have anything to say to you."

Many prisoners declare that this particular counselor calls them sluts. Another prisoner, who killed the man who abused her, comments that her session with the counselor landed her in maximum security. Defending herself against the counselor in an effort to prevent further abuse, she explains:

He [the counselor] calls me into his office. He's sitting behind that desk there like a big shot. He was saying shit about my crime; saying I had no remorse—that I was a coldhearted bitch and all this other shit. And when I felt like crying, he says, "What do you feel like doing right now?" I said, "I feel like ripping everything off your desk and beating the fuck outta you." That's exactly what I said and they put me in the hole for six days—for telling him I felt like beating the fuck out of him. Well, the guards heard me because I was kind of hysterical at the time; they heard me and then they put me back there [in the isolation cell]. I hit the wall so hard about four or five times [that] I almost broke my hand. And, they were going to give me a write-up for that—self-mutilation.[1]

Ironically, this woman was put on Prozac to control her "moods" and "temper tantrums."

Although prisoners experience sessions with this counselor as being far from healing, prison staff have a different view of him. In the words of a staff member, "He's very confrontive; he's really excellent at pushing buttons. He doesn't soft-pedal anybody—that's really good." Furthermore, when one prisoner complained to prison staff about the counselor because "he just sat there and stared at me," the staff "explained" to her that she is uncomfortable with him because he is a man and she was sexually abused as a child. Staff encourage her to continue her treatment with him.

Prisoners deplore the humiliation experienced in counseling sessions. For instance, when Cecilia was in counseling before her transfer to maximum security, she was belittled by counseling staff and prisoners for crying during the sessions. Cecilia, unable to show her real feelings, is perplexed:

> I'm sitting in group and I'm not a big talker. And because I don't talk, when I talk about things that happened, I get upset and cry. When I cry, I'm told I cry to get my way. So, I sit there and try not to cry. I can't talk because if I talk, I'm going to cry. I'm sitting there listening to all these people and I'm getting real angry because I can relate to a lot of things they're going through. And, then I'm told I'm not participating. So, when I do participate and cry, then I'm told I'm a baby. But I attended them because I was supposed to.

Women confined to maximum security do not receive any counseling, with the exception of a group simply called the Behavior Group. According to prisoners, this group is not held consistently and has not met for weeks. The prisoners express this group is really a "bitch session": it is a time when prisoners are allowed to air their anger and grievances without the threat of a write-up. Some Native women do not find this counseling beneficial because, according to them, the facilitator purposely belittles them in front of other prisoners. Native women maintain that the Native counselor is not allowed to visit or counsel women in maximum security; subsequently, they do not attend any counseling sessions. Native prisoners in maximum security are forced to rely upon prison staff for counseling.

All Native women, especially reservation women, are critical of the prison's programs. In the words of a reservation woman:

> They have nothing for the Indian women, and we've been trying to get people aware of that and to have programs for the Indian women. We need our own form of rehabilitation because there are so many cultural barriers. We can go through their recovery programs to a limit here and then we have to start dealing with Indian issues—we have none of that here. I've been one to bring up a lot of

issues here and, of course, I'm not one of the favorites among the administration here—I've become assertive. And when people come in to speak with inmates they [the administrative personnel] make sure I'm not one of them.

When this woman tried to secure culture-specific programming for Native prisoners, the prison branded her a "troublemaker." She was raised immersed in Native culture, has little knowledge of Euro-American culture, and speaks her native tongue. White society makes her feel "ashamed," and consequently she does not communicate well with most white people. She explains that feeling ashamed primarily stems from white people harassing her about the way she talks, thus making her feel "backward." She definitely is most at ease with Native people. She remarks that "[white people] don't really understand what you're talking about." She adds that because Natives are surrounded by white people inside prison, they must learn to "walk a little bit stronger."

Not unexpectedly, imprisoned Native Canadian women suffer the same racialized experiences. Fran Sugar and Lana Fox (1989–1990: 476–477), imprisoned Native women from Canada, discuss the tremendous power of neocolonial racism and their inability to heal:

> For Aboriginal women, prison is an extension of life on the outside, and because of this it is impossible for us to heal there. . . . For us, prison rules have the same illegitimacy as the oppressive rules under which we grew up. . . . Physicians, psychiatrists, and psychologists are typically white and male. How can we be healed by those who symbolize the worst experiences of our past?

Regarding Native prisoners, prison staff explain that most are reluctant to work with white staff members and, subsequently, many do not participate in the counseling and treatment offered at the prison. One staff member adds that she tried to modify treatment programs for Native prisoners. When discussing culture-specific programming, however, she gives an example that leads me to believe she knows very little about Native culture:

> I think you have to be careful when you work with a Native American woman. [You have to be careful not to] destroy her cultural ties because it's important that she keep it. You have to always keep in

mind that she has those ties. I'd say to a white woman who is married to somebody who's abusing the hell out of her, "You need to make a choice—either be abused or move out." I might say to a Native American woman, "Why don't you attempt to move him towards treatment," because it's going to devastate her to break up that family. The white woman has accepted divorce as a way of life, but [the Indian woman] is not going to feel that way about it.

This staff member has a stereotypic perception of Native American families. In precontact Native societies this type of abuse within families was a rare occurrence (see Ackerman 1995; Allen 1985; Etienne and Leacock 1980). Although many forms of abuse are common in contemporary Native communities, it is neither appropriate nor a part of Native culture to abuse one's wife/partner. The staff member has the notion that this type of violence is acceptable in Native culture. Undoubtedly this racist perception, albeit unconscious, interferes with her ability to counsel Native women adequately, particularly those caught in oppressive relationships.

The counseling model focuses solely on individual deficiencies and the building of self-esteem, hence overlooking the social structure, society's deficiencies, or the effects of the prison regime on prisoners' mental health. A proposed outline for mental health at the WCC accents individual responsibility and self-esteem and implies a causal relationship between "unresolved dependency issues" and criminal behavior (Women's Correctional Center 1990, n.p.).

Prisoners experience an arbitrary enforcement of rules, numerous write-ups, and subsequent transfers to maximum security. These actions add to the feeling of being controlled rather than rehabilitated. In fact, it is argued that prison, because the institutional design actually *fosters* dependent relationships, "creates women in need of rehabilitation" (Jose-Kampfner 1990, 123).

RELIGION AS REHABILITATION AND SURVIVAL

Early women's prisons centered on religion as part of the prisoner's rehabilitation (Dobash, Dobash, and Gutteridge 1986). Following that philosophy, rehabilitation at the WCC emphasizes religion. To prison staff, religion is an integral part of rehabilitation for all prisoners. In their view, the issue is not religious preference but involvement of the prisoners in their respective religions.

There are several prison fellowship programs in Montana. One that works closely with imprisoned women is the White Harvest Jail/Prison Ministry and Transition Center and Program. A pamphlet by the ministry states that their program is designed to "teach and train Christian prisoners" (White Harvest Jail/Prison Ministry 1989, 1). Prisoners are encouraged to participate in courses that instruct in "American patriotism, citizenship, community relationships, responsibilities, and obligations, including the proper handling and accounting for their time and money." It is described as a program that will "un-institutionalize ex-prisoners by teaching them how to responsibly make and carry out decisions and peaceably relate to other citizens without taking the advantage of or misusing and abusing them" (White Harvest Jail/Prison Ministry 1989, 1).

This organization published an ex-prisoner's narrative, "Lynda's Success Story and Testimony: Lynda's Escape from the Serpent's Spells, Snares, and Shambles" (White Harvest Jail/Prison Ministry 1989). This story depicts a young woman who had been "in trouble" since age thirteen and was confined to mental hospitals, drug treatment facilities, and juvenile and correctional centers. She described herself as a "drug addict/alcoholic, liar, thief, and immoral" (1). She was immersed in a life of crime, leading to imprisonment at the WCC, where she was eventually saved by God through the prison fellowship program. This ex-prisoner said, "I was in a prison of my own making. I was in bondage to sin" (1).

Emotionally moved by a patriotic, Christian ceremony on Independence Day, Lynda revealed: "During this service we sang national songs, said the Pledge of Allegiance to our flag and country, and gave thanks to God for our freedom" (28). This motivated her to learn more about the United States, which she accomplished by reading a history book suggested by the pastor:

> As I from time to time read of the faith that our founding fathers had in God, I would again and again be moved to tears of joy. I learned about the price the signers of the Declaration of Independence paid to obtain our freedom and of the wars which were fought

to keep it. . . . Oh, how we loved to share all the wonderful things around the battle for freedom and the founding of our country and the Christian Americanism of our founding fathers who accomplished it all for us. (29)

This simplistic, one-sided interpretation of history presents a narrow view of the world, especially considering the violence involved in the "founding" of a country once belonging to Native people. It is reminiscent of numerous "freedom" battles, rationalized by religious ideology, waged against indigenous peoples worldwide. It is doubtful that many imprisoned Native women would find comfort in such teachings.

Although some prisoners enjoy the company and teachings of these ministries, individual failures are stressed and prisoners are led to believe that their only salvation is Christianity. Christianity of this sort, rather than liberating anyone, can be an opiate. This is a bitter pill to swallow for women who are imprisoned for killing abusive spouses, or those incarcerated for property crimes when their "crime" springs from poverty.

Although prisoners have full access to prison fellowship groups and both Catholic and Protestant clergy and services, few attend religious services. Due to informal prison rules, Native prisoners have minimum access to religious leaders from their communities. As an important part of their survival and rehabilitation, Native women requested from the prison administration the opportunity to have Native spiritual leaders come into the prison to pray with them. According to Native prisoners, the prison administration supposedly welcomes Native leaders from Montana's reservations, yet the prisoners must select them from a preapproved roster to which they are denied access by prison staff, effectively preventing spiritual leaders from visiting the prison.

An article written by Little Rock Reed (1990) is critical of existing prison programs, which he perceives as Judeo-Christianity in the guise of rehabilitation. Reed suggests that many Native Americans view rehabilitation differently than those from Euro-American culture. In recognizing that substance abuse, amid other ills, is a serious problem among Native people, Reed advocates the cultural specificity of all prison counseling programs. Especially important and central to rehabilitation for Natives is, according to Reed, the purification ceremony or sweat lodge; Native women prisoners, however, are denied access to a sweat lodge.[2]

Reed (1990) and Grobsmith (1994) argue that without Native American spirituality, imprisoned Natives cannot effectively be rehabilitated. Furthermore, Reed notes that prison programs modeled for Euro-American society are another way to control Native people. Rather than focusing on the societal structure as the primary problem, Native prisoners are diverted by rehabilitative programs that search for internal, personal deficiencies.

Lenny Foster, director and spiritual advisor for the Navajo Nation's Corrections Project, concludes that a spirit-based model of rehabilitation is the only answer for incarcerated Natives (Reed 1993a). Foster argues that Native American programs have been exceedingly successful in changing negative prisoner behavior. Moreover, he maintains that the positive changes are taken back to Native families and communities. Because Native teachings are viewed as strengthening and healing, many Native prisoners who either fell away from Native cultures or never knew traditional Native ways seek out their culture while imprisoned (see Cardozo-Freeman 1993; *The Great Spirit within the Hole* 1983; Grobsmith 1994; *To Heal the Spirit* 1990). Noted journalist Tim Giago says that Native American prisoners relate that wardens frequently see their return to Native religion while imprisoned as "a step backward, a return to the 'savage ways' rather than a true religious awakening" (1984, 327). Similar to other imprisoned Native people, Native prisoners at the WCC search for Native culture as a way to survive prisonization, and Landless women rely upon traditional reservation women as mentors.

Reed (1989) suggests that the United States historically subjected Native people to colonial rule and continues to exercise this domination by denying them the right to practice their religion. Crucial to understanding the experiences of imprisoned Natives are the disruptive events brought about by assimilationist policy and prohibitive legislation mandated by the federal government. At one time, as part of the stripping of Native sovereignty via the denial of their culture, Native American religious practices were forbidden by the federal government. Those Natives who dared openly to practice their religion were incarcerated, and subsequently the religion was forced underground (Beck and Walters 1977). Indeed, Native American religion was banned by the U.S. government from the late 1800s until 1934. Years later, discrimination still continues, and not all Native people are allowed to practice their religion openly. To remedy this, the American Indian Religious Freedom Act was passed by Congress in 1978. This act specifically states that Native prisoners cannot be denied the right to practice their religion.[3]

Unfortunately, the act has not been enforced. Many imprisoned Natives continue to be denied the right to practice their religion, despite a U.S. Supreme Court ruling in 1972 that specifies that all prisoners have the right to exercise religious freedom and despite the passage of the American Indian Religious Freedom Act. As an example, Reed (1989) claims that Native prisoners in the Southern Ohio Correctional Facility cannot use the religious service facility for worship, are segregated from one another so they cannot meet for religious activities, and are denied access to sacred objects. The same denial of religious freedom, with accompanying attitudes, was found at the WCC until 1995, when a prayer leader was permitted access to the prison.[4] Prior to this, the rejection of Native culture permeated the prison and was glaring in all rehabilitative programs.

Native men incarcerated in the state of Montana have fought long and hard to have Native American religion recognized as credible, and in 1983 a sweat lodge was constructed inside the men's prison. At the women's prison, though, the situation is much different. Imprisoned Native women maintain that although they submitted a formal proposal, the prison administration refuses to allow them a sweat lodge.

Healing experiences for incarcerated Native women are seldom acquired from prison programs, but rather arise from friendships with other women prisoners and people outside the prison, or from support from Native women's groups within the prison (Sugar and Fox 1989–1990). The Native women's society at the WCC is paramount to their survival. On 20 February 1991 imprisoned Native women, under the leadership of Native women branded as "troublemakers" by prison personnel, presented to the prison administration a proposal to establish a Native women's society within the prison walls. The goals included culture-specific counseling, instilling of cultural pride and improvement of self-image of Natives, availability of spiritual leaders, and the involvement of Native people in all aspects of the criminal justice system. There was no reply from the prison administration. On 15 March 1991 the prisoners resubmitted the proposal, which led to the establishment of a Native women's group. They are now allowed by the prison to meet for one hour every Sunday. The women view this spirit-based group as part of their rehabilitation and survival, although, tellingly, the prison classifies it as "recreation."

Native prisoners convey that one hour of group prayer is not long enough, but prison staff will not extend the time, although various Christian groups are allowed longer time for their prayer meetings. After much prodding on the part of Native women, the prison allows them to burn sweetgrass during prayer time, if they reside in the general-population building. Similar to imprisoned Native Canadian women's experiences (Sugar and Fox 1989–1990), sweetgrass is not perceived in a positive way by prison staff because, in their opinion, it smells too much like marijuana and they fear it might be a drug. Although white women confined to maximum security or isolation cells have full access to their religion, Native women in these units are not allowed to smudge (bless) themselves with sweetgrass. Fran Sugar poignantly clarifies the significance of sweetgrass to her as an imprisoned Native Canadian woman:

> At times when I'd burn my medicine, when we had sweetgrass
> smuggled in to us because sometimes it was seen as contraband,
> the sweet smell of the earth would create a safe feeling, a feeling of
> being alive even though the cage represented a coffin, the prison a
> gravestone, and my sisters walking dead people. Those medicines
> were what connected me as a spirit child. One time when I was close
> to suicide I was told by Mista Hiya that my spirit was alive and it
> was housed in my physical shell. And from that hard time I learnt
> that my spirit was more important than my body because my body
> was controlled by the routine of life in prison. It was then the con-
> nectedness to being an Aboriginal Woman began. I began feeling
> good about myself even though I had only a few reasons to feel good.
> I understood there was a spirit within me that had the will to live.
> (1989–1990, 467)

According to imprisoned Native women, it will be advantageous to both prisoners and the institution if a Native counselor is hired full-time and treatment programs are modified to be culture-specific. At a meeting in the spring of 1992 between Governor Stephens and Native prisoners (both men and women), the prisoners proposed that the prisons

hire Native religious leaders and Native counselors. Native prisoners argued that they would be better served by their own people. On
21 April 1992, in a statement on a local television news broadcast, the
governor stated that he would implement this plan if the tribes in the
state assisted in the financing of the positions. This is another example
of unconscious neocolonial racism: the governor did not approach various white communities in the state and ask them to finance white counselors who work in the prison system. And he was asking the poorest
people in the state to finance programs for which the state typically
pays. Furthermore, the burden would fall most heavily on Landless Natives and the one PL 280 reservation that is forced to use the state prison
system. Why should other reservations contribute to the funding when
they may have few or no tribal members in the state prison system?

In a desperate act of resistance, Native women prisoners, tired of
discriminatory treatment, issued a position paper (Native American
Women Prisoners 1993). They requested from the prison administration Native spiritual advisors to guide them, access to a sweat lodge, and
an end to a racialized prison system. Prompted by reports from prisoners, in April of 1993 the ACLU filed a class-action lawsuit regarding the
inhumane conditions for women imprisoned in Montana. An excerpt
from the press release read: "Solely because of their gender, women
prisoners are subjected to invidious discrimination with respect to education, employment, vocational training, visitation, recreation, religious
and other programs" (Crichton 1993). The lawsuit regarding Native
women prisoners and religion read: "No Spiritual Leader is available
for Native American women and they do not have a Sweat Lodge. Male
prisoners have the opportunity to participate in weekly religious services and Montana State Prison has a Sweat Lodge" (*Many Horses et al.
v. Racicot et al.* 1993, 18; see also Chapter 5, note 7).

There are fundamental problems with the prohibition of religious
freedom for Natives at the WCC. One is that the denial of this right
for imprisoned Native women is illegal. Imprisoned Native men in this
state are permitted to practice the sweat lodge ceremony, and white
women have access to their religion. Another issue is that Native American spirituality has helped Native people survive the brutal dynamics of
colonization and prisonization. The sweat lodge ceremony, which operates on the concept of interdependence and the notion of helping others, is crucial in an environment that produces bitterness and hatred.

Native American spirituality is not seen by prison staff or many
white prisoners as credible, although as Grobsmith reports, "Montana

prisons indicate that Native American culture and religious practices have helped encourage a law-abiding lifestyle, prohibiting the use of alcohol and drugs among inmates" (1994, 164). If the value of Native culture has been recognized by criminal justice officials in Montana, why are imprisoned Native women still denied their culture and religious freedom? It is curious that prison officials oppose programs for Native Americans that promote good conduct, bolster self-esteem, and possibly reduce recidivism (Fordham 1993).

Although some Native women maintain their innocence, most of those who admit they transgressed determine that they are incarcerated because they fell away from their culture, because they were living in a world that was unholy, unbalanced. To many Native prisoners spirituality is the answer to their well-being, not tranquilizers or "confrontive" counseling sessions with a counselor who has a fancy for the word *slut*. This is not to suggest that all imprisoned Native Americans pursue their culture or religion as a method of rehabilitation or as a way to resist being broken and thus survive the prison experience. For those who do seek solace in their culture, however, there should be no barriers. Concurring with Elizabeth Grobsmith, I believe Native prisoners have the "right to remain Native American despite their incarceration" (1994, 2). Grobsmith suggests that the criminal justice system has been coerced through litigation to promote Native worldviews. Indeed, but it was not until 1995 that imprisoned Native women in Montana had access to a prayer leader.

Native American women in Montana's prison system are decolonizing and rehumanizing. They are resisting domination and the imposition of another culture—as Native people have for centuries. In this way, imprisoned Native women can be viewed as revolutionaries. By conserving a Native worldview within an oppressive institution, these women are, truly, activists. Although these women would not define themselves as radicals, they are engaged in a struggle to transform a racist, sexist, and classist institution. They should be applauded, not punished, for their efforts, especially since becoming engaged in such a struggle is in itself an important aspect of true rehabilitation.

UNMANAGEABLE WOMEN

Euro-American society discourages women from expressing anger. In prisons scant attention is paid to the anger women feel about being imprisoned and separated from loved ones. When they do express anger, even by means of oblique acts of resistance, many are sent to maximum security for rule violations (Faith 1993b; Jose-Kampfner 1990).

Women housed in maximum security can be described as women pushed to their emotional edge who have become extremely angry and vulnerable. Native women are disproportionately represented in maximum security: out of eleven women, six are Native. Three women, two white and one Native, are in isolation cells. This overrepresentation of Native women in maximum security relates directly to Native prisoners' relationships with white guards, because generally the guards issue write-ups. (Additionally, the warden, treatment specialist, and recreation director have the authority to issue write-ups.)

Whereas a typical day in general population and on the floor of maximum security start at the 6:30 A.M. count,[5] with the freedom for prisoners to go back to bed if they do not have GED classes or in-house jobs, the typical day in a lockup cell in maximum security begins at 5:00 A.M. At this time, prisoners are to arise; three times a week they are permitted to shower. (The bathrooms did not have privacy curtains until March 1990.) Prisoners are allowed outside for fresh air for ten minutes to one hour per day. According to prisoners, prison policy specifies that the length of stay in maximum security is not to exceed six months, although the duration ranges from one to fifteen months. The length of stay in isolation ranges from three days to six months.

Prisoners have restricted visitation and are denied access to any programming, with the exception of GED classes. With little programming available, it is nearly impossible to acquire good-time credit in this unit. Several women specifically mention the need for sexual-abuse counseling, but they are denied access. Furthermore, women in maximum security and isolation are not permitted religious services of any kind and are not allowed to talk with each other.

Confinement is especially difficult for prisoners in isolation. Not only is their regime strict, they are not allowed visits from family and friends. This treatment pushes these prisoners to the rim of insanity. Prisoners in isolation resolve that the prison is trying to break them and relate the breaking process to severe readjustment problems they will encounter when they are released. They reason that because their self-esteem is driven to such a low level by lockup time and general prison treatment, it will be impossible for them to survive on the outside.

One recently incarcerated Native woman is in maximum security not because of any write-ups she received but because the general-population building is full. She contends that the prison staff lied to her when they told her she would only be in maximum security "a few days," although she has been there for over one week. When asked why she is in maximum security, she discusses the consequences of the "tough Indian" image she evidently projects to prison staff:

> I'm taking it personally. Maybe they think I'm a bulldog,[6] but I'm not. I've never lied to these people and I won't lie to them. . . . But they think, probably because of my size and tattoos or something, that I'm a bulldog—I don't know. I don't appreciate being lied to. If they want a reason to keep me over here, I'll give them one; that's stupid to think that way but I don't like being lied to. People say they don't think you're going to make it. Why do they have to lie to you? Why can't they just say, "We don't think you're going to do very well so we're going to keep you here for a couple of months."

When asked about appealing her classification, she remarks that prisoners seldom win their appeals, so it is "a hopeless battle." A Native woman who has been in maximum security for nearly one year is afraid to appeal her lengthy stay. One frustrated prisoner, who portrays the appeal system as designed for the convenience of the staff rather than the prisoners, asks, "Why try to do anything?"

Native women in the general-population building are a close-knit group and have formed a spiritual organization to further that bond. They relay that their unity appears threatening to prison staff. As a consequence, several Native women, perceived as "bulldogs" or troublemakers by prison staff, have been reclassified to Close status and transferred to maximum security under what the women consider trumped-up charges. For example, a Native prisoner was transferred to maximum security for calling a white prisoner a "used-up whore"—behavior interpreted as "sexual misconduct" by prison staff.

Sometimes a transfer to this unit occurs under the guise of health reasons. One Native woman was transferred from the general-population building to maximum security because she was in an accident prior to incarceration and walks with a cane, and the general-population building is not handicap accessible. Prison staff decided that living in maximum security would be easier for her because that building does not have stairs. This soft-spoken prisoner is a middle-aged, traditional, reservation woman. She commands the respect of Native and non-Native prisoners and is a cultural leader among the Native women. In the opinion of the Native women, her transfer was designed to break up the closeness of the Native women. Although most white prisoners are not aware of this discrimination, one white prisoner views the transfer in the same way as Native women:

> [The prison staff] has been real shitty too about the Native Americans. I know somebody's prejudiced up there [in prison administration]; somebody's got to be prejudiced because that lady [with the cane] would not be over there—she did not deserve it. She never had a write-up or anything. To deserve to go over to hell; that is hell over there. They call it the hell-hole.

Women who were abused prior to their incarceration, especially those who were locked in small, dark spaces, have a particularly difficult time in maximum security. One woman, who had been confined "in the closet for days at a time" as a child, says,

> When they put you in a room in here [in maximum security], and it's dark, automatically I start thinking I'm not going to get out of here. When I was little, I'd gone without eating for a long time. I'd get sugar-water from him [her abuser]. And this is a bad habit that I have: I lay on the floor and look out [under] the door and look at the light all the time. And these people think I'm crazy. . . . Sometimes I lay down there and they [prison staff] give me a Tranxene. . . . It was suppose to knock me out and make me sleep, but it didn't do that. . . . I start sweating and I know that damn door's locked. It really freaks me out.

Another prisoner, raised in a similar violent household, would have to beg her uncle to let her out of the closet to use the bathroom. This experience followed her into prison:

> When I was on room restriction, [a guard] locked the door on me. I used to go to the bathroom in my pants at my uncle's house because he didn't let me go to the bathroom. Well, I had to go to the

bathroom real bad. I was just screaming in there. I couldn't handle
it. I said, "God, let me out of here!" I was really kicking on the door,
"I have to go to the bathroom." It just reminded me that my uncle
would just laugh. He'd say, "Well use it!" And I'd piss all over the
place and I'd be in those cold clothes for days. See, these people
don't understand that kind of stuff. And they think you're doing it
to get your door open. . . . When I go to my room, I can't shut my
door and they [the guards] go and slam it. I sit on the floor and I'd
have scratch marks on my face. See, I had a nightmare last night and
I bit myself.

Interviewing women in maximum security and isolation is particularly problematic. Oppressive conditions and medications produce ram-
bling, unfocused conversations. These women are almost exclusively
concerned with their personal survival of the prison experience; they
are not afforded the occasion of thinking about other issues, and perhaps
some are too medicated to concentrate.

SEXUAL MISCONDUCT

It is well known that Montanans suffer from homophobia. On 27 March
1995 the *San Francisco Chronicle* reported that the state of Montana had
proposed a bill that would classify gay adults as "violent felons." Additionally, when I give public lectures in Montana regarding imprisoned
women, I am invariably asked about the "homosexual" prisoners. Mirroring attitudes outside the prison, homophobia is rampant inside the
prison, and not just with prison staff but with prisoners also.

Media images fuel prejudice, and the general public, confusing fact
with fantasy, see the imprisoned woman as the "hardened bull-dyke"
lurking in the halls, waiting to rape her next victim. Edna Walker
Chandler provides such a picture in her "factual" account of imprisoned
women:

Jo's mannish looks, low-slung belt and masculine-style vest told
only part of the story. The rest was in her strong, well-built body,
her iron-muscled arms that could beat with a towel-wrapped bar of
soap until her victim was unconscious, with never a bruise on her
entire body. . . . As an attractive, high-grade butch she could have

any "turned-out" woman she wanted as her homosexual partner. . . .
Now she was about to pave the way for trying out another "fish" as
she had tried out dozens of others. . . . She smiled knowingly and
put her hands on Mary's breasts caressingly. (1973, 26 and 29)[7]

Contrary to the picture Chandler presents, Lee Bowker (1981) argues
that although men are more likely to be raped (by heterosexual men)
while incarcerated, imprisoned women are more likely to be raped on
the outside.[8] I would add that women are more likely to be victimized by heterosexual men rather than by "homosexual" women. Also,
Bowker suggests that when intimacy does occur between imprisoned
gay women, it "occurs in a context of a loving relationship so that it is
integrated into a total interpersonal experience" (1981, 414). As Karlene
Faith points out (1993a, 1993b), early studies on imprisoned women
(Giallombardo 1966; Ward and Kassebaum 1965) were instrumental in
the development of stereotypes of imprisoned women as masculine,
violent, and lesbian, and many films about prison life perpetuate these
stereotypes.

A prisoner explains that, in an effort to degrade and control her,
prison staff told her that being a lesbian is a violation of state law. Gay
prisoners suffer discrimination because they are labeled "sick" by prison
staff and some other prisoners. Although many prisoners are not homophobic, several characterize gays as "disgusting." When one prisoner
was in jail awaiting sentencing, other prisoners warned her not to touch
them and then they physically beat her. Since then, she has been beaten
in prison for being gay and subjected to humiliating jokes about gay
people. She is regularly called an "animal" and "stupid" by other prisoners. Other prisoners harass her by making sexual comments "and grabbing at me when the officers aren't looking." Because she is seen as "sick,"
some prisoners are reluctant to engage in conversation or friendship
with her.

While prison personnel supposedly focus on building self-esteem,
prisoners express that the reality is the opposite—the continual lowering of self-esteem by prison staff. An example by Delphina reveals how
sexual preference influences treatment and self-esteem issues for a gay
prisoner in lockup in maximum security:

I don't know why they think they're building self-esteem. An officer
told me, the one that wrote me up for sexual misconduct, that I was

sick; that I didn't deserve to have kids. How's that going to build my self-esteem?

The predominant view in the United States is that gay women are "unfit" mothers.[9] Delphina maintains that prison staff not only tell her she does not deserve children because she is gay, they also deny her visits with her children.

Although several prisoners relate that one guard resigned because she was "in love" with one of the prisoners, most guards are characterized as homophobic. Barbara comments that the guards at the WCC tell her on a regular basis that she is "sick" and "abnormal" because she is gay. When she was incarcerated in another state, however, she had a sexual relationship with a female guard. Barbara entered into the relationship to gain more privileges, while the guard did it for "her own needs." While incarcerated in another state prison, male guards would try to touch her sexually to see if she was "really" gay. When she asked one guard about this behavior, he told her that he bet the other guards she was only gay when imprisoned.

According to Delphina, some prison staff members admit that she is in maximum security because she is gay, although other staff maintain that it is because of multiple write-ups. Delphina voices, "They say the reason I'm in max is because I got found guilty of three Class II write-ups. I know the reason why I'm in max is because of my sexual preference."[10] Delphina received a Class II write-up during Christmas when her mother brought her two young children to visit. Delphina wrapped gifts for her children, and when her family was leaving, she gave the gifts to her children. While Delphina was present, a guard took the gifts from the children and told her the gifts were "confiscated." At that point, according to Delphina, her mother "went off on this guard" and Delphina received a write-up for her mother's behavior. Additionally, prison staff would not let her see her children for sixty days.

Delphina's second write-up was issued when she was caught touching another prisoner's leg while sitting in the dayroom:

> They considered it sexual misconduct. To me, sexual misconduct is having sex—not touching somebody on their leg. But come on, if I touch somebody—beating the hell out of them, or doing something like that—I can see going to a max cell. But just because I touch somebody's leg I cannot see sitting in this cell. That is wrong.

Delphina was issued another sexual misconduct write-up soon after that for the same behavior—touching another prisoner's leg. According to prison staff, sexual misconduct is defined as having sex, kissing, or touching private parts. Staff further comment that "holding hands" and "hugging inappropriately" can also be problematic—it depends upon individual prisoners.

At a woman's prison in Great Britain, "any show of affection between women in prison is in danger of being reported as 'lesbian activity'" (O'Dwyer, Wilson, and Carlen 1987, 180). Similarly, prisoners at the WCC suggest that they are not allowed to physically display feelings toward each other, which creates anger and bitterness toward prison staff. According to Barbara, because she is gay the guards watch her constantly, waiting to write her up for sexual misconduct. Other prisoners are afraid to be too closely associated with someone labeled as "homosexual" because their behavior may be misinterpreted by prison staff as "sexual misconduct." Subsequently, prisoners are not encouraged to reach out to each other emotionally and are propelled into painful isolation.

Barbara maintains that because she is watched closely, she cannot touch anyone in any manner, and other prisoners must also watch their behavior with her. She says that

> If somebody in my family died while I was here and I was crying, upset, freaking out, there isn't an inmate in here who could come up and touch me and say, "It's going to be okay."

According to a prison staff member, behavior is heavily monitored because of the increase in the "cycle of lesbian activity," in which many prisoners are "situationally" gay. Both institutional staff and prisoners make a clear distinction between "true" and "situational" lesbians. True lesbians are those who are gay in any circumstance, whether incarcerated or not, while situational lesbians are women who take on a new sexual behavior only when incarcerated. While some prisoners characterize themselves as bisexual, Barbara remarks that many imprisoned women are "wannabe" gay. This is a situation she does not condone:

> People get hurt when they get into a situation like that. They don't plan on falling in love; they don't plan on being together on the outside. So they're here together and then a husband comes to visit and they ignore the other person while the husband's there. And when he's gone they get back with this woman. I hate that.

What angers another prisoner about "wannabe" gays is that "they think it's part of being a convict, part of being a bad guy."

A staff member explains that an increase in lesbian activity leads to much fighting among prisoners. In a local newspaper article on the dangers found inside prison, guards are quoted as saying that because the prison is understaffed, there is "an increase in lesbian activity among inmates" with the implication that this causes a "dangerous" situation for prison guards (Shirley 1991). This staff member views the rise in "lesbian activity" as disruptive and tension producing among prisoners. She adds that this activity is not easy to control, and once a prisoner is written up for sexual misconduct, she is "hit hard" by the hearing officer.

Barbara senses that the prison is trying to break her and, similar to Delphina, relates her confinement to her sexual preference:

> They put me in a max cell where I can't see nobody; can't talk to nobody but the guards. Come on [crying]—what are they trying to do? Destroy me? And that's what's going to happen. You know, if they're trying to kill what I have going for me and people think that being gay is wrong, and a lot or people don't agree with it but it's just the way I feel. And, I don't push it on anybody, so they shouldn't push back. It's not like I'm pushing to hurt anybody. Yeah, this place reminds me of [the drug treatment center] where they take you and tear you apart and build you back up. Only this place don't build you back up—they just tear you down.

The *Bozeman Daily Chronicle*, in a story about the overcrowded conditions at the women's prison, reported a litany of problems as defined by the ACLU. One of the issues was the arbitrary enforcement of prison rules. Using the situation of a woman in maximum security, the ACLU director, Scott Crichton, commented:

> One example is, there is a woman in isolation in the maximum security unit. She is a Hispanic lesbian and doesn't know why she is in isolation. She is on the verge of going crazy being locked away. We have been asking for some time what she has to do to get out and [Warden] MacAskill can't be specific. (18 March 1990, A8)

Gay prisoners spend lengthy time in maximum security and, additionally, worry about being paroled. According to one prisoner, prison staff make it clear that she will not be released from prison unless she gives up her relationship with her lover. When asked about her parole date, she responds:

> I went to the parole board and they told me that if I could go four months without a write-up, they would let me out in April. Well, I didn't make it. I don't see myself getting out anytime soon because of my sexual preference. They already told me if I don't give up [my lover], we aren't letting you out.

Faith (1993b) concludes that homophobic Western societies have constructed three paradigms to explain "homosexual" behavior. Various religions see same-sex preference as "sinful," social scientists argue that gays are "deviant," and the medical profession classifies them as "sick" individuals who can be cured through various treatments, including drugs and psychosurgery. Faith argues that all three models are used to justify the persecution of gay people:

> All three discourses, which collectively identify same-sex activity as sin, deviance or sickness, have been applied interactively in setting policies for persons who are locked up for legal infractions which have no relevance to their sexual preference. What all these discourses have in common is a foundation of fear toward anyone who rejects the gender norms of conventional social order, and a shared (as well as competitive) propensity to underscore the controlling authority of professional judgement against the lived experience of human subjects. Within the prison environment, to be saved, rehabilitated or cured is singularly experienced as punishment. (1993b, 214)

In theory, the "remedy" at the WCC for being gay is "counseling" and "medication"; in practice it is harassment, overuse of mind-altering drugs, and lengthy time in maximum security.

As in the past, contemporary prisons are powerful, dehumanizing institutions. Regardless of the rhetoric of rehabilitation, prisons create an environment that is not conducive to regeneration (Dobash, Dobash, and Gutteridge 1986; Faith 1993b; Sugar and Fox 1989–1990). Prisons are organized to discipline and punish, not to ready the supposed transgressors for reintegration into their communities. The conditions in women's prisons many times result in prisoners' fending for themselves, in whatever way they find best (Carlen 1985; Dobash, Dobash, and Gutteridge 1986). It is no wonder that some prisoners rebel as a way to maintain their integrity as human beings. On the other hand, it is also understandable when some comply in order to do "easy time" as a way to survive. The WCC creates an oppressive environment. This atmosphere structures the prison subculture and provides the foundation for the relationships among prisoners and between prisoners and guards.

Seven

PRISON SUBCULTURE
"IT'S ALL A GAME AND IT DOESN'T MAKE SENSE TO ME"

There is little systematic research on how women experience prison and very few studies devoted to the institutional culture of imprisoned women. The first studies of imprisoned women in the United States centered on behavioral responses to prison and prisoner solidarity (Giallombardo 1966; Ward and Kassebaum 1965). These early studies proposed that imprisoned women, rather than developing antistaff norms, construct supportive subcultures that are viewed as mock families operating within prison. However, in agreement with research conducted in Great Britain (Carlen 1985; Dobash et al. 1986), I found little evidence of family-type relationships existing within the WCC. The prison views this type of relationship as inappropriate and generally discourages such associations.

PRISONER-PRISONER RELATIONSHIPS
Native Prisoner Relationships

Similar to imprisoned Native American men (Cardozo-Freeman 1993; Grobsmith 1994) and imprisoned Native Canadian women (Sugar and Fox 1989–1990), imprisoned Native women in Montana are unified by their culture, religious beliefs, and the struggle to remain Native. Prisoners in maximum security, whether Native or non-Native, are not allowed to congregate and, subsequently, an environment is produced that does not permit any cohesiveness. Native women in the general-population building, however, are a close-knit group, and the newly formed spiritual organization furthers that bond.

Reservation Native women are admired and respected by off-reservation and nonreservation (Landless) Native women. Off-reservation and nonreservation women mention that they do not know as much about Native American cultures as they wish, and they request knowledge and guidance from reservation women. Reservation women graciously accept this role, although several characterize themselves as "real" Indians, implying that as reservation Natives they are "more" Indian. The distinction is indicative of the history of the vicious discrimination waged against Landless Natives in Montana. While historically it was the full-bloods versus the mixed-bloods, this has been transformed in Montana into a split between reservation, off-reservation, and nonreservation Natives. Within the prison, the division does not appear to be operating in a malicious way.

White Prisoner Relationships

Unlike Native women, white women are not connected in any cohesive manner. Similar to patterns revealed by Kruttschnitt (1981), these women, although not united as a group, share an opposition to prison staff. When they adjust to staff expectations, they make it clear that they do so to benefit themselves, to reap any rewards possible in a bleak situation. As one white woman says, "I'm in here to do my time and get out; I ain't taking any of these women with me."

The loneliness most white prisoners experience is overwhelming. They are cut off from their families and from each other. Joan, for example, has received only one visitor since her incarceration nine months ago:

> I've been lucky. The last time I was in here I did not have one visitor in the six months I was here—not one. I didn't have to care about the visiting rules and regulations because I never was going to get a visitor anyway. This time I've been blessed. This church lady that comes in here, she said, "Well, I've got some good news for you. A lady in our congregation is from your home town." She turned out to be my baby-sitter when I was little. I was very happy. She's quite a bit older than me. . . . She said, "I brought you some shampoo and toothpaste." I said, "Thank you—I've got lots of shampoo." And, she said, "You can trade it or something." I said, "No, whatever you bring me nobody will get to touch it. I don't even let them touch

the bottle. I'm going to be very protective over anything you have for me." I still have the same toothpaste. I'm going to hold on to the same shampoo bottle. It's something to remind me that I do have somebody that cares. Even a shampoo—isn't that silly? It's sentimental.

White prisoners complain about how other white prisoners treat them badly, perhaps modeling the sometimes vicious behavior of the guards and other prison staff. Karen, who was abused prior to incarceration, says other white prisoners "pick on" her frequently because she is a passive person. They call her "stupid" and other belittling names, which results in Karen "blowing up" at them. She is vulnerable and contends that in this kind of environment, it is best if others do not know your weak points because they can be used against you. Because of their isolation, white prisoners are vulnerable and rarely express emotion openly. Prisoners are afraid most of the time, which may contribute to their low self-esteem.

Many white prisoners maintain that in this environment it is difficult, if not impossible, to show support for other prisoners. Aside from being leery about showing any weaknesses, prisoners mention that they never know how other prisoners will react when they do show compassion toward them. Jonna, a white prisoner, describes a tense exchange begun with an attempt to show support:

> There's too many games in here—on the emotional side. If you're ugly they'll pick on you. I even catch myself doing it. This one girl makes herself, not on the physical side, ugly as sin. She had a better heart than what she does now. Her heart isn't as kind as it used to be; she got sarcastic with me the other day. I was just worried about how she was feeling—I saw her crying. As an individual that would probably be crying in her situation, I said, "Are you okay?" [The other prisoner said,] "Yeah, why do you want to know?" [I said,] "Excuse me for asking; go on, cry your ass off. I don't care what you do—just go ahead and cry. Go cry your woes to somebody else because I'm not going to listen; I'll never listen." You put up a wall; that's not the human being inside of me—that's not me.

Jonna explains that offers of kindness are rarely returned and that other prisoners are unpredictable. Similar to other prisoners, Jonna relates this behavior as akin to an abusive relationship with a man: "I've been a victim in my abusive husband-wife relationship. It's time that I stand up on all sides—as a part of my rehabilitation." Yet this is difficult: Jonna never knows what is going to happen, "even minute by minute." She proposes that if a prisoner has one good friend inside the prison she can survive. Many white prisoners are still searching for that friend.

White prisoners say that prisoners steal from one another, in addition to abusing each other emotionally and physically—"little fights like little kids." Trust between white prisoners is at an extremely low level, and when victimized by other prisoners the last people they want to contact are the guards, whom they see as similarly abusive and untrustworthy. Furthermore, most prisoners, Native and non-Native, determine that prisoners' crimes do not affect their relationships with each other. Nevertheless, most also say that women convicted of crimes against children are not liked nor trusted by other prisoners. These women, those convicted of victimizing children, are the most lonely of all within the prison.

Native-White Prisoner Relationships

Cultural pluralism has not worked in Euro-American society and undoubtedly does not operate inside prison. Wright (1973) argues that within prisons, as a technique of control, racial/ethnic groups are encouraged to foster antagonistic relationships. Prisoner relationships are definitely tense at the WCC, and ignorance of Native American culture spills over into the interactions between Native and white prisoners. For instance, one Native woman's religion is ridiculed by her three white cellmates, who call it "voodoo." The term *voodoo* is also used by a guard in a write-up issued to a Native prisoner who threatened to "hex" the guard. While voodoo is a recognized and credible religion, in this instance the designation is used as a racial slur.

Several Native women voice that when they finally won the right to burn sweetgrass at prayer meetings, several white prisoners told the guards they were mixing marijuana in with the sweetgrass. This not only resulted in several shakedowns of rooms occupied by Native women but also increased existing racial tension between Natives and whites. The Native women felt insulted when they were accused of using marijuana with sweetgrass; in the Native American way, the mixing of prayers and drugs or alcohol is seen as sacrilegious.

Native women successfully arranged for a drum group from one of the Indian reservations to come into the prison, and many white prisoners were upset, although they were invited to attend. Some non-Native prisoners perceived this event as "special treatment" for Native prisoners, despite the fact that Native women paid for the event and white prisoners have events tailored for their culture. Moreover, Native women say that when programs about Natives air on television, some white prisoners make snide remarks during the programming.

According to Native prisoners, racial strain between Native and white prisoners increased when Native prisoners secured their own counselor. Again, some white prisoners perceive this arrangement as extraordinary care reserved for Native prisoners. A Native prisoner, challenged by a white prisoner about the therapy reserved for Natives, declared angrily, "Jesus Christ don't you think we're due? After hundreds of years of genocide and now we're in prison. Not only that, Indians need different counseling." This confrontation not only typifies the racist feelings some white prisoners have toward Natives but also exhibits the lack of counseling and treatment programs for prisoners in general. Many white prisoners appear to be desperate for treatment and are jealous of anyone securing additional counseling. Moreover, the tension between Native and white prisoners reflects poorly on the effectiveness of the available counseling.

Most white prisoners do not have a positive perception of the spiritual group formed by Native women. One white prisoner says most white prisoners do not relish the idea that Native women have their own group. She insists that their ignorance about Native American spirituality and culture is the reason many white women prisoners are prejudiced against the formation of the group. This prisoner acknowledges that many white women call Native American spirituality "voodoo." Unfamiliarity with another culture is turned into repulsive racism.

To Native prisoners, especially reservation women, culture is the key to friendship. For example, Mary prefers the company of Natives because they understand each other:

> If there's a bunch of white women in the dayroom, we don't really care to sit in there because, you know, like Agnes said, "They talk too much." So, what we do is find a corner and sit and visit. Although it offends some of the white women in here when we do that, but sometimes we just like time to ourselves. We can relate to one

another and be ourselves—be Indian. Where[as] in here [prison], you have to compose an image with these white women.

It is culture, not race per se, that divides the prisoners. White women knowledgeable of Native American culture, those whose spouses and children are Native, accept and are accepted by Native women. Additionally, these white women, marginalized within their own racial/ethnic group, meet with the Native women for their prayer group on Sundays.

One consequence of the racial tension is that Native women feel they cannot reveal their real emotions around white women. Many Native women insist this is a way to preserve their image of being hardened, tough Indians. They are protected by this image; most white women will leave them alone and not harass them. However, as Mary states, by "putting on an act" she is not honestly involved in rehabilitation. In her view, this act is part of the game demanded by the prison's social environment; ultimately, she feels, it will not benefit her, because she is not disclosing her true feelings, not functioning as an honest person. In Native cultures, honesty is extremely important. Indeed, in precontact tribal societies, the word was considered sacred and lying was a major crime. Although dishonesty affects all people and cultures, to traditional Native people it is regarded as a sin.

A white prisoner delivers her own definition of racism, and displays the cohesiveness of Native women, when she explains how "racist" Natives are toward whites. When she tried to physically beat a Native prisoner, she was faced with the entire population of Native women in the general-population building, at which time she backed down. She explains, "Yeah, I called her on and when we met in the rec room, the whole goddamn tribe was there. So, I just left—now that's racist."

These examples illustrate how cultural ignorance, coupled with the prison's environment, pits different groups of women against each other, operating as yet an another way to dehumanize and control them.

PRISONER–STAFF RELATIONSHIPS

One way to cope with prison life is through solidarity among prisoners, sometimes including the establishment of a prisoner code of ethics that exhibits hostility toward prison staff. Several early studies (Jensen and

Jones 1976; Tittle 1969) proposed that a prisoner code of ethics existed among incarcerated women, as it did among incarcerated men. Nevertheless, another study, conducted by Candace Kruttschnitt (1981) on prisoner solidarity, discloses that although prisoners are in opposition to staff expectations, they are not necessarily cohesive with each other either. The findings of this study reveal that when prisoners do conform to prison staff expectations, they do so in order to benefit themselves and subsequently serve their sentences doing "easy time." According to Kruttschnitt, those conforming are more likely to be white, older prisoners whose first arrest happened later in their lives, and prisoners in minimum-security units. Moreover, compliance among incarcerated women increases as their stay increases; that is, the longer a woman is in prison past the two-year mark, the more likely she is to conform to staff expectations.

Kruttschnitt (1981) and Jensen and Jones (1976) found that imprisoned women of color show less change in their attitudes toward prison staff than white women. Kruttschnitt proposes that women of color prisoners, usually forced to deal with a white staff, tend to advocate strong opposition toward racist prison staff throughout all phases of their confinement. Moreover, in the Kruttschnitt study, those women who exhibited hostility toward prison staff tended to have a high degree of contact with fellow prisoners, to be in maximum security, to have prior prison experiences, and to be younger. Because many imprisoned women do oppose prison staff but at the same time do not fully endorse a prisoner code of ethics, women's prisons may be described as "containing a subculture of inmates rather than an inmate subculture" (Kruttschnitt 1981, 137).

The WCC is a small prison, with twenty-nine part- and full-time staff members, which permits frequent contact between prison staff and prisoners. The staff members most exposed on a continual basis to prisoners are the guards. Thus, prisoner-guard relationships are an important part of the daily lives of the prisoners. The prison employs twenty-one full- and part-time guards; seven are male and fourteen female. The guards dress in uniform, are called "officer" by prisoners, give "direct orders," and have militaristic ranks typical of penal institutions.

Prison staff members, in interviews and off-the-record conversations, often make negative remarks about various prisoners. For example, when discussing the rise in female criminality and arrest rates, a staff member accused one particular Native prisoner, viewed by prison personnel as "extremely manipulative," of using her gender to sway the court into delivering a lenient sentence. Using a simplistic Adam-and-Eve approach to criminality (i.e., viewing the woman as the real criminal and instigator of the crime), and clearly giving women more power than they have in any arena, one staff member claims:

> There's more of a demand to treat women as you do men. It still isn't equal; women still get a lot of breaks that men don't get. In fact, we have one case here of a woman—everybody I talked to involved in that case made it clear that she was the primary perpetrator; the two other primary defendants, [who] were male, claimed in court that she was the one that pushed the whole thing. She was heavily involved; she got to plea bargain and got forty years and they're on death row.

Such statements are difficult to swallow, because the data show that when men and women are convicted of the same crime, women typically receive longer sentences.

Observations of prisoner-staff interaction demonstrate that generally prisoners are treated disrespectfully. For example, many times when prisoners greet guards in the hall, the guard will either ignore the prisoner or reply with a negative remark, such as "What's so good about it?" An example by Dorine represents the disrespect shown to prisoners. Without explanation, they were ordered to clean the prison for a visit from state legislators, and they were threatened with maximum security if they refused. Dorine confronted prison staff:

> Like I told [a prison staff member] in group this morning. I said, "Hey, when these legislators came through you could've come to us and said, 'We need this whole place waxed and cleaned up because the legislators are coming through.' Instead you came to us and said, 'You know what—if you don't wax this damn place down we're going to give you a direct order. If you don't do a direct order, we're throwing you in max.'" I told [the prison staff member], "When you come on with that attitude, it tends to make us say, 'Hey, screw you; throw us all in max—then who are you going to get to clean this damn place up?'" I said, "That's the attitude that it makes us want to have."

Mirroring trends found in research on incarcerated women in Great Britain (Carlen 1985; Dobash, Dobash, and Gutteridge 1986), many women at the WCC live in fear of the guards and worry constantly about being written up for "bad" behavior. Like the British women, at this prison many women resolve that the guards purposely pick on them. This is particularly true for the Native women, who maintain that because they are a cohesive group they are threatening to prison staff, and for lesbians solely because of their sexual preference.

The WCC is a prison that is, similar to others, "organized to respond" (Carlen 1985, 11) to prisoners not obeying the rules. The environment is viewed by prisoners as a violent, mean game. Many prisoners insist that staff arbitrarily adhere to or ignore the prison rules and regulations manual, which prisoners refer to as the "joke book." The women describe an environment in which the enforcement of the rules changes depending upon who is on duty, to the point that it seems as if staff members make up the rules. A letter from the ACLU to the director of Corrections cited inconsistency in staff enforcement of rules, particularly the arbitrary enforcement of the rules associated with multiple write-ups given to prisoners and their subsequent removal from the general population to lockup.

In a fictional account of incarcerated white women, Patricia McConnel (1989), who has been in jail several times and was incarcerated in federal prison, writes about the relationships between the guards and the prisoners. Her experiences echo those of incarcerated women in Great Britain (Carlen 1985; Dobash, Dobash, and Gutteridge 1986) and incarcerated women in Montana. McConnel details the physical and emotional abuse found in jails and prisons—abuse that McConnel believes to be an approach that is tacitly sanctioned throughout the criminal justice system. McConnel relates this kind of cruelty to the subsequent decrease in an already low self-esteem found in many prisoners.

In describing a power relationship between a prisoner and a female guard named Garth, McConnel acknowledges that this type of interaction actually happened to her:

> Garth is a specialist at the power/humiliation game. She knows that every instinct in the marrow of my bones is rebelling. . . . I've been insubordinate and she can throw me in the hole, and there goes some of my time off for good behavior. . . . She's ordering my every movement as if I were a robot. I'm dammed if I do and dammed if I don't. It isn't a decision I can take time to ponder over, and the main thing in my life right now is to get out of here on the earliest

possible day. If Garth doesn't get my self-respect today she'll get it tomorrow anyway so what's the use? (1989, 180–181)

Regardless of race/ethnicity or sexual preference, women in Montana's prison report the same belittling experiences from prison guards that McConnel describes. Prisoners proclaim that most guards scream at them rather than speak in a normal tone. On one occasion, the guards in maximum security ate the cookies left by a church group for the prisoners. Although this may appear minor, to women in maximum security who are never allowed such treats, it was a major event.

Most guards are characterized by prisoners at the WCC as stirring up trouble:

> [A guard] invites it; she entices it, and that's part of her control. She'll come up to you and you'll be reading the newspaper, and she'll rip it out of your hand. And if you do anything, you can get written up for it.

Other women describe guards as "evil" and are fearful of them. Prisoners are seriously intimidated by these guards. In the words of one prisoner,

> And this one officer, the minute she hits the floor [arrives on the job] everybody heads to their rooms because she's just on the prowl. She's like what the Bible describes—the devil as an angry lion ready to pounce on you at any minute. That's the way she is. She's angry about the whole world.

Some prisoners experience guards as "petty." For instance, one prisoner was issued a write-up for running up the stairs two at a time. Additionally, prisoners assert that some guards engage them in tedious tasks. For example, Winona remarks that one guard "had us moving furniture back there—first you put the table over there, then you put it back over there." For Winona, menial tasks of this sort give her the feeling that everything she does is wrong. Furthermore, when prisoners do these tasks without getting angry, the guards then become incensed. The guards seem to be deliberately provoking prisoners and perhaps baiting them to justify time in lockup.

Winona offers another example: she and other prisoners worked for days to ready the prison for a visit from state legislators. A guard came in and remarked that the prison was not clean enough; they needed to work harder. At this point, Winona "blew it":

> I said [to the guard], "What? What did you say? I've been working my ass off on this place, and now you're telling me after I've done all this for my fifty-cent pay today, to get my ass in there and scrub those bathroom walls? I'm not going to do it unless you give me a direct order." I was crying and I said [to the guard], "You can't look at the good that we've done and say, 'You guys did a good job'? You have to pick out the bullshit and say, 'You didn't do enough'? 'You gotta do more'? Or 'You gotta do this or that'? Why can't you just once say, 'You did a damn good job'"? I was crying, embarrassed, humiliated. It was like the last straw. The girls looked at me like *ooh*. I got mad and grabbed the rags and the Purex fell and I said, "Furthermore, they don't give you anything to clean it with; that piss has been on those walls for years, and you give me one bottle of disinfectant!" I got in there and took my anger out on the wall [laugh].

Prisoners realize that if they try to save their self-respect, they risk a transfer to maximum security. On the other hand, guards do not respect prisoners no matter what they do—even if they comply.

Another prisoner reports that many male guards are especially hard on assertive women, demanding that they be submissive:

> If anybody that's got a little bit of heart and backbone, as far as projecting that—holy jeez! [The guards will] ride you; they'll make sure your room gets shook down. They'll make sure you get write-ups; they'll follow you around the institution. They'll stand outside your door and listen to what you're talking about.

Some prisoners portray guards as "cold." For instance, when Linda was first incarcerated she thought she could relate to several guards in a mutually respectful way. It was not long, though, until Linda discovered she was wrong:

> Another [guard], she violated my trust. I was just hurt the other night; she discounted me. I was talking with her, and then she got a phone call and I sat there for about ten minutes. She was still on the phone and she says, "Oh, you can go now." It was like, "Goodbye, and I think we will keep on the basis that we're on—cop and inmate.

You be the cop that you are and watch me wax my floors when I get extra duty, and you be the cold one." I put her on a pedestal.

Not all guards are viewed negatively. Prisoners describe one guard as "respectful," "humorous," and a "good Christian man." They say he will write up prisoners for infractions but in a "respectful" and consistent way; in turn, they respect him for his behavior. Several guards, generally lower ranked, are described by prisoners as "okay" or "nice" and "respectful."

There are two guards that one prisoner, Allison, feels she can talk to; nonetheless, she is cognizant that she must manipulate them in order to be heard. For example, one night when Allison was too stressed to perform her in-house job, she asked the guard for time-out in the gym:

[I told the guard,] "I'm so glad you're on." I will butter them up so much after they give me something. I will thank them, "Thank you from the bottom of my heart," because I feel it. It's the truth—if they give you something, be thankful for it . . . hang on to them and praise them, because otherwise if you say it was something little— no, you'd better expect that it is one of the big things.

The preceding quotation describes the deference required of Allison in order to obtain something she desperately needed. Although Allison sees the guard as "good," she was still manipulated by the guard and definitely learned how to play the game, which includes stereotypic ladylike behavior—one of deferring. Moreover, the interaction is evocative of an emotionally abusive relationship in which the prisoner is forced to beg for a favor and to be thankful for it when it is delivered. Even the "good" guards are aware of the us-versus-them attitude that exists. The strict separation conclusively divides guard and prisoner, and the line is not to be crossed. Prisoners experience that they are discounted by guards and not treated with the respect they deserve as human beings.

RACISM AND PRISON STAFF

Previous work on imprisoned Native Canadian women (Faith 1993b), imprisoned Native American men (Cardozo-Freeman 1993; Grobsmith 1994), and imprisoned women of color in Minnesota (Kruttschnitt 1983) confirms that the race/ethnicity of the prisoner affects treatment by prison staff. Other research on prisoners in the United States (Flanagan 1983; Goetting and Howsen 1983; Mann 1993; Ramirez 1983) reveals that racism is directly related to the reporting of prisoner misconduct. Prisoners of color are more likely than white prisoners to be written up for rule violations.

Native women at the WCC are viewed negatively by some prison staff solely because of their race/ethnicity. For instance, when I mentioned to a prison staff member that I would like to interview one particular Native woman, he responded that she would be a good candidate for the study because she "represents everything bad in Indian culture." He never expressed anything similar about white prisoners and white culture.

Native women profess that their race/ethnicity influences the white guards' treatment of them. For example, Agnes, a Native woman, comments that the prison's administration pegged her as a "troublemaker," and because of this most guards treat her harshly. Agnes views both the labeling and the ensuing treatment as racist, and she claims that guards purposely bait her in order to confine her in maximum security. Agnes remarks that the guards are worried about her possible affiliations with legal groups. In fact, Agnes is documenting the prison's treatment of Native prisoners and sending the information to the ACLU. Evidently, this proves threatening to the prison. According to Agnes,

> Some of the officers go through my mail to see if I'm getting any kind of mail from Native American groups—who's corresponding with me. I don't know what they're afraid of. Why are they so afraid to address these issues? What scares them? What's so threatening about it?

Agnes has written multiple letters to Native American newspapers and organizations expressing the negative treatment Native women receive at the WCC. She describes the prison's reaction to her:

> So, therefore, I was labeled a "radical," like I discriminate against white people. And, of course, they don't even understand that term, yet they hear someone else say it so they say it. They say I'm prejudiced in some ways because I want to help the Native American.

Prison staff warned me about Agnes, whom they describe as "a manipulator—even the Indian women hate her" and as one who "hates white people." Agnes finds it odd that she is labeled a racist: "I mean, they call me a racist and here I am in a white prison, run by white people, based on white values."

Other Native women write letters to local newspapers criticizing the prison system and offering potentially cost-effective alternatives to imprisonment and existing prison conditions. These women declare that prison staff subsequently develop a negative perception of them and treat them badly. Winona, who wrote several letters to newspapers, says a prison staff member told her, "Either knock it off or you're going to be here for the rest of your life." Thus, when Native prisoners are assertive and try to help other prisoners, they face a threatening environment.

Not only are Native prisoners denied the right to fully practice their religion, they also find it difficult to be allowed to view films about Native people. For example, several Native prisoners remark that it took them months to secure several movies, including *Soldier Blue*, which depicts the Sand Creek massacre of Cheyenne and Arapaho women and children. According to prisoners, the staff thought it was too controversial to be shown. One member of the prison staff did manage to show the prisoners *War Party*, a feature film about racism in modern-day Montana. This staff member was supposedly reprimanded for showing them the film because the prison administration thought it would incite the Native prisoners to riot.

> We saw *War Party*; they got mad at [the staff member] because he took us over and showed us that movie. [The prison administration] thought we were going to riot. All of us little band of Indians were going to riot [laughs]! The guards got real upset because he showed us that movie.

Deciding what is appropriate for prisoners to view is another way to control them. The assumption that Native prisoners will riot (another Indian uprising) if shown these films demonstrates that prison staff are intimidated by Native prisoners in a racist manner.

When guards conduct shakedowns of Native prisoners' cells, they often carelessly touch their sweetgrass and medicine bundles. One traditional Native woman is extremely upset over this kind of disrespect:

> I tell them [the guards], "These items are sacred to us. We have respect for them; that's all we ask from you—show a little respect. Is it any different from you going in there and jerking the Protes-

tant's Bibles? And throwing them around? Is it any different from you running in there and telling the Catholics or jerking their rosaries away? Tell me," I said, "don't Protestants have their own sacred items? Do you dump the Catholic's holy water out just to check if they have chemicals in them?"

When Native women managed to secure a Native spiritual leader to come into the prison, according to Winona, the prison administration was upset. In the view of Winona, who arranged for the spiritual advisor, the Native prayer leader did not understand that he had to notify the prison of his arrival date; he simply showed up one day. The prison administration apparently saw this as Winona manipulating the system because she arranged the visit. Winona says:

> [A prison staff member] said, "Well, [the administration] sees that as a threat—here Winona's got these Indian people coming in and they're not asking if they can come in, and they might see stuff that we don't want them to see." [The prison staff member] said, "That's why they had us police the place for the legislators."

According to Native prisoners, the prison staff perceive prisoners who organize cultural events as prisoners with "behavioral problems."

The image of the "savage Indian" thrives at the WCC. Seldom do white prisoners threaten to physically harm Native prisoners. Native prisoners mention white prisoners never "push" them because they know to leave them alone. This image, grounded in the neocolonial racism in Montana, hampers total prison solidarity.[1]

Racialized oppression continues, not only in the state of Montana but throughout the United States, because of powerful ideological justifications. Part of this racist ideology is the development and maintenance of negative stereotypes. White prisoners may fear Native prisoners because they see the racist image presented as the truth. As well, this very image may be the reason prison staff use heavy control mechanisms with Native prisoners: much use of "medication" and lockup in maximum security. They are all afraid of "the Indians." Perhaps this is why prisoners were not allowed to see *Soldier Blue*. The complexity of neocolonial racism is illustrated by the tough, "savage" image that protects Native prisoners from white prisoners yet jeopardizes them with prison staff.

SEXUAL INTIMIDATION

Another way to control incarcerated women is through sexual abuse (Rafter 1990). Sexual abuse of female prisoners by male staff is, unfortunately, very common in the United States (Faith 1993b). Incarcerated women of all races/ethnicities are victims of this kind of violence. On 16 November 1992, *USA Today* reported that fourteen correctional workers at a women's prison were indicted on charges of sexual abuse. Ninety women imprisoned in the state of Georgia filed affidavits filled with tales of sexual coercion. It was also reported that the staff involved in the sexual abuse, not unexpectedly, went to great lengths to keep the molestation hidden.

Prisoners at the WCC claim that they are sexually intimidated by male guards. One form of intimidation is male guards on night duty "peeking" at them in their cells when they are undressing for bed. Regular bed checks are part of prison policy and are to occur at scheduled times, but prisoners maintain that some guards arrive early and surprise the prisoners. This is alarming to the women, because most of them are in the middle of undressing and not fully clothed. Many white women have an attitude very different from that of Native women concerning this violation. White prisoners may say, "Oh, so what—if he wants a show, let him look. I ain't got nothing anyway." Although both Native and white women are sexually intimidated, generally Native prisoners are modest and have a particularly difficult time coping with this violation. Their solution is to undress in the closet, and many wear sweatpants and T-shirts to bed. Prisoners also report that one of the bathrooms has a window with no curtain, and some male officers frequently watch them when they are sitting on the toilet. Again, an unneeded stressful situation is created—a situation of control and Peeping Tomism.

An incident recently took place in which a guard fondled a prisoner. Whereas several prisoners contend that the prisoner "enticed" the guard and was a willing participant, other prisoners are incensed that it occurred at all. Cecilia witnessed this sexual assault: "He [the guard] just put his hands all over her; he kissed her. He didn't screw her or whatever you call it, but he was touching her and he's not supposed to." Cecilia comments that this particular guard is either fondling prisoners or "roughing them up." The guard, on duty with pay during the inquiry, was found not guilty of sexual assault by an investigative team from outside the prison. The prisoner involved was represented by a local county attorney. Several days after the investigation was completed, the prisoner was transferred to maximum security. The prison staff argued that she was not moved because she filed charges against this guard but for other reasons. Prisoners, however, conclude she was transferred to maximum security specifically because she filed charges. In Cecilia's words, "She's sitting in max. We all know where that stems from; we're not stupid. We know that their reasons for max are not the reasons they give!" Whereas the guard had his hands slapped for his behavior, the prisoner was punished by lockup in maximum security. Surely, this punishment for reporting the guard's behavior will deter any prisoners from pressing charges against prison staff for sexual assault or intimidation.[2]

In the United States there is a history of violent sexual attacks on women of color. Laws against rape were designed to safeguard only "respectable" white women; other women, including Natives, were left to fend for themselves (Friedman 1993). Native women were afraid of white men because of the violence waged against them and the absence of protective laws. Albert Hurtado suggests that there were no secure places for Native women—not even Indian reservations: "In 1856 the San Francisco *Bulletin* carried a story of a reserve where 'some of the agents, nearly all of the employees' were 'daily and nightly . . . kidnapping the younger portion of the females, for the vilest purposes'" (1988, 181).

Hurtado argues that during colonization, the rape of Native women by white men was typical. Citing another article from an 1858 California newspaper, Hurtado writes that when a white man could not get a Native woman willingly, he would "'drag off the squaw' and 'knock down her friends' if they interfered" (1988, 180). Violations of women operate effectively as a way to terrorize and control them. Today, violence based on attitudes of the past continues.

All women encounter the virgin/whore paradox. Native women have been reduced to the depraved squaw or the Indian princess (Green 1976; Smith 1990). The princess image was recently repopularized by Disney's release of *Pocahontas*, in which we see a very sexy, and very young, Indian princess. The princess is noble, virginal; the squaw is savage, whorish. The princess, of course, is too noble to ravage—only squaws are raped.

While none of the white women disclose being raped while incarcerated (which does not mean they were not sexually abused), two Native women say they were raped in jail by white male jailers. One of the women, Agnes, was raped multiple times by the same jailer. This happened just prior to her conviction and subsequent transfer to prison. The other woman, Winona, was raped several years ago when she was in a county jail. Both women maintain that the rapes occurred because they are Native American women. Although Winona decided to bring her rapist to the attention of the authorities, Agnes is intimidated by the criminal justice system and has decided, in part because of her attorney's attitude, only to process her rape emotionally, not legally. Her attorney, in a response indicative of his attitude toward Native women as "squaws," told her not to press charges against the jailer because she has had sex with many men and is "no angel." Agnes explains that because she was raped as a child, and later as an adult, the sexual intimidation that occurs in this prison nauseates her.

Several prisoners mention that when the prison had a smaller population, some prisoners traded sex with guards for marijuana and alcohol. A Native prisoner agrees that this happened but insists that only white prisoners exchanged sexual favors with the guards. Citing cultural differences in reactions to abuse, she explains:

> To me it's a violation of your being. I guess it's just a different type of raising. With these white women here, you know probably because they roamed the streets so many years, it doesn't bother them—they've become immune to it.

Prison staff agree that the most common difficulty for prisoners is prior sexual abuse. They estimate that 90 percent of the prisoners suffer from sexual abuse. In light of the nefarious conditions in which these women were raised, sexual intimidation of prisoners should be of paramount concern.

PRISONERS' RESPONSES TO CONTROL

Prison subculture is a depraved culture. In the words of former prisoner Eugene Delorme, "This system works hard to turn us all into monsters. This prison is a jungle and makes good men turn back into savages just to survive" (Cardozo-Freeman 1993, 130). Prison life is a violent game in which the rules are arbitrarily decided by others. According to Carlen (1985) and Dobash, Dobash, and Gutteridge (1986), this cruelty may lead to violence on the part of prisoners as they attempt to maintain some form of self-respect. This type of violence can be seen as one way to survive a socially sick environment. The staff's response to this survival tactic, however, is lockup in the maximum-security unit, where prisoners are isolated in order to learn their lessons. Lengthy time in maximum security seemingly strips prisoners of any integrity and dignity. Additionally, knowing that they will be thrown in lockup if they do not conform usually keeps prisoners in their places (Carlen 1985).

Psychological violence and lockup are only one kind of threat. Other threats to survival include isolation, provocation by guards, institutionalization, and boredom, plus the use of mind-altering drugs to control imprisoned women (Carlen 1985). At the WCC, one way prisoners cope with prisonization is to take the prescribed mind-altering drugs. Although not all prisoners are required to take these drugs, some do so because they are not strong enough to refuse them. Others use prescribed medications, as they did prior to incarceration, to survive the evil prison environment. Generally, prisoners who use drugs to cope are subjected to lengthy stays in maximum security and lockup.

Carlen (1985) and Dobash, Dobash, and Gutteridge (1986) maintain that guards deliberately manipulate and force imprisoned women to their emotional edge. Some imprisoned women are pushed to that edge earlier than others because they are extremely vulnerable when they enter prison. Prison guards, therefore, have complete control over prisoners. Consequences of this kind of control, other than prisoner violence, include suicide, self-mutilation, and insanity. It is no wonder some elect to comply with prison staff in an effort to survive. Other survival tactics, according to Carlen (1985), include forming close friendships with fellow prisoners or attaining a "top-dog" position in which prisoners manipulate the system to ensure that nobody, neither staff nor prisoners, will bother them.

Many prisoners at the WCC employ manipulation as a method to resist prisonization. Prisoners dialogue about "playing the game" as a way to survive. A prisoner explains how she plays to her advantage:

> In prison I call all the male officers "sir"; I call all the female officers "ma'am." I'd like to call them what they act like, but I don't. Other prisoners say, "You're kissing their ass." I'm going to play their game to get out of here and I don't care what other inmates say.

Although this prisoner does not like the guards, she knows she cannot display her true feelings. To do so could possibly land her in maximum security. She plays the game for her own benefit.

Another woman, Dorine, refuses to manipulate the system because she believes that ultimately such behavior would prove detrimental to her. She clarifies this by stating that she is in prison because she played games on the outside. Whether outside or inside prison, the core of the game is dishonesty and manipulation. Dorine says, "There's a time when a person's got to be honest with themselves. If you don't have that, you don't have anything." She explains further:

> [The prisoners who manipulate are] going to fail. Since I've been here, I'll bet there's been five or six girls come back. They will come back because they've played the game. . . . they weren't being real. You can tell when a person's lying and when they're not. I'm too damn old to get out there and play the game again.

Prisoners allege that the penal system theoretically insists upon truthfulness from the prisoners, yet representatives of the system lie and manipulate prisoners. The following words of a Native prisoner express the sentiments of many prisoners:

> It's all a game and it doesn't make sense to me, because they want you not to be manipulative to get what you want. They don't want you to play games but they're playing games with you, so you have to be a good player. It doesn't make sense. This place doesn't make sense.

Many prisoners become master manipulators in order to survive, yet once released from prison they have difficulty unlearning this behavior. Many prisoners note that this alone affects recidivism. To a certain extent, everyone must play the game—a game in which only the guards know the rules. The use of manipulation and games by staff and prisoners contribute to the sickness of the prison's social environment. Prisoners are trapped in poisonous surroundings and believe this causes mental and physical maladies. Moreover, they claim that when they resist the diseased environment, prison officials negatively label them and try to break them—a serious threat to prisoner survival. The other option is to conform to staff expectations.

None of the prisoners express that *they* conform to staff expectations, although they comment about *other* prisoners, "snitches," who conform. Snitches are seen as allying themselves with prison staff, reporting various rule infractions by other prisoners. Most prisoners detest snitches; nevertheless, Winona has a different perspective:

> There are a couple of girls in here who are having a hard time be-cause they run to the guards and tell them everything. One of the girls that does that has never had anybody that really stood up for her, or with her. She has a real low self-esteem—worse than most of us. I feel sorry for her.

Prisoners considered staff "pets" are not viewed by other prisoners as totally conforming. Other prisoners simply see these individuals as pre-ferred by staff for the coveted prison jobs. Regarding a certain prisoner, one prisoner said, "Oh, she's just the warden's little pet; she was in re-form school when he was working there." The condescension toward "pets" increases the already existing tension between prisoners and fur-ther prevents any possibilities for prisoner solidarity.

Following trends shown in previous research (Dobash, Dobash, and Gutteridge 1986), suicide attempts are not taken seriously at the WCC, and many times they are defined by prison staff as an "assault." Under those circumstances, prisoners are written up and put in isolation as pun-ishment. A prisoner says:

> My friend came and said, "I'm going to kill myself and you can't stop me." She's a tough con; I'd never seen her even cry. So she told the guard she was going to kill herself. He just sat there. She tried to kill herself; she cut her arms and nothing was done. Plus, she got wrote up for it.

According to prison staff, suicide attempts seldom occur. When they do happen they are characterized as "attention-seeking" behavior rather than as a symptom of stress and anxiety. A staff member offers the ex-ample of a young Native woman who swallowed a piece of plastic and placed a rubber band around her neck "just to get attention—she was not serious." Prisoners, on the other hand, maintain that attempts are frequent. Prisoners say that those who attempt suicide are often transferred to maximum security, although in some cases they are transferred to the forensic ward of the state mental hospital.

A former director of Montana's only women's pre-release center remarks that suicide attempts are frequent in pre-release, especially among Native women. This pattern is comparable to the Canadian women's prison system (Faith 1993b; Grossmann 1992; *To Heal the Spirit* 1990). The former pre-release director places the blame directly on depression that results from living in a foreign, white environment. She recommends that the recognition of cultural differences be incorporated into all aspects of the criminal justice system, particularly prisons and pre-release centers.

A recent study on imprisoned Canadian women links childhood violence to subsequent suicides while incarcerated:

> When a woman has been sexually abused as a child, she's going to behave in certain ways as an adult. She'll have problems with trust, with feelings of personal control. She tends to take responsibility for everything that goes on around her, assuming it's her fault and she's bad. She'll have incredibly low self-esteem, and may self-injure. She's at a high risk for suicide. (Heney 1990; quoted in Grossmann 1992, 409)

Another Canadian study (Shaw et al. 1989) reveals that 90 percent of the Native women sentenced to a federal prison are victims of physical abuse and 61 percent were sexually abused. Native Canadian women are 7.5 times more likely to commit suicide than the general female population. Native women, "due to their personal histories, are already at greater risk for suicide than non-aboriginal female inmates" (Grossmann 1992, 409).

Grossmann (1992) argues that social isolation is crucial in the examination of incarcerated Native women and custodial suicides. The author offers that whether the isolation is separation from families or the removal of a prisoner from general population to maximum security, the isolation stems from prisonization. Emphasizing familial and cultural importance, Grossmann proposes that

> separation from families, communities, and culture is a disturbing event for all inmates, but particularly for aboriginal women.

Geographic distances from families often preclude the possibility of regular family visits. This is a significant problem as the majority of these women are mothers . . . and have major concerns about the effects of incarceration and separation on their relationships with their children. (1992, 410)

When racism, direct or institutionalized, is attached to the above conditions, an intensely gloomy predicament exists for imprisoned Native women—an environment conducive to depression and suicide.

Suicide is not always the consequence of internalized oppression. Suicide can be an act of freedom, an act of defiance. The following statement about suicide and Native Americans, in the context of colonialism, provides additional insight:

It reflects the hopelessness of trapped and imprisoned souls. It is an unwillingness to continue suffering. . . . According to many American Indians, whose lives have been affected by the government goal of assimilating them into the general ethos of American life, suicide could be construed as the ultimate act of freedom. It is an act that defies governmental control and challenges the dominant society to face up to its irresponsibility in meeting treaty agreements for health, education, and welfare. (LaFromboise and Bigfoot 1988; quoted in Bachman 1992, 109)

RECOMMENDATIONS FROM THE PRISONERS

When asked what alterations they desire in the penal system, prisoners produce a long list. Most prisoners want a female warden because they believe a woman will understand the problems and needs of women and, accordingly, structure the prison to fit incarcerated women.[3] Prisoners remark that this is especially crucial because of the lack of privacy and because of sexual intimidation on the part of some male guards. While a prior study (Shaw 1992) reveals mixed views from female prisoners regarding the employment of male guards in women's prisons, most prisoners at the WCC suggest that male guards do not need to work the night shift: prisoners are locked in their rooms and therefore do not pose a threat that may require stereotypic male strength to quell.

As demonstrated by prior studies (Grobsmith 1994; Shaw 1992), prisoners want to be treated with respect by prison staff. All prisoners aspire to be seen as human beings instead of "kids" or "animals." Prisoners also recommend consistency in rule enforcement. Some prisoners recommend a more specific definition of sexual misconduct, so that comforting someone or showing appreciation through behavior such as hugging will not be considered an infraction of the rules.

Prisoners in maximum security urge that confinement to that unit be limited to one month. Several prisoners who claim to have been in that building for over one year believe the prison is deliberately trying to break them. Prisoners also suggest that women with medical problems, those waiting for beds in general population, and pregnant prisoners should not be punished by undeserved transfers to the maximum-security unit. Whereas some prisoners discern that the prison deliberately abuses them with inadequate health care, others determine that neglect occurs due to financial difficulties within the Department of Corrections. Prisoners endorse the upgrading of the health care, decreasing the amount of mind-altering drugs prescribed, and the hiring of additional health-care practitioners.

Prisoners advocate more counseling and treatment programs, and the employment of qualified staff. Most white prisoners request more one-on-one counseling, rather than group counseling, due to tension between prisoners. A common grievance is that there are too few counseling and treatment programs. Women serving long sentences are especially critical and burned out on existing counseling, and they maintain that short-timers are selected first for counseling programs. Traditional, reservation Native women desire traditional Native counseling for mental health problems. They undoubtedly feel the type of counseling they need is not available to them. Agreeing with incarcerated Native American men (Grobsmith 1994), all Native women prisoners and several white women prisoners recommend that the prison staff enlighten themselves on Native culture, especially the American Indian Religious Freedom Act. These women conclude that if ignorance is replaced with knowledge, perhaps some racist behavior will disappear.

Several reservation women who are serving long sentences mention they are estranged from their culture and worry about becoming "white" and alienating themselves from their Native communities. Native prisoners urge the prison to offer cultural activities tailored for

Native prisoners. Furthermore, due to existing interpersonal problems between Native prisoners and white staff, Native prisoners want Native staff in any capacity employed at the prison. Native women also desire the freedom to form a group that will allow them to share feelings and resources with each other.

Native prisoners argue that the state government must recognize the overt and covert discrimination operating in the criminal justice system. They propose that the Native nations create a liaison position between the prison system and Indian reservations. After release from prison, tribal members could be served by a liaison concerning job placement and reintegration into their communities. A liaison could also help Native prisoners write support letters to the parole board and aid them in locating funds for educational purposes.

Although most Native American nations in Montana are helping Native prisoners with educational needs, Landless Natives are jeopardized by not having the tribal structure that typically provides such services. They are particularly worried about transition from the inside to the outside and believe the Indian Affairs coordinator's office should assist them upon their release from prison. The Indian Affairs office could also serve as a watchdog agency, especially with regard to sentence disparity, Indian Child Welfare Act compliance, and religious freedom issues. Landless Natives, citing another issue of sovereignty, suggest that both the Indian Affairs office and individual tribes exercise more authority regarding Native prisoners.

Prisoners recommend more On the Job Training positions and an expansion of the prison industries program, and they advocate an increase in pay for these positions and for in-house jobs. Furthermore, several prisoners suggest that, to lessen the tension among prisoners, all jobs have the same pay. One prisoner offers that the more prisoners are involved in employment, educational, and counseling programs, the less likely they will be to "play the games."

Many prisoners resolve that prisoners' relationships with each other will be eased if the prison is segregated between long-timers and short-timers. Prisoners believe the overcrowded conditions contribute to poor interprisoner relations and recommend either a larger prison or fewer women sentenced to prison.

Prisoners also propose a raise in the gate-pay. Reflecting a sexist bias, as well as a possible violation of the law, men incarcerated in Montana receive two hundred dollars' gate-pay, whereas women receive only ninety-five dollars.

Prisoners endorse another pre-release center for women because they believe many incarcerated women do not belong in prison—the punishments do not fit the crimes. There is minimal assistance from the Montana Defender's Project and public defenders, and prisoners propose increasing the access to attorneys and legal information. Because some prisoners file their own appeals and do not have access to a copy machine or carbon paper, the legal process is especially cumbersome. Many prisoners are forced to handwrite letters of appeal to legal officials.

The most important wish of the prisoners, however, is not a program. Prisoners hope to survive the belittling and humiliating experiences of prison with their sanity intact. Prior to prison, most prisoners led lives that can be characterized as precarious at best and horrific at worst, and anyone would be chronically depressed in the social environment produced by prison.

Eight

MOTHERHOOD IMPRISONED

IMAGES AND CONCERNS

OF IMPRISONED MOTHERS

The most damned women in our society are those classified as "unfit" mothers (Mahan 1982). Mothers may be judged incompetent due to substance abuse, general lifestyle, sexual preference, or race/ethnicity. Mothers who are offenders and thus violate the stereotypic image of the "good" mother are treated particularly harshly by the courts (Beckerman 1991; Carlen 1988; Farrington and Morris 1983; Pollock 1995).

This kind of labeling is most obvious when courts officially judge women to be "unfit" as mothers, as occurs in child custody hearings. Despite anecdotes that women are more likely than men to receive custody of their children, when the fathers want the children, mothers lose custody battles 70 percent of the time (Schafran 1990). Moreover, failing as a mother has far-reaching consequences. Forced to live with the label of being "unfit" for a role that may be central to her self-image, a woman may internalize the label and question her own adequacy as a parent and as a woman (Baunach 1985b; Henriques 1982; Stanton 1980).

If we consider the definition of an "unfit" mother as one who does not care about her children, then studies on imprisoned women and their children reveal that most imprisoned mothers do not warrant that description (Baunach 1985a, 1985b; Beckerman 1991, 1994; Bresler and Lewis 1983; Clark 1995; Henriques 1982; Mahan 1982; Stanton 1980; Zalba 1964). Most, in fact, maintain a great love for their children. Because of the powerful influence of mothers in the lives of their children, incarceration has obvious negative consequences on the mother and her children (Henriques 1982). In many families, the mother is the core, so her absence creates a family crisis. The longer a woman is imprisoned, the less likely it is that her family will remain intact or that her children will later live with her (McGowan and Blumenthal 1978). The presence and maintenance of family stability are critical factors in an incarcerated woman's successful adjustment after release from prison (Henriques 1982; Stanton 1980; Zalba 1964).

Unfortunately, imprisoned women are essentially forced to be unsuitable as mothers because, by virtue of their prisoner status, they are incapable of providing for their children (Mahan 1982). Although incarceration is not allowed to be considered as evidence that a parent is "unfit," some states have statutes that permanently terminate the parental rights of an imprisoned parent regardless of the crime (Feinman 1986; Mann 1984; Stanton 1980). Fortunately, only five states operate in this manner: Florida, Illinois, New York, Wyoming, and Montana (Stanton 1980). In some states, the nature of the crime itself is used as the major criterion for child custody; in other states, ambiguous standards are used to determine custody.

Although most states no longer use a mother's incarceration as grounds for legally terminating her parental rights, an imprisoned mother with children in foster care is in a precarious position. Childcare authorities expect her to comply with rules of conduct that are prevalent for natural mothers, yet the circumstances of her imprisonment restrict her capability to fulfill these expectations (Beckerman 1991), thus potentially jeopardizing continuation of her parental rights. Contact with her children is most likely minimal, and, like many incarcerated mothers, she may not be made aware of pending custody hearings (Beckerman 1994). The effect on imprisoned mothers is that they endure "double punishment" for their crimes: "a prison sentence and the threat of the termination of parental rights, continuing a historical pattern of societal bias against, and hostility toward, imprisoned mothers" (Beckerman 1991, 180).

Seldom do we hear men characterized as "unfit" fathers, even if they are incarcerated. In Euro-American society, the burden and joy of parenting has been borne primarily by women. This speaks to the notion of "true womanhood" and the proper role of women as "good" mothers. The assumption is that responsible women bear, rear, and protect children. Those who stray from this path are characterized as deviant and unfit. The cases of three women incarcerated at the WCC for being "unfit" mothers illustrate this point. All three were convicted of "failure to protect a child." In all cases, the women's husbands actually committed the crimes, and both the women and their husbands served time.

In two of the cases, the men sexually abused foster children placed in their care, and in the third case a man physically abused a foster child. Three different judges alleged that the mothers not only knew about these crimes but had the power to stop their husbands. These women were perceived as "irresponsible," failures as mothers, and were given prison sentences because they were unsuccessful in protecting these children from abusive men.

MOTHERHOOD, GENDER, AND RACE IN SENTENCING

Prisoners are aware of race/ethnicity and gender issues and have strong beliefs about the role those issues played in their sentencing. One gender-related issue is pregnancy. Several women conclude that a court appearance before a judge while pregnant is damaging. Darla, a white woman pregnant and addicted to drugs at the time of her sentencing, comments:

> He [the judge] said that was why I went to prison—because I was pregnant. And they were afraid I'd use the drugs. I was pregnant and hooked on drugs; soon it's going to be a crime to take drugs when you're pregnant. You're going to be getting twenty years. I thought the pregnancy would go for me, too, when I got in front of him, but it went against me. No, I didn't receive a lighter sentence. That's *why* I went to prison.

Darla's assessment is correct: in some states, pregnant women addicted to drugs can be arrested for child abuse or neglect (Pollock-Byrne and Merlo 1991).

Another white woman, from a conservative middle-class background and not an addict, also believes that her pregnancy was used against her by the judge:

> [The judge] said he was sending me to prison in spite of my kids. And my youngest was born during that time—she was two months old when I got sent here. So I had gotten pregnant and had the baby between getting arrested and getting sent here [prison]. I was accused of getting pregnant on purpose. He was using my kids against me.

This mother concludes that because she was perceived as "devious," as using her pregnancy to gain sympathy, she received the maximum sentence for her crime.

Many believe the myth that women receive lighter sentences than men and that mothers receive exceptionally lenient sentences. One prison staff member at the WCC, however, realizes that mothers may often receive harsher sentences than men or than women who are not mothers. In his words,

> I don't think that the fact that they're mothers really contributes to a lighter sentence. In some cases I've seen it contribute to a heavier sentence—where a judge will get mad at the person and say, "You're telling me you're a mother and you ought to be with your kids but look how you're mistreating them. So it's better off to get you away from your kids." It can work to the detriment [of the female offender].

A Native woman who was convicted of mitigated deliberate homicide compares her sentencing to that of a man convicted of the same crime:

> At the time I was sentenced, he [the judge] did state that "Because you are young and pregnant and have a child at home I'm going to be lenient on you. Therefore, I'm sentencing you to thirty years." Well, when he said "lenient," I was waiting for him to say, "suspended," and he didn't. After that there was a guy who was Native American also, who was up for killing his girlfriend around the same time I got in trouble. This was not his first time in prison; he had three prior assaults, and his fourth one he ended up killing his girlfriend. He got twenty-five years for mitigated deliberate homicide, two years for the use of a weapon, and twelve years suspended. So I don't believe that women receive lighter sentences. He had priors and this is my first felony in my life. It was the first time I'd even been in a courtroom. It's a myth.

Another prisoner agrees that mothers do not receive lighter sentences:

> I have seen women that got some real heavy-duty sentences. We've got a woman that got a "dangerous" put on her for writing bad checks! You know, what does she have? A violent pen? We have a

lady here that's doing a hundred years. Five years ago you never heard of that. One of the judges that I saw made it very plain—a mother's place is in their home taking care of children and not out in public and not out in the community writing bad checks.

Studies on the gendering of sentence length disclose that the severity of a woman's sentence is related to family background and marital status (Carlen 1988; Farrington and Morris 1983; Kruttschnitt 1982). The presence of a male figure, either a father or husband, in a woman's life results in a less severe sentence (Kruttschnitt 1982). The assumption appears to be that "strong" men provide control over "weak" women's behaviors.

Failure to comply with gender stereotypes may also have an effect on sentencing. A woman imprisoned multiple times maintains that after the 1970s women's sentences started to lengthen, especially for nonconforming women involved in male-type crimes, regardless of whether those women had children. Feeling that this additional punishment was applied to her, she recalls her sentencing:

He [the judge] didn't care about me being a mother because of my crime. Back then it was like I was Ma Barker—women carrying guns. That was really the clincher for me because I was a known felon. I was known for criminal activity and I was known for carrying a gun. So being a mother didn't matter at that point. My case was pretty severe and they didn't care if I was a woman or not. They had to make an example out of me. At that time, crime was escalating with women. Women were starting to take a front row to criminal activities rather than sitting at home waiting for hubby to come home with his partner and count the money. I've never been that way anyway. I'd just as soon answer to myself and have my own weapon and do my own thing than have a man take care of me.

Women involved in male-type crimes are seen as less "female," as the role is constructed in Euro-American society. Challenging traditional beliefs about the proper female role, these women do indeed receive harsher sentences than men (Chesney-Lind 1981; Erez 1992). As threats to the social order, they are also given longer sentences than women who are involved in female crimes or who display stereotypic feminine behavior. Moreover, being a woman of color complicates the issue. As Lewis (1981) argues, women of color generally do not fit the image of what a woman should look like, nor do they exhibit "acceptable" behavior. This deviation from the "ideal" can result in oppressive treatment by the criminal justice system. To survive the prison experience, women may need to adopt stereotypic "ladylike" behavior.

Ben Pease, who volunteers at the women's prison in Montana, believes that Native women are especially jeopardized in the Euro-American court system because they have culture-specific behaviors that criminal justice system officials do not understand. In addition, often they are naive regarding Euro-American courts and lack the financial resources to secure an accomplished attorney (Shay 1996). Many Native women reason that race/ethnicity was more important to their sentencing than gender or motherhood. They conclude that they received the maximum sentence because they are Native Americans. One Native woman relates that the judge, a white woman, did not even ask her if she had children. This imprisoned mother sees the judge as a racist:

> She was my judge before. She was racist toward Indians and I felt that's how she was sentencing me—according to my race. She does not like Indians. I figured that out. I watched the way she treated a couple of these Indian guys right before I got sentenced. I watched how she reacted toward them; how she looked at them. She was trying to be professional but she was also being like, "Oh God, another Indian is standing in front of me—these Indians." She didn't say anything about my daughter. She just started telling me, "This is what we're going to sentence you to—you have a lengthy sentence." That's all she ever said to me. I felt her hostile vibes and I watched how she sentenced Indian people.

Native Americans are stereotyped as (among other negative images) drunken, suicidal, lazy, primitive, and criminal. At best, the image is one of the "savage," backward Indian—the Indian who must assimilate, be "rehabilitated" into the dominant society. Partially this is due to the poorly conceived representations of Native people that endure today (see Berkhofer 1978). Natives' lack of social and economic power work together with negative stereotypes to elicit more severe societal reactions, including within the prison system. Specifically referring to

Native Canadians, Michael Jackson (1992) argues that stereotypic images do affect the way Natives are treated by the criminal justice system:

> Put at its baldest, there is an equation for being drunk, Indian and in prison. Like many stereotypes, this one has a dark underside. It reflects a view of Native people as uncivilized and without a coherent social or moral order. The stereotype prevents us from seeing Native people as equals. The fact that the stereotypical view of Native people is no longer reflected in official government policy does not negate its power in the popular imagination and its influence in shaping decisions of the police, prosecutors, judges and prison officials. (quoted in Faith 1993b, 192)

PRISON STAFF AND IMAGES OF MOTHERHOOD

Staff at the WCC describe imprisoned mothers in a variety of negative ways: as irresponsible, manipulative, selfish, immature, uncaring, lacking discipline, and suffering from low self-esteem. These judgments are not necessarily an assignment of blame; they see these characteristics as behavioral manifestations resulting from years of sexual abuse, co-dependent relationships, dysfunctional families, and substance abuse.

Although prison staff determine that some mothers, "unfit" mothers, do not care about their children, others are perceived as "women . . . who truly love their kids and were as good as mothers as they knew how to be when they were out there" (Adams 1991, 8). While staff see some mothers as frequently expressing concern for the welfare of their children, they accuse others of acting superficially and using the role of mother to gain status and attention. Prison staff often remark that one woman or another really does not care about her children; she was neglectful of them in the past and is now "putting on a show" for others. The concerns of these mothers frequently go unnoticed or unanswered because they are seen as insincere.

According to prison staff, "responsibility" is the most desirable trait for imprisoned mothers. In their view, the majority of imprisoned mothers never exhibited responsibility prior to incarceration, and the onus for child care fell onto relatives, friends, or the state. This acceptance of assistance by the mothers before incarceration is interpreted by prison staff as evidence of uncaring attitudes toward their children.

Of course, there are important exceptions to the systemic pressures to stereotype, blame, and punish. One individual who works closely with mothers regarding foster care and adoption believes that the stereotypic image of imprisoned mothers as "unfit" is grossly unfair. He believes imprisoned mothers are generally concerned with the welfare of their children. He also observes the mothers as incapacitated by a number of situations, including poor parenting skills, dysfunctional family structures, relationships with abusive men, and early pregnancies. Furthermore, he characterizes imprisoned mothers as fearful of state service workers and uninformed in matters relating to the custody of their children. He understands that many of the prisoners are afraid of him: "When I show up at the prison, I am the guy from the state here to steal your baby from you."

The parenting class facilitator and imprisoned women share a mutually respectful relationship. The facilitator finds the mothers receptive and eager to learn about parenting issues. At the onset of her work with imprisoned mothers, she was stunned by their willingness because she had been influenced by unfavorable notions of imprisoned women and the prevailing societal belief that this group is "bad." In her words, however, "They are not—they're wonderful, caring women who've had horrendous things happen to them."

Recognizing that imprisoned mothers' relationships with their children may be an impelling force for personal transformation, the facilitator perceives the mothers as aware of changes they need and want to make for themselves and their children. She sees the women as mothers, not prisoners, and views them as kind, respectful, and responsible individuals learning and maturing from their experiences.

THE EFFECTS OF PARENT-CHILD SEPARATION

Although most incarcerated women are single, more than 75 percent of all women in prison are mothers, and the majority have children under the age of eighteen (Greenfeld and Minor-Harper 1991; Snell and Morton 1994). Four out of five imprisoned mothers were living with their children prior to incarceration (Greenfeld and Minor-Harper

1991). The separation of incarcerated mothers and their children is per-ceived as temporary, and approximately 85 percent of the mothers with children under age eighteen hope to reunite with their children follow-ing their release from prison (Greenfeld and Minor-Harper 1991). Fifty-three percent of imprisoned mothers with children under eighteen re-port that their children are now living with a grandparent, usually the mother of the incarcerated woman. Twenty-two percent have children living with the fathers, and 22 percent have children living with other relatives. The remainder of the children are in foster care or another in-stitutional setting (Greenfeld and Minor-Harper 1991).

Because children most often lived at home with their mothers prior to incarceration, the separation is generally the first major parting from their mothers. As previous research would predict (Baunach 1985a, 1985b; Greenfeld and Minor-Harper 1991; Henriques 1982), most mothers at the WCC were living with their children prior to incarcera-tion and identify their primary concern in prison as separation from their children. The problem is both emotional and legal, and often the two are related. Some studies (Baunach 1985b; Henriques 1982) have conveyed incarcerated mothers' perceptions that separation brings on or worsens their children's emotional, physical, or academic problems. Delores, a Native woman at the WCC, fears that others will taunt her son because of the serious crime of which she was convicted; imagining what people might say to her son drove her to two suicide attempts. Separation from their families also produces intense apprehension and emotional distress for the mothers. Prior studies (Baunach 1985a; Hen-riques 1982; Ross and Fabiano 1986) found that women prisoners often internalize the separation and experience depression and loss of self-esteem. At the worst, imprisoned mothers exhibit self-destructive be-haviors (Mann 1984), such as Delores's suicide attempts.

Native and white mothers use dissimilar coping strategies for the dis-tress separation causes. Many Native mothers find comfort uniting to-gether in their culture. Their spiritual prayer group apparently provides a therapeutic setting in which to display their grief. Given that white women do not form a cohesive group, it is perhaps not surprising that some cope with separation by isolating themselves from other prisoners. Prison conditions teach them not to express their emotions publicly; other prisoners and prison staff would view such displays as a sign of weakness, which would lead to further victimization. One young white mother describes her way of coping with the pain of separation from her child:

I wait until everybody's sleeping and put my face in the pillow and cry my eyes out. I don't let anybody see me cry; I keep it to myself. You can't do anything around here. You can't even show your anger. You can't show your fear—you can't show your depression.

While some white mothers cry alone at night for their children, others try to elude their feelings. One white mother voices: "If I can avoid it, it's better for me because then I don't have to feel the pain. I cope by avoiding it; I cover up with my silliness."

The prison environment does not allow mothers to fully express their feelings of loss and offers little support for grieving. This repression and lack of support almost seem to be an unwritten part of the punishment. Furthermore, mothers' distress about issues regarding their children makes them vulnerable to manipulation by prison staff.

All mothers express that the separation from their children has negative effects on them and their children. Mothers are apprehensive that their children, especially the younger ones, will not remember them or will become detached from them. As previous research demonstrates (Baunach 1985b; Henriques 1982; Ross and Fabiano 1986), the age of the children is indeed a critical factor affecting estrangement. Mothers in maximum security—who are allowed minimal contact with their children—and mothers with lengthy sentences are especially concerned. Delores says she has been in prison so long that she is totally estranged from her entire family.

Mary, similar to many mothers, is disturbed about the length of time she must spend away from her children, especially from her youngest:

It's been years now; it is a long time to be away from your children. My baby was two years old when I was arrested and she's going to be seven this year. Now I look at the years that I've missed through her growth. And then there are my sons. My son turned seventeen and I missed his graduation from the eighth grade. My second son's going to graduate from the eighth grade and I'll miss that. But I try really hard to show them that I'm still there with them.

Linda is especially troubled about her youngest child. Like others with small children, she is fearful because her child does not know her as a mother, so it will take much work for them to develop a mother/child relationship. This mother remarks that younger children have a difficult time with separation not only because of their young age but also because they misconceptualize prison. When asked if her children have difficulty conceptualizing the reality of prison, this mother tearfully responds:

> Yes, mainly with my son [crying]—he's seven now. He pictured me behind bars and he was really amazed that we have TVs here. He stole a bike last spring and the cops came. He decided last fall that if he stole a bike, they'd put him in prison with his mom. Well, actually he was doing it to get sent here because he thought he would get to be with his mom. It was really hard to explain to him that that's not the way it works and that he shouldn't be doing it.

Another mother, with five children, has a similar problem with her young son's conception of prison:

> My three-year-old boy doesn't realize this is a prison. He tells me, "Mom, how come you can't come to my house for dinner? How come you can't come to my house and spend the night?" Because he has to come over here [to the prison] to visit me—he comes and spends the weekend here with me. He doesn't understand why I can't go to his house. I take him upstairs and show him my room. He doesn't understand why I can't go to his house so I can see his room—he gets angry. The last time my husband picked him up from a visit, he was crying and throwing a fit, which I can understand. He was saying he wanted to stay at Mom's house and live with Mom at her house. He didn't want to go back to Dad's house. He doesn't comprehend this. He looks at it as Mom's house—an apartment building.

"Behavioral adaptation" refers to the negative behaviors and associated feelings children experience toward their imprisoned mothers. Mothers are troubled that their children may develop negative attitudes toward them because of their imprisonment. Many mothers sense their children are angry at them for being imprisoned. Their children manifest this hostility in negative behavior. Julie conveys her concerns about her oldest son, who is five:

> He's very mad at me. Whenever I call, I try to talk to him first— before he gets upset. We usually talk and, after a while, he'll just

drop the phone; he doesn't want to talk anymore. When he's here, he just goes nutty when it's time for him to leave—he kicks, he scratches, he bites. When he's here, it's like he doesn't have any problems and he gets along with his brother. As soon as you get him home, he tries to hit his brother and choke him.

Like many women, Julie was pregnant when she entered prison. She says her oldest boy, now five years old, related the pregnancy to her imprisonment rather than to the crime itself. He now manifests his anger in negative behavior against his baby brother:

My oldest son believes that in order to get a little brother he had to give up his mom. I went through my entire trial through my pregnancy. I got here and one month later, I had my child. During that time, I let my oldest rub my tummy and would tell him that he was going to have a brother or sister, and he was all excited. When I came here and had the baby, and he came, he was excited about the baby. When they came to visit me that day and it was time to leave, he thought we were all going and he kept saying, "Come on, Mom, let's go." And I kept telling him, "No, I can't—Mommy wants you to be really nice to the baby and take care of your little brother, okay?" He was excited at first and then I think he thought, "If I get my baby brother, I have to give up my mom." I had my mom tell me, and my husband too, that on several occasions he said, "Take him back and get my mom." So right now I'm going through a hard time with my oldest. He's becoming very rebellious. He looks forward to the visits, but when you first ask him he'll tell you "no," that he's not coming.

Victoria also determines that her children are mad at her because of her imprisonment:

I know that my children are mad. I know my oldest daughter is especially, and she'll come out and tell me, "I hate you," and things like this. I'll tell her, "That's all right to hate Mom. Mom still loves you; Mom's sorry and Mom's here. She's trying to get better." That's about all I say, and that's what I tell her every time she tells me, "I hate you." And it happens a lot; she has a lot of anger.

Another mother has a different perspective. She focuses on her son's sorrow about their separation rather than on his occasional anger. She tearfully comments, "He's not mad—he's more hurt. He wakes up in the middle of the night crying for me."

Behavioral adaptation issues differ not by race/ethnicity but by placement type. Women with children placed formally (in foster care or adoptive homes) attribute their children's negative attitudes to the influence of the guardians. For example, Suzanne directly blames her children's foster parents for the negative attitudes her children developed toward her. She believes that the foster parents tell her children negative things about her:

> When I didn't come home at Christmas, my son asked, "Why not?" and "Where's my mom? She said she was coming home after Christmas. Santa Claus has already been here." Well, the foster parents told him his mommy wasn't coming home. So now he refuses to talk to me due to the fact that he thinks Mommy ain't coming to get him at all.

Most mothers with older children are fearful that their children will act out by breaking the law and become involved with the criminal justice system, another form of behavioral adaptation. Judy articulates what many mothers feel:

> The worst thing I could ever think of that could happen from here on out is that my kids would have to go through what I have. Unfortunately, the chances are higher for them than for other children— that's a reality. The only thing I can do is educate them and let them know.

Victoria is also anxious about her children following in her footsteps and possibly ending up in prison:

> I don't want to see my kids end up where I've been. My stepdaughter ran away; we don't know where she's at. I just don't want my children growing up like that. I don't want my kids to go through what I had to go through—running away trying to survive out there— especially when you're working the streets. You get into all the crap; I don't want my kids to have to go through it.

The narratives in this study show that the major concerns of imprisoned mothers who are housed in the WCC's general-population building involve issues regarding their children. In contrast, the primary concern of all mothers in the maximum-security unit is their own emotional survival of the prison experience. These mothers, overwhelmed with their personal survival, are distracted from concerns about their children. When interviewed, mothers in maximum security, in which Native Americans are disproportionately represented, deliberate at length on their prison experiences and have difficulty concentrating on questions regarding their children. When directly questioned about family and children, however, these mothers do emotionally and sincerely address issues regarding their children. Like most imprisoned mothers, they usually weep when they talk about their children.

In addition to the difficulties that separation entails for both parents and their children, imprisoned mothers have other major concerns. These concerns include placement and custody of children, visitation arrangements, anticipated readjustment problems with children after release, and, in some cases, current pregnancy.[1] These concerns are discussed in the next chapter.

Nine

DOUBLE PUNISHMENT

WEAK INSTITUTIONAL

SUPPORT FOR

IMPRISONED MOTHERS

The Indian Child Welfare Act, just to be totally honest, is kind of a pain in our side . . . because we have to go through the tribal court system.

STATE EMPLOYEE

There is a complex, but ultimately weak, system of institutional support for incarcerated mothers as they attempt to fulfill their role as mothers. There are special problems associated with prisoner pregnancy, and all imprisoned mothers face the challenges of child placement and visitation. Mothers who have lengthy sentences or difficulty arranging visits with their children are particularly jeopardized. Imprisoned mothers are expected to conform to the same standards as other mothers, which ignores the important differences in their lives (Beckerman 1991).

In this study, two prison staff members, one contract employee (the parenting class facilitator), and a state employee described in their interviews the role undertaken by the prison and the state to support the family life of imprisoned mothers. In addition, this study gathered interview data on the mothers' perceptions of the prison's attempts to strengthen the mothers' ties with their children. These narratives indicated that sentence length, children's residence prior to their mother's incarceration, race/ethnicity, and location of confinement are important issues.

IN-PRISON PREGNANCY AND BIRTH

Approximately 6 percent of the total female prisoner population in the United States is pregnant at the time of incarceration (Snell and Morton 1994). Conforming with the conclusions of a previous study (Baunach 1985a), pregnant women at the WCC face special emotional difficulties when they are forced to surrender their newborns to other caretakers without being allowed time to bond. Pregnant women who have not made a placement decision struggle with the decision of locating their babies in foster care near the prison or with relatives far away from the prison. Although foster care affords frequent visitation, this placement type evokes mothers' fears of losing custody of their children.

One pregnant woman, confused by conflicting information, explains:

> The prison staff told me that I could put the baby in a foster home in a nearby town, and they'd bring the baby once a week so that we can bond. Then I was told by prison staff I could pick my baby up the day I'm released. Now I don't know how valid this stuff is. I talked to Child Protective Services and they said that's not the way it'd be when I'm released. I'm worried about custody and I'm two months from my delivery date and I still haven't made up my mind.

Supposedly, prison rules specify that a mother can bond with a baby for three days after delivery. Darla, whose husband is also in prison, was not afforded this opportunity by prison staff. She professes that she was singled out and punished by prison staff for having used drugs during her pregnancy. Darla was allowed to spend a mere fifteen minutes with her baby at birth and has not seen her since. One of the mothers interviewed reflects on the emotional struggle of pregnant prisoners:

> I've seen women have babies in here and it's really hard on them. I think they should be allowed to keep their babies for a certain amount of time to bond, but prison rules don't allow it. They're over at the hospital as long as they have to be. I saw one woman have a baby one day and she was brought back here the next day; she had to say goodbye to her baby in the hospital! And she might not see it again for a while.

Many women and the parenting class facilitator comment that bonding between mothers and newborns is crucial and recommend that the prison provide a six-week period for bonding.

A state employee charged with representing the best interests of the children relates that imprisoned mothers who have babies while incarcerated have particular emotional difficulty deciding where to place their children. In these cases, he must make the decision for the mothers. Pregnant prisoners face other problems in addition to placement decisions. Imprisoned mothers and the parenting class facilitator consider it essential to have more resources for pregnant women. For instance, no one is allowed to help these women through labor. The facilitator is aware that this causes much fear on the part of pregnant women because "they would like to have someone close to them help them through the delivery." Mothers report that they are driven to the hospital and dropped off. They are on their own, with the exception of the matron who stands guard over them.

Mothers also desire classes offering prenatal and birthing information. One mother, with two children and Lamaze training, faced resistance from several guards when she decided to offer advice to one young and naive mother-to-be:

> For pregnant women in here they offer no Lamaze or prenatal or nothing. We have a young girl in here, she's nineteen years old, who's pregnant with her first child. She has no concept of what pregnancy actually is other than just giving birth to a child. She knows nothing about feeding, burping, or what's expected in the delivery room. One of the officers got real upset because I was explaining it to her one day. I was teaching her some things I learned, and that made the officers real uptight. One of the guards made the statement that I wasn't licensed to be giving her advice. I said, "Maybe you ought to bring her a video." It made me very mad.

This particular pregnant prisoner cannot join the parenting class because the current session had already started when she arrived at the prison, and by the time another session starts she will have already delivered her baby.

Several mothers mention that prison staff propose new a prison policy dictating that all pregnant women be relocated to maximum security upon reaching their ninth month of pregnancy. This transfer is supposedly recommended for reasons of safety and health; the staff see the burdensome stairs in the general-population building as a hardship for pregnant women. These mothers conclude that if this policy is approved, they will in effect be punished simply for being pregnant.

The parenting class facilitator says that after giving birth, most imprisoned mothers are exceedingly depressed and require time to grieve. She adds that women with lengthy sentences and children in adoptive homes also experience a tremendous mourning period. Her parenting classes do not deal with the issue of grieving; in fact, the prison offers no structured grief therapy.

CHILD PLACEMENT

A substantial number of imprisoned women have children in foster care (Barry 1985b; Beckerman 1991; Henriques 1982). As the incarceration rates for women skyrocket, prisons and social service agencies must adequately address the complicated task of maintaining family stability when the mother is imprisoned.

At the WCC, once women are sentenced, child-care responsibilities are assessed. Children are then either placed formally in foster care or adoptive homes by state welfare offices or by the mothers or placed informally with relatives by the imprisoned mothers. Placement issues vary by type of placement, race/ethnicity, reservation status, the mother's marital status, age of children, and the number of children to be placed. For all mothers, regardless of race/ethnicity, additional difficulties arise when there are more than two children to be placed.

In general, few women have children formally placed. Of those who do, more white and nonreservation (Landless) Native mothers than reservation and off-reservation Native mothers place children in foster care or adoptive homes. Mothers whose children are in foster care or adoptive homes are generally anxious about placement. Formal placement can have devastating emotional effects for the mothers. One study participant spoke of a woman with a lengthy sentence whose two children were placed in an adoptive home by the state. This mother, who never saw her children again, "grieved for them as though they were dead." Mothers in this study with children placed informally are more satisfied with custody and quality-of-care issues than mothers with children placed formally. Each type of placement, however, entails a special set of problems.

One of the most important issues in the placement process is decision-making power. Decisions to place children in foster care may be made without consulting the imprisoned mother (Baunach 1985b; Stanton 1980). Regardless of the outcome, a noninvolved mother experiences much more anger and grief than one involved in the decision (Baunach 1985b). Not unexpectedly, some studies (Henriques 1982; Zalba 1964) disclose that many imprisoned mothers express distrust and distaste for state social service agencies in charge of placing their children. Moreover, imprisoned mothers with children in foster care are anxious about their own financial status in possible competition with foster parents, who are typically from higher class backgrounds (Baunach 1982). From the imprisoned mother's perspective, the foster parents are more secure and competent in their parenting skills and more able to provide material comforts for the children. Some mothers, however, see possible advantages to formal placement. Darla, whose parental rights to her son were terminated, is aware of the problems she caused her son through drug use and neglect. Wrestling with the decision of whether to put her infant daughter in adoptive or foster care, Darla says:

> I feel that I have to make a decision in here—for her sake. I don't want her to go through what my son's gone through emotionally. He's all messed up. He chokes children, chokes cats; he killed a cat and was happy. He killed it and walked off; he's messed up. He could be a convict himself because of my dumbness. I want to make sure my daughter's got a better life. I've got to make a decision and if she doesn't get down here pretty soon, I'm going to have to do the right thing and adopt her out. Other girls in here say, "Fight for her." Her being in another city isn't doing me or her any good. She doesn't know me. If she was to come down here, it's going to be hard because she doesn't know me and will cry. But I'm willing to take that chance and go through that hell so we can be together.

On one hand, Darla wants to be a mother and near her children. On the other hand, she recognizes that because she is a drug-dependent imprisoned mother, it may be in her children's best interests to be in stable homes.

Nationally, arrangements for child care for imprisoned mothers vary by race/ethnicity: women of color tend to place their children with relatives more often than white women (Baunach 1985b; Bresler and Lewis 1983; Henriques 1982). For example, the Baunach study (1985b) reveals that 39 percent of incarcerated white mothers place their children with nonrelatives, whereas only 13 percent of incarcerated African

American mothers have children residing with nonrelatives.[1] Baunach's research revealed that although all imprisoned women are concerned with the separation from their children, the extended family network within African American communities aids the imprisoned mother, and these mothers seemingly have fewer difficulties concerning placement of children.[2] In this study of WCC women, the same strength of extended family structure was found within the lives of the reservation Natives, dwelling both on and off the reservations, but not among nonreservation Natives or whites.

One cannot understand Native women in prison without understanding the family structure from which these women have been removed. The extended family network operates as a natural support system within many cultures in the world and within many racial/ethnic communities here in the United States, including the Native American community. When this family structure is fully functioning, members of the extended family are responsible to and for one another. In this way, when a biological parent is removed from the home or community for whatever reason, the children have numerous relatives who can assume the role of primary caretaker. The extended family, thus, is a flexible network. Although women in Euro-American culture may face the role of mother as a devalued woman, this is not true in other cultures (Andersen 1988). For example, in African American culture (Collins 1991) and Native American culture (Allen 1985; Powers 1986) the role of mother is accorded high status. Additionally, in the dominant American culture of the nuclear family, many women face the responsibility of parenting alone. In extended family networks, however, many people are involved in child care.

Racism shapes the organization of family for people of color, molding it for survival in the midst of oppression (Caulfield 1974; Powers 1986). In Native communities, relatives in the extended family are expected to ensure the preservation of the family because it is the foundation of the tribal structure. Furthermore, it is the women in these communities who have taken the lead to keep families together. Extended families prevail in Native communities, providing Native women with support and strength to endure stressful life events. Although women of color are jeopardized in many ways, in the area of familial support they are "privileged" by their race/ethnicity.

Although imprisoned Native mothers do not have as much contact with their children as white mothers, these women, regardless of reservation status, are generally closer emotionally to their extended families than white women, even though their families can often be defined as dysfunctional. Native women also have a community, rather than a nuclear family, that they call home, and most sense that they will be welcomed back into their tribal communities upon their release. There is, however, one important exception to this: reservation and off-reservation women involved in violent crimes against tribal members are not welcomed back into their reservation communities. This is an example of traditional tribal punishment in which social ostracism is implemented. Traditional discipline of this type operates today in many tribal communities, especially within traditional reservation families.

There is a tendency for people, including well-meaning scholars, to treat all women as a homogeneous demographic group. They assume that all Native women have substantially similar life experiences and problems—similar to one another and similar to other groups of women. These assumptions are all highly misleading for research. For example, reservation status has an important influence on the major concerns of imprisoned mothers and on institutional support available for mothers. Mothers connected with reservations usually place children with extended family members and are generally satisfied with those placements. Most nonreservation mothers, on the other hand, have children placed formally in foster care and have no knowledge of the Indian Child Welfare Act. Because of their lack of connection with a reservation, they are disadvantaged.

To realize why nonreservation Natives are particularly punished within Montana's prison system, one must first consider the historical context. Native Americans are different from other racial/ethnic groups because of their unique status within the United States. The special relationship they "enjoy" with the federal government stems from the hundreds of treaties signed between Native American nations and the United States, and from the fact that Native American nations were legally defined in an early U.S. Supreme Court decision, *Worcester v. Georgia* (1832), as sovereign, independent nations. Landless Natives, the nonreservation Natives who either refused to sign treaties or had their reservation status abolished by the federal government, have been disenfranchised and consequently have less power. They are controlled by the federal government and treated similarly to other racial/ethnic groups without treaties—as second-class citizens. The fact that Landless Natives have less power is another example of the effects of colonization and social control exercised by the federal government. It is not surprising that nonreservation imprisoned mothers are more troubled about issues of child placement and custody than are reservation and off-reservation mothers, who have the protection of their tribes and access to tribal courts and social services. Furthermore, nonreservation imprisoned mothers are more concerned about children placed within their own families, because the stresses and strains on their extended families due to colonialism have taken a toll.

WCC Formal Placement

Formal placement, for the purposes of this study, is defined as foster care or adoptive settings. Women at the WCC with children formally placed encounter overwhelming problems.

Although various social service agencies represent the children of imprisoned mothers, one prison staff member is charged with advocacy on behalf of the mothers. Unfortunately, most mothers, especially those in isolation and maximum security, do not consider the staff member delegated as their advocate to be truly representing their concerns. It is possible that these women are principally seen as "unfit" by prison staff and thus not worthy of assistance.

According to a state employee charged with representing the best interests of the children, children in formal placements are generally doing well. This individual tries to place children with caretakers of the imprisoned mother's choice. Although he prefers that the children reside with relatives, many women want them located in a county near the prison to facilitate frequent visitation. He attempts to involve mothers in the decision making, but many times he is forced to make the determination for them.

Placements work best for imprisoned mothers when they know the foster or adoptive parents, and the state employee attempts to acquaint the foster parents with the imprisoned mothers. In cases of very young imprisoned mothers, he attempts to promote a good relationship between the mothers and the foster parents because he believes the foster parents may have a positive influence on the mothers. Not all foster parents, however, are amenable to such a relationship.

An event of special concern to imprisoned mothers is the transfer of their children from one foster home to another. Although such transfers

are not frequent, when they do occur the mother is typically not allowed to participate in the decision process. The state informs mothers
of such decisions by mail after the decision is final. To many imprisoned
mothers, it does not matter how infrequently transfer from one foster
home to another occurs; that transfers happen at all is alarming because
of the stress they know such dislocation will cause their children. Con-
versely, being powerless to encourage removal from an unhealthy foster
home is also a painful situation for a mother.

The state seems to have little communication with imprisoned mothers and much power and control over them and over their formally
placed children. As indicated in prior research (Barry 1985b; Beckerman
1994; Henriques 1982; McGowan and Blumenthal 1978), communication between social workers and imprisoned mothers is limited, and,
consequently, the mothers are perplexed about their familial obligations
and legal status.

Only six mothers in this study, four white women and two nonreservation Natives (out of twenty-seven interviewed), have children in foster
care or adoptive homes; however, for them, the problems are overwhelming. Few women, even among those who do not have their children formally placed, convey anything positive about this type of placement. Some were in foster care themselves as children and do not have
positive memories; hence, they bring their experiences into their present thinking regarding formal placement. Common concerns regarding
formal placements are custody issues and the quality of care the children are receiving.

THE RISK OF LOSING CUSTODY

Since imprisoned women are more likely than imprisoned men to be
the primary caretakers of their children and are more likely to be the
custodial parent prior to incarceration, they are also more likely to face
extensive legal problems and emotional distress related to child custody
(Beckerman 1991; Haft 1980; McGowan and Blumenthal 1976; Zalba
1964). Some women experience an enormous fear that they will permanently lose custody of their children as a consequence of imprisonment.
Placement and custody issues are special concerns to those mothers at
the WCC who are single parents, have absent spouses/partners (who are
often themselves incarcerated), have no family members able take their
children, are nonreservation Native mothers, are pregnant, and/or have

very young children. To complicate their situation further, following a trend discovered by previous research on prisons (Beckerman 1991, 1994; McGowan and Blumenthal 1978), the WCC has a serious shortage of legal advice for mothers concerned with losing custody of their children. Little legal information is available, and, due to overcrowding, the law library was transformed into a cell.

At the WCC, mothers with children placed formally relate that custody is a primary concern. These mothers frequently fear that they will lose legal custody of their children. Their fears are well founded. For example, Victoria, whose story appears below, lost custody of her children because the prison failed to pass along to her some legal documents. In addition, sometimes the system puts pressure on mothers to relinquish custody. Suzanne, who had all three children living with her prior to incarceration, has two of her children in foster care in another state. Her baby is informally placed, residing with her fiancé and his mother. Suzanne was not allowed to participate in the decision to place her other children, who were relocated to foster care on the day she went to jail. Several social workers from state welfare offices continually pressure her to give up her children for adoption, accusing her of having been neglectful toward her children when they were in her care.

Victoria had placed her five children legally with her mother-in-law when both she and her husband were sentenced to prison. Shortly thereafter the children were placed in foster care because, according to Victoria, her mother-in-law could not handle the responsibilities of five children. When Victoria's husband was released from prison and went to live with his mother, the children were returned to that household and he regained legal custody. But at this point a major error occurred. The prison failed to give Victoria the legal documents that had been sent to her in care of the prison. These documents were returned to the county attorney's office unread by Victoria. Also, the prison failed to pass on to Victoria notification of the pending hearing. Unaware of the hearing, she was unable to avail herself of the prison staff's willingness to provide transportation. At the hearing, which she could not attend, Victoria's children were placed in foster care and both she and her husband lost custody.

Sentence length is a critical factor in determining whether the child is placed temporarily or permanently. According to a state employee, adoption is only a consideration if the mother receives a lengthy sentence or if she requests this type of placement in lieu of foster care. Even though Montana law specifies that if a woman commits a felony the state can legally take her children and resort to adoptive home placement, he claims that the law is not enforced. On the other hand, other employees of the WCC contend that the state has the power to terminate a woman's parental rights after she has been incarcerated for one year. One prison staff member further explains that for those serving lengthy sentences, the child will be placed in foster care for two years and then the mother will be given the "chance" to relinquish her parental rights. If she does not voluntarily concede, the court will terminate her parental rights.

Although permanent placement of children is not an immediate threat for most imprisoned mothers, the "relinquishment of parental rights" is a common procedure with a similar effect on the parent. With this process, the courts give the state "temporary investigative authority" for ninety days. This enables state social workers to submit imprisoned mothers to psychological testing to identify problem areas, which usually relate to substance abuse. Social workers then assess the test results and request that the mother follow a specific treatment plan. After a ninety-day period, social workers report to the court on the imprisoned mother's progress. If the social workers find the progress unsatisfactory, they can request temporary legal custody of her children. Another evaluation of the mother is made after six months. At the end of that time, if the mother has made no improvement, state social workers can ask the court to terminate her parental rights. For example, Darla's parental rights to her four-year-old son were terminated because of her multiple arrests, child neglect, and involvement with drugs. She has had no contact with him since her incarceration; with her rights as a parent terminated, visitation and telephone calls are prohibited, although she can write letters.

Illustrating the procedure for removing a newborn from an indecisive imprisoned mother, a state employee offers the following example of a pregnant teenager:

> In [the pregnant teenager's] case, the fact that she is incarcerated, is a teenager—these all raise issues. But as far as our ability to impose a treatment plan on her, assuming she may be abusive in the future, we can't get away with it legally. So in her case—when we go in to take the child, if it gets to that point—if it looks like the state is going to have to care for the child, there's one of two things that can happen. We can have her sign a parental agreement, which is

good for six months. That simply . . . authorizes us to spend state money to take care of her child; that's a voluntary act on her part. We are just asking for substitute care. The other option, if she doesn't want to do that, we have to have some way to authorize spending the state's money. If we don't have that, we have to go to court and get a temporary investigative authority for ninety days. It's just a court order. We go beyond the wishes of the mother.

In addition to sentence length as crucial in determining the type of placement, removal of children prior to incarceration is an important criterion. Women whose children had been removed from their care prior to incarceration are at increased risk of losing custody upon incarceration and are more likely to be pressured by the state to put their children in adoptive homes. Many reservation and off-reservation Native women have the support of their extended families and tribal social services; if their children were removed prior to incarceration, they reside within the family or tribe. As a result, white and nonreservation mothers are more affected by a child's residence prior to incarceration.

Nonreservation mothers often have special difficulties with placement and custody issues. One example is Judy, a nonreservation mother in maximum security. One of her four children was adopted by her brother and his wife, who are both substance abusers, and another is living with his father on an Indian reservation in the state. Judy goes to court in several months to determine whether her parental rights for the remaining two children will be terminated. Her mother originally had the children, but when she suffered a stroke they were placed in foster care. Judy's sister retrieved the children from the foster home and was awarded custody. Recently, however, Judy's sister said that she could no longer care for the children and turned them over to the state welfare office. Judy is thoroughly frustrated with the current situation. Sobbing, Judy says that she is helpless and tries not to think about her children because it will drive her insane. Judy believes that the criminal justice system in general offers no support to her concerning her children and custody issues. She relates,

The system has always held my kids over my head. My parole officer, the last time I came here and this time, really shoved it in my face. She said on my parole papers this time that I showed no interest in my kids.

Her parole officer's stance makes her feel that the criminal justice system is adding punishment upon punishment by formally reporting that she never cared for her children, increasing the likelihood that she will lose her parental rights.

Other prisoners advise Judy to secure a Native American organization to intervene on her behalf. Yet because she is a Landless Native, there is no specific tribal social service program for her to contact. She is frustrated and has no idea whom to notify. The only prison staff member available to help her has her office in the general-population building, which is inaccessible to Judy in maximum security. This woman, who wants her children in a Native American family, is, like many non-reservation women, unaware of the Indian Child Welfare Act of 1978, which prevents the unwarranted removal of Native children from their homes and communities and specifically states that Native children can no longer be placed in non-Native adoptive and foster care homes.

Imprisonment compounds problems for nonreservation mothers, because they are not exposed to legal information or adequate advice regarding placement and custody issues. Another nonreservation woman whose child was placed in a white adoptive home by the state repeatedly seeks help from prison staff to change this placement. This mother insists that her child relocate to a Native American home; to her, culture is everything, and she wants her son to grow up Native. She claims that her pleas are ignored by prison staff.

When working with Native American prisoners, all social service agencies and their workers, state or otherwise, need to be knowledgeable about the Indian Child Welfare Act. Although Montana state employees and prison staff at the WCC are working with a prison population that is 25 percent Native, they are not thoroughly versed in the act. One prison staff member, who theoretically represents the needs of imprisoned mothers, has no knowledge of the act. Citing a specific case, she expresses:

> That's what we don't know anything about. Well, our county attorney said, "I don't know anything about that act." I don't know how to proceed, so for me to fill these papers out is nonsense. This is a part-Indian baby. It will be registered [enrolled in a tribe], so it needs to be done in the tribal court. We will help and assist with getting her [the prisoner] before a judge and letting her sign those papers in front of a judge.

One state employee, who is aware of but not well versed in the act, admits: "The Indian Child Welfare Act, just to be totally honest, is kind of a pain in our side. We have to be very careful about how we do things; it's increased a lot of work for us." When asked why he perceives the act as bothersome, he replies:

> Because we have to go through the tribal court system. We have to place the child in an Indian home even if they're, I think one-fifth Indian. It's easier to take somebody up the street to former foster parents and say, "Hey Joe, here's one—please keep an eye on them."[3]

He relates that although he has no direct experience with placements under the act's regulations, he has heard that the act slows down the process because of the lengthy forms involved.

At the WCC there is, additionally, ineffectual interagency coordination between the various tribal and urban Indian social service agencies and the prison. Revealing the complications of federal law, a prison staff member describes the case of an off-reservation mother who received a lengthy sentence and wants to put her child up for adoption:

> If I could ever get this worked out. . . . I've been trying to get hold of the [certain tribe] Tribal Court for two weeks and I can't get anybody to answer the phone. She wants to adopt her baby out; she has an excellent home for it. The tribal court has agreed to the home, but what they did was send me blank adoption papers and a letter saying take her to a judge and get this signed. There are so many laws for reservations, which are under federal law, and this is under state law but our county attorney won't touch it. He said, "I don't know those federal laws." It gets real complicated. What I need to do is get back to them and tell them, "You need to fill the papers out and all you have to do is send them to our county attorney requesting that she sign those in front of the judge."

THE RISK OF LOW-QUALITY CHILD CARE

Another major concern for imprisoned mothers with children placed formally is the quality of care their children are receiving. This issue mainly affects white mothers and nonreservation Native mothers, who feel that guardians are economically motivated and not properly caring for their children.

Suzanne is distraught over her children's placement in foster care. In such situations, any contact with the children must be cleared with the state welfare office; this slows down the contact process with her children. Additionally, many times her children do not receive her letters and gifts because the foster parents do not deliver them to the children, and the foster parents also do not allow the children to communicate with their other relatives (their fathers and grandparents). Furthermore, regarding the quality of care, Suzanne—similar to other mothers— fears that foster parents are only in the business for the money:

> My kids are not being taken care of properly. The foster parents
> get six hundred dollars a month for having my kids. Plus my ex-
> husband has to pay three hundred dollars a month in child support
> to these jerks. And my grandma has been called, and the social
> services has been called that my son and daughter go to school in
> shoes that are just holding on by the strings. They're using my kids'
> money to support their own stupid family.

Suzanne's children report to her that the foster parents "spank them a lot," which is a type of discipline she clearly does not condone. Even more alarming, she adds that her five-year-old daughter was sexually molested in this home by the foster father. Suzanne declares that the foster father has been charged with child molestation before but that her pleas to remove the children fall on deaf ears. Her daughter has been seriously injured by the foster father:

> She was in the hospital for a week and a half. He had hurt her so
> bad that she had to have stitches on the inside and outside and they
> put her right back in there [the foster home]. My daughter, until
> I was arrested, had never been in the hospital. She's been in there
> twelve times since I've been up here [in prison] in seven months.

Regarding the nightmarish care her children are receiving in this foster placement, Suzanne communicates the damage done to her family:

> My daughter has been hurt so much emotionally. She is hurt so bad
> mentally that she has to see a psychiatrist—at the age of five. It's

getting real bad; it's getting out of hand. I feel I'm going to have
a lot of problems now because of all the emotional stuff that the
kids have been through. It's going to take a lot more of Mommy
around to calm them down and to do all kinds of stuff. Last Friday
my kids called and my son wouldn't talk to me. I asked my daughter,
"What's wrong with him?" She said that the foster father told him
that his mommy wasn't coming to get him, that his mommy didn't
love him. She said, "Mommy, do you love us?" I said, "Of course
I love you."

Although Suzanne hired an attorney to have her children relocated
to another home and to gain visitation rights for her family, she is frustrated because her imprisonment slows and limits her efforts to protect
her children. Consequently, she is consumed with worry over the quality of care her children are receiving in this placement.

Darla, like most of the mothers, is uneasy about the quality of care
her baby is receiving in foster care primarily because she has not met
the foster parents. She is fairly content with her son's placement because
she knows the foster parents. To Darla and other imprisoned mothers,
this acquaintance is vital:

I worry about both of them. I worry about him being adopted out—
abusive homes, sexual abuse. There's too much abuse now; you even
worry about women molesting children. I don't know what kind
of home my little girl's in—that's why I want her closer to me. I
know the family she goes to is the same one the other girls have gone
through. They love this foster family. They've been only good to
their kids. I don't know who they are, but if she's closer I can get to
know them. I would like to know the foster people. The lady my
boy's with, I got to know when I was on parole—good people. I'm
striving for him to stay where he's at.

None of the white mothers mention the race/ethnicity of foster or
adoptive parents as a concern. Native mothers, however, consider race/
ethnicity to be a major determinant of the quality of care their children will receive. For example, although Judy is distraught over the
placement of her son in an alcoholic household, she is additionally disturbed because her brother's wife is white and, given their different backgrounds, not a person with whom Judy can comfortably communicate.

Citing cultural reasons, Judy, like other Native mothers, wants her children raised by Native people and in Native communities. Another non-reservation mother, with her only son in a white foster home, remarks:

> The foster home my son's in right now refuses to let him know about his culture. I went to court and requested that my child be placed with American Indians who are spiritually active, because that's my religion and that's his.

Given the long history of the federal government's removal of Native children from Native homes and communities to boarding schools, and the state government's systematic removal of Native children to white foster and adoptive homes, it is understandable that Native mothers would resist foster and adoptive placements in white families. In the historical and cultural context, Native mothers would tend to see such a placement, regardless of its specific merits, as an expression of colonialism. Undergirded in some cases by an antipathy toward white people, this perception would naturally lead Native mothers to conclude that the race/ethnicity of the caretakers is a critical factor in regard to the quality of care their children will receive.

WCC Informal Placement

Mothers, whether Native or white, prefer to place their children informally with relatives because it allows them some association with their children. Mothers with informally placed children, though less distressed about custody issues, may nevertheless be apprehensive regarding the quality of care and may initially feel some insecurity about the placement. Even though the mothers favor informal placement, this arrangement is not without problems.

Reservation and off-reservation women have the security of the reservation as a safe place for their children. They also feel fortunate to have a tribal court to assist in informal placement of children. The tribes in Montana have the power to ensure that parental rights of imprisoned mothers are not terminated. Thus, mothers connected to reservations are less anxious about custody and quality-of-care issues than nonreservation mothers and white mothers.

Mary, a reservation Native, is very comfortable with the placements of her children with her various relatives. When she was first arrested social workers came to see her in jail and demanded to know the whereabouts of her children. Mary notes that being a tribal member, with the protective efforts of her tribal status and culture, benefited her:

> When I was first arrested, you should've seen the social workers! They were just running around! They wanted to know where my kids were. I told my sister to get them back on the reservation, get them back home. The social workers came down to the jail and said, "Where's your kids? We understand you have kids. Where are they?" And I said, "They're just fine—just leave them alone." I was getting some horrendous charges on me and so the state was trying to intervene. They were trying to take my kids, but they were already in tribal jurisdiction.

Mary's tribe organized placement with various relatives, so she does not worry about losing custody of her children. Two of Mary's children are with their father in another state, two with Mary's sister on her reservation, and the youngest with the aunt who raised Mary, also on Mary's reservation. Mary is satisfied with the placement of her children with her extended family. Her aunt is a highly respected spiritual and cultural leader on the reservation where three of her children live. Her ex-husband and their two children live with his parents on another reservation, where his mother, a woman Mary trusts and highly respects, is a community leader and a medicine woman. Having a good family to rely on, a family that will pass on Native American culture to their children, is important to Mary and other Native mothers.

Julie, an off-reservation mother, has her two children placed with their father—her husband, who lives with his mother off the reservation. Her husband and her mother share legal guardianship of the children. Comparable to many women whose children live with relatives, Julie is not worried about custody.

Although several Native mothers do not have agreeable relationships with the extended family members who have their children, they are nevertheless usually satisfied with the placement. For instance, although Delores does not get along with the aunt who is caring for her son (the tribe has legal custody), she believes he is well taken care of and consequently is secure with his placement. She specifically mentions that he is getting much love—the one thing she did not receive as a child.

Only one Native mother with children placed informally is concerned about the quality of care her children are receiving. Julie is uneasy about her children, not when they are with her husband and his mother but when they visit her family. Julie explains:

> It was her [Julie's mother's] brother who sexually molested me, but I've taken steps and he's moved to another state. My family refuses to believe it because they worship the ground he walks on. Whenever he comes for vacation, we make arrangements so that my kids will stay with my in-laws. I told my mom and grandmother that I will not have my kids under the same roof with him. They don't like it and my kids have never met him; I refuse to allow my kids to do so without me being present. I don't trust him.

Linda's three children are with her husband. Although she is generally satisfied with the placement, she voices concerns that are typical for women who have children living with their husbands:

> Sometimes [I worry], probably not as much as before because he's been doing it for so long. My parents watch the kids while he works so he doesn't have to worry about baby-sitters, and they're there if he needs anything. But I mean, it's just not the same as Mom. You have to learn to let go of it, though, because you have no control at all.

The preceding quotation illustrates that many women do not feel totally comfortable with their husbands filling the role of primary caretaker.

Comparison of Placement Types

Race/ethnicity and reservation status thus affect placement type in two ways. First, reservation and off-reservation mothers have tribal support concerning placement and custody, whereas nonreservation mothers do not. Nonreservation mothers, in this way, are affected more by colonialism because their Native communities have less sovereignty, and thus less power to determine the fate of tribal members. Nonreservation mothers are more likely than other Native mothers to have children placed formally. Second, because of placement type, reservation and off-reservation mothers are more satisfied with the quality of care their children are receiving than nonreservation mothers or white mothers, regardless of placement type. In addition, reservation and off-reservation women generally have the support of their extended families, whereas white women and nonreservation women are more likely to rely on formal placements and state social-service agencies to care for their children.

Generally, women who place children with family members, whether informally or formally, do not worry as much about the quality of care. Nevertheless, in this study one nonreservation mother, Judy, is troubled about her two children who were unsuccessfully placed with her sister and had to be removed. Judy also is fearful about the quality of care her son is receiving, having been adopted by her brother and his wife, who are both substance abusers. We can see that even though mothers are generally more satisfied with placements when they know the caretakers, there are exceptions.

VISITATION

Although most imprisoned mothers desire frequent visits with their children, many are not afforded this opportunity (Baunach 1985b; Barry 1985b; Beckerman 1994; Henriques 1982; Stanton 1980). This may be the consequence of state laws' declaring some mothers "unfit," long distances between prisons and the children's homes, financial difficulties (e.g., lack of money for gasoline and overnight accommodations for the drivers delivering children), guardians' not bringing the children to visit, or the prison visitation policy itself. Nationwide only 9 percent of all imprisoned mothers receive regular visits from their children. Many mothers, particularly exceptionally poor women whose children live a great distance from the prison, endure their entire sentences without seeing their children, although 46 percent speak with minor children on the telephone at least once a week, and 45 percent have contact with their children at least once a week through the mail (Snell and Morton 1994). Nevertheless, as seen in previous research (Stanton 1980; Zalba 1964), mothers determine that although visits prove difficult for their children, they desire contact because they fear that otherwise their children will not remember them. Most mothers stress the need to see and touch their children; hence, visitation is paramount.

WCC Visitation System

At the WCC there are three possible forms of contact: telephone calls, letters, and visitation. Mothers view interaction with their children as significant because it is the primary avenue for maintaining the parent/child relationship. Regardless of race/ethnicity, most mothers desire more contact with their children, especially with newborns and very young children.

Visitation is, of course, restricted by prison rules. Institutional policy specifies that mothers in the general-population building can have their children who are under the age of thirteen for overnight weekend visits once a month. All mothers must complete an eight-week parenting program offered by the prison and be members of the Parenting Support Group (an informal group composed of imprisoned mothers) before they are entitled to this privilege. Only one mother is allowed overnight weekend visitation per weekend, and these visits are subject to approval by the Parenting Support Group. This means that for the first eight weeks of incarceration, mothers are not allowed to see their children except during regular prison visitation hours, which are on Saturdays and Sundays from 8:30 to 10:30 A.M. and 12:30 to 2:30 P.M.

Newborns are additionally allowed to visit mothers every Monday for one hour—provided the child is in a home that allows for such frequency. Usually newborns living near the prison are in foster care. Additionally, crisis situations with children of any age permit day visits to occur one day a week for three hours. For children living out of state, special arrangements can be made by prison officials to facilitate mother/child visits.

The prison has a special room in the general-population building set aside for mother/child overnight weekend visits. This small room contains a few old toys for the children and a television set complete with a videocassette recorder (VCR) for viewing videotapes. The prisoners attempted to cheer up the room, which has cracked walls, by painting a mural of animals on one wall. This particular room is located directly over the boiler room and is always much too warm and stuffy; the temperature hovers between seventy-five and eighty degrees. The cramped room has two old, single-size beds and can comfortably fit two people. For some women this is too small, because they will have two children visiting at one time. This means that two people must sleep on a single-size mattress.

Montana has specific regulations concerning visitation between parents and their children in foster care. A state employee involved in child placement is supportive and frequently tries to locate children near the prison to facilitate contact. Concerning imprisoned mothers whose children reside outside the state, which affects more white mothers than Native mothers, visitation is problematic. For example, during the school year this state employee deems it inappropriate for the children to travel and miss school to visit their mothers. In addition, he expresses that such visits would upset the children. Yet if mothers and their children plan on reunification after the mothers' release *and* were living together prior to the mothers' incarceration, then he is extremely supportive in bringing the children to the state where the mothers are incarcerated.

Mothers with children in adoptive homes or foster care must obtain approval for visitation. When a child is so placed, state social service agencies have the authority to control visitation. One agency representative remarks that the prison fully cooperates with that kind of power, and he admits to having much control in setting the guidelines for visitation. He explains:

> [The prison staff's] standing is that if we are paying for the child, the medical costs and all that kind of stuff, then we have the say as to how much visitation—when and that kind of thing. We set how many days a week. Our standard policy right now is once a week for an hour visit—for any child [whether the mother is imprisoned or not].

Another visitation restriction is the cut-off age of thirteen for overnight weekend visits with children. Prison staff say they are not firm with this rule, especially for older female children. Illustrating this and giving an example of a crisis situation that warrants a day visit, a prison staff member clarifies:

> We also do day visits that are crisis sorts of things. For instance, we had an inmate here, and her daughter was fourteen and a half and got pregnant out there—living with Grandma. She really needed to talk with Mom, and Mom needed to talk to her. So three different times we allowed her to come in early in the morning and stay until evening, and she was with her mom all day. We make those kind of exceptions, but we do not make them for males.

This staff member explains why male children over age thirteen are not allowed overnight visits with their mothers:

Sometimes we deviate from age thirteen with boys. It depends upon how mature they are. We've had ten-year-old boys in here and we've told the mother no more weekends—he's too involved in the sexual. We see him eyeing all the women and making suggestive remarks and things. So we don't want to put him in that situation, so we say, "no." He's too immature, but the girls are usually all right. The boys, we really have to watch and see how mature they are.

The staff member adds that although boys over age thirteen are aware of sexuality, she does incorporate some flexibility regarding visitation:

Again, if they're over the age of thirteen, there's too much sexual stuff. They just don't need to be involved in that, and we do have inmates that do things like that. So we have to be real careful of that. What I may do, if it's a son who needs to talk to Mom, is that I may allow a four-hour visit. I did when I still had the law library, and they would stay in there during that whole visit. Mom would give him some special help, but virtually we bend all the rules trying to get the bonding—if we can.

WCC Visitation System Problems

As disclosed by the narratives, there are many conflicting factors related to the issues of visitation. Contact between mothers and children is deemed important by all those interviewed for this study. Frequent visitation, however, is hampered by several factors including an overcrowded prison, rigid formal and informal prison rules, and state regulations placed on imprisoned mothers with children in foster care.

Although prison rules specify that prisoners can have their children for overnight weekend visits once a month, due to the overcrowded conditions and the limit of one visitation per weekend, women are only allowed such visits with their children every six to eight weeks. Additionally, prison rules indicate that prisoners can have two children at a time for overnight visits. For women with more than two children, this means that they will see each child every two to three months. Many mothers complain that their children have difficulty understanding why they cannot visit more often.

Although visits are vital to the maintenance of family and provide a setting to possibly alleviate separation anxiety, because visitation takes place inside a prison, it could create new anxieties. For example, during regular visitation hours, mothers must visit with their children in the dining room, where all visitors, including very young children, must sit at a table. An imprisoned mother was threatened with a write-up because her child was sitting on her lap. She later found out that this is an informal rule—that the prison has no specific policy against physical contact with children. In this visiting area there are a few old toys and a chalkboard, although the guards do not allow the children to write on the chalkboard.

The mothers generally feel that prison policy is designed to force the children to become little prisoners when they visit. Inside the prison, the children are expected to follow the same rigid routine as the prisoners. For example, the children must go to count, can only eat when the prisoners are fed, and are expected not to make any noise. Linda discusses this policy:

> It's hard on them because they don't understand the rules. They have to wear shoes all the time and they have to be with you all the time. They can't be running around and stuff. The pool room used to be open three hours a day and they couldn't understand why they couldn't go down and play whenever they wanted. They couldn't even go down to the basement. Sitting and visiting is really hard because they expect the kids to sit at the table. Well, I found out that doesn't work. They expect them to act like little grown-ups when they're not. And, they expect children not to make any noise.

Children visiting mothers during regular prison visitation must be accompanied by an adult who has been cleared for visitation. If visitors are even a few minutes late for visiting hours, the guards deny them entry. There is no flexibility regarding this rule, according to the mothers, and they remark that this is unusually difficult on children who have traveled many miles to see their mothers.

Children are naturally curious about where their mothers live and sleep, but they are usually not permitted by the guards to see their mothers' cells. Children have a need to know that their mothers are safe. Allowing them to see where their mothers live might help alleviate the children's separation anxiety.

Most mothers, especially those in maximum security or with lengthy sentences, feel that prison rules restrict visitation. Prison staff, however, assert that the prison is extremely adaptable regarding visitation and is willing to go so far as to cancel various rehabilitative programs to provide space for mother/child visits. Flexibility, according to some members of the prison staff, means that children of mothers in good standing can visit outside visiting days and hours as long as the need is urgent and the visits are scheduled.

Some staff members' comments on flexible visitation directly contradict other staff opinions, however. One staff member is not supportive of frequent or flexible visits because he determines that it will take time away from needed counseling and "being responsible." "Responsibility" is seen as prisoner programming (involvement in the prison's rehabilitative programs) and working on issues regarding low self-esteem. For example, he comments that if a child visits during the time the mother is in therapy, the mother should not miss the therapy session and "use the child visiting as an excuse."

Some guards share this notion of responsibility and mother/child visitation. For instance, the parenting class facilitator relates that an imprisoned mother brought her baby to parenting class. A guard noticed that the mother had the baby in class and told her she had to leave class — that she was not allowed to take the child to class with her. The mother, according to the facilitator, tearfully explained to the guard that she did not want to miss class *and* she wanted to see her baby. She also explained to the guard that it was the facilitator's idea to bring her baby to class. The facilitator then intervened and told the guard that she had indeed made this suggestion. According to the facilitator, the guard insisted on reprimanding the mother and, threatening the mother with a write-up, forced her to leave the parenting class.

There is a clear communication gap between the prison staff and the prisoners on this issue of flexible visitation. Despite staff assurances that there is a formal regulation allowing day visits, none of the mothers were aware of this policy. One mother who has been incarcerated for one year witnessed only two visits that occurred outside regular visiting hours: one with a mother and her newborn, and the other with a mother and a young child she had not seen for a year who was being placed in an adoptive home. According to imprisoned mothers, there is virtually no flexibility in visiting regulations.

Another barrier to mother/child visitation is that mothers in the maximum-security and isolation units are not allowed overnight weekend visits with their children; only mothers housed in the general-

population building have this privilege. Moreover, some mothers resolve that guards purposely set them up to lose this privilege by issuing
write-ups and subsequently removing them from general population to
maximum security. Only two mothers in maximum security, and none
in isolation, had visits of any kind from their children once they were
removed from the general-population building. In both cases, the mothers had scheduled overnight weekend visits with their children but were
transferred to maximum security before the visits occurred. In these in-
stances, the mothers were allowed day visits with their children, and the
mothers were not allowed by the guards on duty to hug or touch their
children.

Mothers in maximum security, according to prison rules, run the risk
of losing all visiting privileges for six months. Mothers confined to isolation cells are not permitted visitation with their children, and these
mothers are very much affected by the loss of such privileges. A Native
mother addresses the issue of being in maximum security on a charge she
does not consider valid, and how the guard on duty controlled her visit
with her three-year-old son:

> I was really upset. My whole world had just fallen apart. That week-
> end was supposed to be the weekend that I had worked four months
> to achieve for my son to come and spend a weekend with me. The
> prison staff dropped it; they pulled it [the visit]. I was in that back
> area in max and I had to visit him through those bars. I couldn't
> even touch him; I got him for one hour. My family traveled hun-
> dreds of miles to get him here and I get him for one hour. I said to
> the officer, "Can I just touch his hand?" [The guard said,] "No, you
> cannot touch him; it's a write-up if you touch him." Now that's
> ridiculous!

For mothers in maximum security, denial of visitation with children and
the refusal to permit mothers to hug their children turns the "double
punishment" of prison motherhood into triple punishment.

The interviews brought to light one case of a mother who believes
that her visitation was canceled as a punishment for her sexual orienta-
tion. This mother in maximum security labored tirelessly—by attending
the parenting class, joining the Parenting Support Group, and successfully avoiding any write-ups—in order to have an overnight weekend

visit with her young children. According to her, prison staff neverthe-less decided that the only reason she wanted her children to visit was so she could have sexual intercourse with another prisoner. The overnight visitation room is in the general-population building, and prison staff suspected that she would sneak another prisoner into the room. The tearful mother says, "And I'll be damned if they didn't pull my visit. I never got to have my kids, and that was the hardest thing I ever had to do was to call my kids because they were all excited." She was trans-ferred to an isolation cell in the maximum-security unit, where she is not allowed visits with her children for six months. She believes that the only reason she is in isolation is her sexual preference.

A different sort of obstacle that hampers positive visits between in-carcerated mothers and their children is the negative responses from other prisoners. Prisoners contend that witnessing child visits is extraor-dinarily difficult for women who lost their parental rights. According to imprisoned mothers, several women lacking legal custody of their children react with hostility toward the mother whose children are vis-iting or toward the children. Other mothers cry because the children remind them of their own that they may never see again. On the other hand, some women respond to visiting children in a positive manner because it allows them contact with children. Suzanne, who has not seen her children since her incarceration began, says:

> We have women who bring their kids in here all the time. I just love it because it makes me feel good. There's this girl in here, she has five kids and she brings them in two at a time. I'm always with her kids. I say, "Go ahead, I'll take care of them—get lost." It helps too because I can't see my kids. Seeing somebody else's kids, they kind of replace my empty part of me, my loneliness.

For a variety of reasons, not all women who, by prison rules, are allowed visits from their children receive such visits. Some mothers, mostly white mothers with children in foster care, affirm that their chil-dren's caretakers do not allow the children to visit them. Other mothers lost parental rights and are not permitted to visit with their children, and others will not allow their children to visit because it is emotionally difficult for the children. Mothers with long sentences have mixed feel-ings about having their children visit. Like women in earlier studies (Stanton 1980; Zalba 1964), some mothers at the WCC worry about the social environment of the prison adversely affecting their children; therefore, they do not want their children to visit frequently. Imprisoned mothers are placed in a difficult situation: they desire more contact with their children, especially very young children, who they fear will not know them when they are released, yet the social environment of the prison does not permit positive visitation.

Telephone calls are not the preferred method for maintaining contact, since the mothers must call out of the prison collect (i.e., by reversing the long-distance charges). Still, for mothers who are not afforded frequent visitation with children, this is an important way to keep in touch. Only a few women have regular telephone contact with their children. They are fortunate because their children are with their grandmothers, who readily accept the collect calls. Following trends found in prior research (Beckerman 1994), telephone calls are of utmost importance for WCC women who are not allowed visitation by the foster parents (who often withhold letters and gifts mothers send to their children). The telephone, thus, is their only means of communication with their children. Suzanne's children are taken to the local welfare office on a designated date and time to call her at prison. Suzanne is allowed to talk to them on the telephone twice a month for twenty minutes.

Nevertheless, using the telephone and letters as the only means of contact is not very fulfilling. Telephone calls do not allow the closeness that mothers desire. According to Suzanne,

> The phone—all we're doing is hearing voices. I send them pictures and they send me pictures, but there's no closeness—we're thousands of miles away. We have no way of maintaining really close feelings, maintaining all the love. My son really needs it now with his foster parents telling him all this stuff [criticism of Suzanne]. Because it's out of state, there's nothing I can do. I've tried to get my kids moved over here closer to me, but they won't do it because it's out of state.

Furthermore, Suzanne notes that her son's physical condition has deteriorated because she is denied visitation and forced to rely on telephone calls:

> My son's an epileptic. Twice since I've been here, they've had to Life Flight him in order to save his life because he won't pull out of

these seizures. I'll be glad to get home because the doctor says a lot of it is my son's nerves because he can't see Momma. All he gets to do is talk to me twice a month for twenty minutes.

Suzanne's solution to the predicament of not being allowed to see her children? "I'd want a furlough to go see my kids. I have not seen my kids for fourteen months."

Some mothers are subjected to more than the prison or state welfare office controlling their contact with their children. For instance, one woman's biggest problem regarding contact with her children was her ex-husband, who used the children against her when she asked for a divorce. He initially prevented her from having any contact with the children, who are in his custody.

He threatened me, "If you get a divorce, I'll make sure you never see the kids again." That scared me, and it was right in the prime of the trial, and I backed away. I said, "Okay, I won't file for a divorce." Being that I raised my kids by myself, you know, my whole world was falling apart. Everything—I'm losing everything—and one thing that I don't want to lose is my kids because that's all I have in this world. So when he did this, I said, "Okay, anything you want. Just let me see my kids." He can't continue using my kids to make me do the things he wants, to make me be the way he wants me to be. I have my own mind.

This woman was initially intimidated by her husband's threats and agreed not to divorce him in order to maintain contact with her children. Even though she consented to remain married, he did not allow her contact with her children. After months of no communication with her children, she filed for a divorce; months later, her ex-husband finally let the children contact her. This woman is controlled not only by prison visitation rules but also by her ex-husband, much in the same way some mothers with formally placed children are controlled by their children's guardians or state welfare offices. No other woman mentioned this problem with husbands or ex-husbands.

At the WCC, Native mothers have minimal contact of all types due to cultural and social reasons. Given the low educational levels of Native women, the lack of money necessary for travel and correspondence, and their overrepresentation in maximum security, it is not surprising that Native prisoners do not have as much contact with their children as white mothers. Furthermore, telephones are relatively uncommon in Native households on Indian reservations in Montana.

Suggestions for Visitation Improvements

Prison visitation rules, both formal and informal, appear to be controlling and punishing. In my opinion, mothers should be given the clear message by prison authorities that it is beneficial to have physical contact with their children, rather than informal rules that communicate that mothers will be punished if physical contact occurs between them and their children. Additionally, it would increase the quality of the visits if Minimum-status mothers were permitted supervised walks with their children, which would provide some privacy as well as entertainment for the children. Imprisoned mothers and their children could share special times of the year together if the mothers were allowed to plan parties for children on certain holidays (e.g., Christmas, Halloween, back-to-school parties). The men's prison in Montana organizes such events, which seem to benefit the incarcerated parents and their children.

In this small prison there are many rigid formal and informal rules. Most prisoners firmly feel that the prison must revise its policy on visitation, including the limitation of one visit per weekend, to afford women the opportunity of seeing their children at least once a month. The issue of contact speaks to larger concerns, such as the need to restructure the prison's environment or perhaps provide furloughs, as suggested by several mothers, to enable mothers to visit more often with their children.

The Adoption Assistance and Child Welfare Act (PL 96-272), enacted in 1980, dictates that efforts must be made to reunite children in foster care with their natural parents even if they are imprisoned (Barry 1985b; Beckerman 1991). Reunification plans should include frequent visitation between natural parents and their children and regular contact between social workers and natural parents. Neither prison staff nor the state employee involved with child placement discussed the Adoption Assistance and Child Welfare Act. Again, because of their lack of knowledge or noncompliance, we can assume that their advocacy for the mothers and children is impaired.

Ten

REHABILITATION AND HEALING OF IMPRISONED MOTHERS

The separation from their families, especially their children, produces tremendous grief and anger for incarcerated mothers. Some prisons have begun implementing programs to rehabilitate and strengthen family ties. Judith Clark (1995), who offers considerable awareness as a former prisoner at the Bedford Hills Correctional Facility in New York, argues that although there are obvious restrictions when one parents from a distance, mother/child relationships can and should continue despite the mother's incarceration. Prisons absolutely need to address the issues of parenting while incarcerated, a growing problem for the entire society.

Two prison programs at the WCC aimed specifically at strengthening ties between imprisoned mothers and their children are the parenting class and the Parenting Support Group. Nevertheless, the narratives reveal that both the WCC and the state insufficiently assist imprisoned mothers in improving and maintaining family stability.

Once mothers are released from prison, they need to focus their rehabilitation on the readjustment with their families. While most mothers, Native and white, find the anticipated readjustment problems with their children overwhelming, some are primarily concerned with personal adjustment issues and how these will affect their readjustment with their children.

INNOVATIVE PROGRAMS TO FOSTER PARENT-CHILD CONTACT

Historically, children were imprisoned with their mothers until the era of bottle-feeding, when children were placed with other caretakers and imprisoned women had little contact with them (Rafter 1990). Today there is a trend to reverse this, and many women's prisons recognize that mothers should be afforded frequent contact with their children. Efforts are made to implement special programs to preserve family stability. The state of California responded to this need by authorizing four prisons to offer a program that will enable imprisoned mothers and their children to live together (DelVecchio 1996). The proposed facility will house thirty mothers and approximately forty-five children. Eligible mothers must not have a history of violence, and those convicted of drug offenses, other than selling to sustain their habits, are not qualified for the program. Oakland was chosen as one program site; unfortunately, because the state did not actively involve the neighborhood in the planning, they encountered intense opposition (DelVecchio 1996).

There are only a few correctional institutions across the nation that function to maintain regular contact between imprisoned mothers and their children. These institutions have programs that include parenting classes, special visits scheduled for children, and home furloughs (McGowan and Blumenthal 1978). The New York State Correctional Institution for Women, located in Bedford Hills, has a live-in mother/child program. This nursery allows women who give birth while incarcerated to stay with their babies until the children are one year old (Grossman 1984). The women and their babies live in a section of the hospital that has an average of ten mothers and their newborns at any given time. The women involved agree that the program benefits them and the children by aiding in the prevention of family disintegration. In addition, Ohio and North Carolina allow newborns at their prison hospitals, and babies are permitted to stay for as long as eighteen months inside the women's prison in Florida (Stanton 1980). Few women in these states keep their children with them, however, because many prisons are not committed to this policy, which requires prison staff cooperation (Baunach 1985b; Feinman 1986). Most state correctional institutions have general visiting that allows for one-hour visits ranging from daily to twice a month.

Other resourceful programs for imprisoned mothers include Project MOLD in Nebraska and the Purdy Treatment Center for Women in Tacoma, Washington (Feinman 1986; Stanton 1980). Imprisoned mothers on work release at Purdy may have their children for weekend visits in apartments outside the prison. Mothers are encouraged to have maximum contact with their children in an effort to prepare for family life once they are released. Purdy also has a foster care program in which the state works with the prison to place children close to the prison. Imprisoned mothers and foster parents work together to make decisions for the children. Contact with children is a priority, and foster parents bring the children to the prison to visit with their mothers; on occasion, the mother may visit the child in the foster home. This program clearly helps to maintain and strengthen mother/child relationships. A third program at Purdy, a nursery located on the prison grounds, began in 1975. The nursery trains imprisoned mothers in the area of child development (McGowan and Blumenthal 1978). After completing a course in child development, those mothers not convicted of child-related crimes are eligible to work as aides to the teachers in the nursery.

WCC OPINIONS ABOUT REHABILITATION AND ON-SITE FACILITIES

The mothers at the WCC have conflicting feelings about whether the prison should have a facility where children would live near or with their mothers. Darla, a drug addict clearly concerned with her rehabilitation, explains her position:

No, I don't believe in it [separate facility for children]. The weekend visits are nice—that's enough. Not on an everyday basis because there's too many games. The mother has to work on herself. If she has the kids here all the time, she's going to be devoted to her children and she isn't going to be into rehabilitation. When she gets out of here, she isn't going to be into her children; she's going to be into dope or alcohol. She's going to forget about her kids.

Linda, however, has a different perspective:

If they had a separate housing unit for the mothers with kids, I could see it if they were younger. But once they get to school, I think they should be out.

Native women share the general confusion about children living with or near mothers in prison. Cognizant of the prison's social environment, Mary opines:

I think it's a good idea because of the first year of the child's life and they're just developing. I think they should spend that time with their mothers. As for opinions about prison being such a bad environment, it doesn't have to be: if they could build a house away from the prison setting and let it be like a home environment. Having children in a place such as here, I think is going to leave a scar on the children because they make it too formalized. The children become little, tiny inmates themselves. They have to go through rules and regulations just like we do. The guards frisk us, they frisk the kids just the same; that's where I say it leaves a scar on the children. This is what their memories are going to be.

Also influenced by the prison's social environment, another Native woman responds:

A child shouldn't be allowed to stay here for more than a weekend because there's a lot of tension on the floor and children are really sensitive to that. There's a lot of foul language out there. In here it's like a drop of a pin and there could be a fight. It's not a place for a child; it's easy for a child to get hurt. It would be different if we had a nursery across the street; then I would agree to it—like a house or something. But to grow up in a place like this—I grew up in jails and foster homes and it's not a life to live. In here, the children will become institutionalized.

Although one prison staff member appears supportive of frequent mother/child visitation, she is not comfortable with the idea of children living at or near prisons with their mothers. She clarifies:

I'm against having children in prison because every woman who walks in has multiple problems. Women don't get into prison unless they have multiple problems. If they're going to take care of their child, then they're not going to work on those problems.

Addressing the issue of the social environment of the prison as a reason for not supporting children living with their mothers, she adds:

A child up to three years old—the environment is not going to affect them. If they're with Mom and they're bonding, prison is a memory they won't even remember. I don't have any problem with the environment, but in view of that a mother's not going to work—she's never worked on herself. So, I think they should be allowed to visit and do that bonding, but I don't think they should be here twenty-four hours a day, seven days a week.

This staff member, along with other staff members and several imprisoned mothers, focuses on the responsibility of the women for their own rehabilitation. Parenting full-time is not perceived as a positive part of that process. Other mothers and the parenting class facilitator, however, conclude that young children should be near their mothers. The facilitator's appraisal is from a child development perspective, and, in her opinion, the bonding time after the delivery of a baby is especially crucial. She is convinced that much damage is done when a child is immediately taken from the mother. Moreover, she notes that to become good parents, mothers need contact with their children in order to practice good parenting skills. In her opinion, children should reside in a separate facility near the prison, not inside the prison; she suggests a halfway-house setting.

THE WCC PARENTING PROGRAM

Parenting information and training are identified by WCC staff as a necessity for imprisoned mothers. It is the opinion of prison staff that parenting education is essential before most imprisoned mothers can effectively parent. One staff member at the WCC says:

The parenting issue is so critical to women's corrections. It's not terribly critical to men—most of them who have kids don't know who they are because they never functioned as a parent. If we don't impact these mothers, both themselves and how they deal with their children, we're spawning a whole other generation [of criminals]. They're going to be here [in prison]. The parenting issue is absolutely vital. I see children coming in for visits and they're kids like my kids. Their chances of ending up in prison is multiplied many more times than somebody else's; it's a race against time. You've got to get Mom so she's an effective positive parent to eliminate damaging the kids.

Institutional staff perceive the parenting program as vital and are supportive of family stability.

One staff member who embraces the parenting program definitely blames deviant behavior within society in general on dysfunctional families and considers the mother's behavior to be the most important influence on children's deviance. Bad parenting is not only linked to crime; it is seen as "spawning" criminals. This staff member adds:

> These [imprisoned mothers] are primary caregivers who are raising another generation of children. It may be a little late for the woman who comes to prison at age forty, but if we can work with her on parenting skills maybe we can impact the next generation of kids. Can we help these children to break this cycle that's gone on for generations? There, I think, is the main answer to the crime problem.

The one prison program aimed specifically at strengthening familial ties is the parenting class. This class is held three times a year. Each eight-week session meets once a week for three hours, for a total of twenty-four hours of instruction per session. Because the mothers assist in the definition of the goals for the course, the topics change with each group.

As defined by the facilitator, the basic goals of the parenting class are for imprisoned mothers to obtain information about child development; learn to increase their understanding of parent/child interactions; share with one another in group; and establish a philosophy about parenting. Additionally, the facilitator offers what she terms "empowering" legal information on parental rights while incarcerated, although she cannot find much information on Montana law and depends heavily on literature from the state of California.

White mothers experience the classes in a positive way and enroll in the course several times. One white mother especially approves of the current facilitator, whom she sees as respectful of imprisoned mothers. To this mother, respect is extremely important:

> I think [the facilitator] is really a great person. She's very intelligent. . . . She really cares, she listens. She even talked to us in between classes and after class. And I got a lot out of parenting and

when the class was over, I wrote her a note telling her how much I enjoyed the class. She treated us like human beings.

All of the white mothers are enthusiastic about the class and the facilitator. Not only is the class informative and empowering to these women, and potentially empowering to Native women, it provides a setting where the prisoners are treated with respect and given a sense of some control.

Native mothers have vastly different perceptions of the parenting class, however. Most Native mothers do not attend the parenting class for several reasons. For one thing, it is scheduled at the same time as the group specifically designed for them. Also, many are in maximum security, which prohibits them from attending the class. Others see the classes as culture-bound and thus of little interest. Many Native women, particularly those from reservations, are uncomfortable around white people and perceive the class as "just another white program" facilitated by a white person. The criminal justice system is seen as "white," and Native women are isolated within this system. Most Native mothers say that the white staff do not understand their issues, and the parenting facilitator, although trying hard to please Native mothers, is prejudged simply because she is white.

Most Native mothers conclude that the parenting program is advantageous for white mothers because those women are unskilled as parents. In contrast, Native mothers see themselves as strong mothers due to the extended-family support system. One reservation woman, who was raised in a traditional Native household, remarks:

> That kind of bugs me—white people trying to tell me how to raise kids. I was taught by my mom how to raise kids. Indians are just different—they're closer I think. I'm not putting them [white people] down; it's just that that's the way I was brought up. That's what I believe—Indians are stronger. They know things.

Especially important is the knowledge these women gained from the women in their families. A reservation mother explains:

> I've come to find that the majority of [white] women who come to prison have never been taught parenting skills. Whereas you and I

have been taught by our mothers or aunts or grandmothers; we were
taught these things when we were growing up. There's one [white]
lady that was in here—she did not know how to do laundry,
basic things. Just think about it. She didn't know how to do that,
let alone care for a baby.

Many of the white mothers at the WCC were raised in dysfunctional
nuclear families, foster care placements, or reform schools and did not
receive the benefits offered by an extended family. It is possible that this
background does affect their parenting skills and produces relatively
weak mothers.

Some mothers also express other reasons for avoiding the parenting
class. Native mothers with older children surmise that the curriculum is
designed around the parenting of younger children; because their children are teenagers, they do not attend the classes. Some Native mothers
who took the course from another instructor expressed frustration that
this particular parenting class did not effectively deal with the issue of
coping with the separation from their children. Furthermore, several
white and nonreservation mothers who lost legal rights to their children avoid both the parenting class and the Parenting Support Group
because both are painful reminders that they are not seen legally as
mothers.

Although few Native mothers determine that they benefit from parenting classes, one Native woman, who took the class from a previous
facilitator, has only positive things to say about the facilitator:

She's excellent—she can tell you so many things, and she gets real
close with the women. She builds trust; girls just pour out to her.
I've taken her assertive classes twice, her TA [transactional analysis]
classes, her anger classes—she was great. Now we don't have any of
that anymore. All we have is parenting, whenever they can get that
lady here—that's it.

Mothers grieving for deceased children feel a need for grief therapy,
which is not a part of the parenting class. Several Native women reveal
that the death of their babies was directly linked to their drug use during pregnancy, and that their drug usage increased after the deaths. The
death of their children is the primary concern of these mothers, and

they desperately need psychological counseling to help them to work through their loss. In the absence of such counseling, these women direct their desire for grief counseling toward the parenting class facilitator, who is not qualified to perform that function. In the words of one Native woman who took the class from a previous facilitator,

> You know, we can't go too far into any problems because she's only the parenting teacher. So, you don't want to start talking about your inside feelings; about how you might feel about losing a child because it could be dangerous—it could be detrimental. So there's no real backstop in this institution, as far as counseling goes, if I wanted to talk about the guilt I have about my daughter dying. I would like to talk about it—let me put it that way. But at this point I'm afraid to; I'm afraid to start feelings that may never stop. I don't know—I'm afraid. Because I don't have anything to fall back on.

The new facilitator has no contact with Native mothers; all mothers enrolled in her course are white. When she expressed this concern to prison staff she was told "not to worry about it." The staff explained to her that the Native women have a group they attend during the time class is scheduled. Native women meet once a week with a Native woman counselor. That the two groups are scheduled at the same time, inadvertently or otherwise, prevents Native women from attending the parenting class. None of the Native women, however, object to the inaccessibility of the class. Nevertheless, a parenting class focused on the unique cultural issues of Native parenting might be welcomed by the Native population and could be quite beneficial for the mothers and their families.

THE PARENTING SUPPORT GROUP

The Parenting Support Group is comprised solely of imprisoned mothers. It is an anomaly within a system that presents itself as controlling: the imprisoned mothers are given the power by prison authorities to approve overnight weekend visitation. This group could be an important tool for the empowerment and growth of its members. However, many mothers are critical of the support group, naming prisoner hostility toward other prisoners or their children as their main concern. In addition, members do not always participate with the purpose of receiving and offering support: some only attend so they can obtain weekend visitation privileges with their children.

Because most prisoners would have little prior experience serving on decision-making committees, it is predictable that without guidance by an expert in team processes, problems would exist. The committee has the authority to select a leader from its own membership to facilitate the group meetings. This authority is theoretically empowering, but empowerment means nothing without the skills and training to use that power wisely. Some mothers say that the group is not structured enough, and others remark that it is what happens within the group that irritates them, not the structure. Both problems stem from the same source: the basic rules of respectful interaction that would be central to the success of any team are not enforced by the facilitator, because the proper training and coaching has not been done to ensure the facilitator's, and the group's, success. In the words of one mother:

> I'm in the support group so I can have my kids here, and I've noticed that there's a lot of women in here who are not supportive—they more or less cut each other down. It's just awful. I've seen them really verbally beat up some of these women about what they've done with their kids, and it's usually the ones who don't have their kids anymore. They've had them taken away for some reason, or they've done the same things, or they just don't like the woman, and they'll take it out on the kids.

This mother suggests there is much anger on the part of some prisoners that is misdirected at an undeserving mother or child. Here we have further evidence that some mothers, who lose their children through the courts or through death, are not afforded the opportunity to process their anger and grief either in parenting class or elsewhere.

It is a sad irony that, because the Parenting Support Group must approve all overnight weekend visits, the prejudices of some women who are struggling with their own psychological problems become inflicted on other women. For example, mothers involved in crimes against children almost never gain approval from the support group for overnight visits with their children. One prisoner conveys that these mothers, although few, are subsequently estranged from their children and drop out of parenting classes and the support group. Another prisoner explains why mothers who have committed such offenses are not liked by other prisoners:

> One lady is in here because of what happened to a baby. And my friend brings her little boy in here for visits, and this lady wants to play with him. I wanted to hit her! I wanted to say, "Get the hell away from him; don't even come near that child!" I have a hard time with that because I was abused as a child and even if they're not my children, I'll be damned if I'm going to let someone abuse them.

Mothers who committed crimes against children, apparently perceived by members of the support group as "unfit" mothers, are therefore punished for the type of crime of which they were convicted. It is possible that because prison authorities agree with this perception, the support group is allowed to misuse its power in this way. Because of the vast number of imprisoned women who were victimized as children, it is understandable that they would harbor anger against women who were convicted of crimes against children. On the other hand, the women so convicted may be rehabilitated. Moreover, their children could well be suffering more from the separation than from the original crime, in part because the child might feel guilt over providing testimony that may have helped to convict and remove the parent from the home. Every case is unique, and evaluation of such a situation requires sophisticated guidelines and guidance that should be provided by prison staff.

In general, then, the WCC parenting program is ineffective. Staff demonstrate minimal efforts to adapt the program in ways that could truly strengthen the relationships between imprisoned mothers and their children. Poor coordination among various prison staff and programs also creates problems. For example, although one white mother enjoys the parenting program, she notes certain restrictions that put imprisoned mothers in no-win situations. When she was in maximum security, prison staff told her she would be moved to the general-population building, where she would be entitled to visits with her children, *if* she joined the parenting program. She agreed; however, the prison scheduled a dentist appointment for her for the day the parenting class met. She refused to go to the appointment because of the stipulation that she attend parenting class. Then, she claims, the nurse became angry at and abusive toward her for missing the dental appointment. She felt damned if she attended the parenting class and damned if she went to the dentist. This incident illustrates how the controlling environment becomes a self-perpetuating system that is incapable of supporting the maintenance of family ties.

In an era of reclaiming family values, prisons and social service agencies must remember the children, invisible and often forgotten, of imprisoned mothers.

READJUSTMENT AFTER RELEASE

Several studies (Henriques 1982; Ross and Fabiano 1986; Stanton 1980; Zalba 1964) conclude that a mother's incarceration causes disorder in her children's lives and many times results in a less stable family after the mother's release. Other research (Baunach 1985b; Henriques 1982; McGowan and Blumenthal 1978; Stanton 1980) proposes that some imprisoned mothers believe their children will not remember them, will lose respect for them specifically because they are in prison, and will not want to live with them once they are released from prison. These feelings are particularly strong among women who do not receive frequent visits from their children. Other mothers, whose children cling to them and closely watch them during visitation, worry their children will be more emotionally dependent upon them after release than they were before incarceration.

Imprisoned mothers at the WCC are concerned with the readjustment process once they are discharged from prison and reunited with their children. Concerns regarding readjustment problems with children differ by race/ethnicity and the extent of absence from the children. Other important factors are the age of the children, number of children, and the mother's history with substance abuse. The issue of readjusting as a parent is compounded by anxiety regarding the personal adjustment to life outside the prison. Minimum pre-release counseling and no post-release family-counseling services are available to help mothers readjust to family life or prepare for that readjustment. The parenting class facilitator hopes to implement an aftercare program for imprisoned mothers. In her view, such a program would help mothers relate to their children during the transition from prison to the outside. She suggests an additional support system designed specifically for the children of imprisoned mothers, which could enable the children to learn to deal with the issue of having an incarcerated mother.

Women who were previously incarcerated have a comprehensible understanding of the difficulties of readjustment with children. In prison for the second time, Darla conveys her problems with her son after she was released from prison the first time she was incarcerated:

> The first day I was out, he just loved me. But then, the next day, it was like he would watch me everywhere I would go but he wouldn't talk to me or anything. It was like he was afraid I was going to leave again. It was really hard to get that bond I had with him before I left.

Other mothers relate imprisonment and older children's anger over this type of separation as preventing readjustment of any kind. A white mother, imprisoned for the fifth time, fears that because of her son's anger, there is no mother/child relationship to which to even readjust. She communicates what other mothers with lengthy sentences or multiple times in prison indicate: "I'm afraid to think about that because I want a relationship, but I don't know if he'll ever be able to forgive me."

Women with more than one child are anxious about balancing their time between children, especially if they have very young children. For example, Julie has two children, the younger one born while she was in prison. She seems aware of the work entailed in developing a relationship with a child who does not know her. Additionally, Julie is nervous about how working outside the home will affect her readjustment with her children:

> I'll be having to readjust with my oldest, and I'm going to have to get to know my youngest, who is bonded really bad to my mom. When they left him for his visit with me he freaked out. I've got to get used to that and, in the meantime, make sure my oldest doesn't think I'm devoting all my time to my youngest. At the same time, I need to work toward a career—it's going to be real difficult.

The concerns of substance abusers, Native and white, focus somewhat more on their personal adjustment after release from prison, although they also connect their substance abuse to possible problematic readjustments with their children. For instance, Judy's family was falling apart before her incarceration. Acutely aware of her addiction to alcohol and how this affects her parenting, Judy, a Native mother, explains:

> It's clear-cut: I don't know if I'm going to be able to take care of my kids. I think that I'm going to have to get more responsible— enough to take care of myself because of my long-term addiction— because I know I need intensive treatment. I'm not getting treatment here. I think that I've got that to conquer first, because I think I'd be a fool if I tried to take my children right now.

Many Native mothers additionally worry that obligations to extended family members might interfere with their personal adjustment, which could also complicate readjustments to children. This is Judy's second time in prison, so she has a clear idea about what is involved in the readjustment process. Reflecting upon her previous experience with parole, Judy describes an impossible situation:

> This last time I was out, they gave me a hardship parole. My mother had a severe stroke. My stepdad had some DUI [driving under the influence] charges and he couldn't work, but he needed to go to work to pay off his fines. Somebody had to be there twenty-four hours a day to take care of my mother. Then the welfare got mixed up in this because my sister has a foster care license. The welfare slapped all kinds of stipulations on me—what I'm supposed to do to get my kids back. They let me out of here in order to take care of my mom. But, I couldn't do all those things at once. Welfare wanted me to go to parenting classes every Thursday and attend chemical-dependency meetings. My parole officer wanted me to go to three AA [Alcoholic Anonymous] meetings a week and report to the parole office twice a month. Plus, I had to be there with my mom all the time. Plus, trying to get my kids back in my home— you know, to get them used to me. It just kind of turned into hell. And then my stepdad, he kept drinking, and I couldn't handle arguing with him; it was getting my mom pretty upset.

Judy had difficulties concentrating on her children while taking care of her mother, arguing with her stepfather, and trying to support herself and her extended family. All this proved to be too much for Judy, and she started drinking again. Violating her parole by drinking and leaving the area without authorization, she was soon arrested and returned to prison.

Talking specifically about being released and reunited with her children, and in general about being fresh out of prison, Judy further discusses the process of readjustment with children as compounded by her personal readjustment:

> The social workers don't understand that when you're incarcerated you just can't come out and say, "Well, here's your kids; take care of them." They don't realize how you feel. You're jittery when you get out. You're not used to being in an open place with all these people. With my parole officer this last time, I was nervous the whole time. Both times when I went and seen her, I was just like this [shaking]. And she said it would take six months to recover from being out of prison—six months to get back into society. I walked around this store and I looked around at these people. I thought for sure they knew I was in prison—like it was written all across my face, you know. I felt guilty; I felt just awful. I was nervous and walked around that store like this [shaking]; I just knew those people knew.

Although not a substance abuser, another Native prisoner is anxious about the influence of her extended family on her personal adjustment and judgment. She has been in prison nearly four years and will be eligible for parole in one year. She worries about being back in her old neighborhood and confronting relatives of the person she committed a crime against:

> I come from a fighting family—that's what I was taught. I know if I go back and continue to be close to them, I'll be right back here. If I run into my victim's sister, I'll be right back in prison. You know, "Are you going to let her talk to you like that?!" And bam, I'm going to be fighting again, and I can't have that, especially when I'm going through problems with my children.

Considering the socioeconomic status of most imprisoned mothers, who have led oppressed and depressed lives, their readjustment to society after imprisonment can be overwhelming. Life for these women before prison was already difficult. These mothers, with multiple problems, require helping agencies that aid, not hinder, their adjustment to the outside and readjustment with their children and families.

Native mothers—indeed, all Native women—readjusting to life after incarceration face an especially formidable task. Truly, indigenous peoples suffer today from poverty, high rates of suicide, substance abuse, and family breakdown, which are seen as direct indicators of the stresses connected with being Native in an oppressive society (Allen 1985; Antone, Miller, and Myers 1986; Bachman 1992). These negative conditions in Native communities, symptoms of colonialism, have been termed "ethnostress" (Antone, Miller, and Myers 1986, 9).[1] Feelings of despair and powerlessness have disrupted our lives as Native people. Since we are emerging from a dehumanizing experience (see Forbes 1992 and Freire 1970), we must immerse ourselves in what Antone, Miller, and Myers label a "rehumanization process" (1986, 24). To be a whole person is to be humanized. Native women, because of racism, sexism, and classism, must be empowered, and women recently released from prison are conclusively not in a position to assist in that effort. These women require time to adjust to life outside prison as individuals—time for a healing before they can contribute to empowering families and communities.

Although one could speculate that it is tremendously difficult for women to lead productive lives after incarceration, a few manage this achievement. Despite the odds, some ex-prisoners are contributors to their families, communities, and tribes.

<table>
<tr><td>*Eleven*</td><td>

NARRATIVE OF A NATIVE WOMAN ON THE OUTSIDE

GLORIA WELLS NORLIN

(KA MIN DI TAT)

</td></tr>
</table>

> *Oppressed people resist identifying themselves as subjects, by defining their reality, shaping their new identity, naming their history, telling their story.*
>
> BELL HOOKS, Talking Back

> *Every woman has a well-stocked arsenal of anger potentially useful against those oppressions, personal and institutional, which brought that anger into being. Focused with precision it can become a powerful source of energy serving progress and change.*
>
> AUDRE LORDE, Sister Outsider

In one of the few essays published about Montana's Landless Natives, Verne Dusenberry (1958) lists the names of Pembina Chippewa recorded in 1850. These are names we recognize today in Montana: for example, Azure, Belgarde, Caplette, Cardinal, Grandbois, Houle, La-Fromboise, LaRocque, Laverdue, Monisette, Montreau, Pappin, Peltier, Plouffe, St. Pierre, Trottier, Valier, Valle, and Wells. This last family name, Wells, belongs to Gloria Wells Norlin, who was imprisoned at the WCC in Montana.

Gloria's story illustrates issues presented in earlier chapters.[1] Gloria, who did not commit the crime of which she was convicted, had great difficulty finding an attorney interested in appealing the decision. The interconnected issues of race/ethnicity, gender, and class are glaring in

Gloria Wells Norlin in her store, "Indian Uprising." Photo by Shane Ross.

her experiences with the criminal justice system. After her incarceration, Gloria continues to struggle in an effort to regain self-respect and family stability.

The youngest of six children of Agnes Kucera and Lawrence "Blacky" Wells, Gloria was born in 1955 at Fort Benton, Montana. She was raised in small towns in central Montana, including Lewistown, one of the original settlements of the Little Shell. Once a Native community, Lewistown is now a white town. Reflecting on days of old, Gloria says:

> The small retirement town I lived in consisted mostly of white
> John Birch–type citizens. It was surrounded by the beautiful Judith
> Mountains, the Snowys and the Moccasins. Thinking back on how
> our early ancestors must have been in awe of the panoramic view,
> to this day, sends chills down my back. I can see the twenty-five
> Chippewa families that ran from the Turtle Mountain Reservation
> coming up on these mountain ranges and making the decision to
> settle.

Gloria is well versed in the history of her tribe, passed down by relatives. Her grandfather ranched not far from Lewistown in an area known as the N-Bar Ranch, in a community once called Tyler. Gloria says of the land her family lost to white people: "It is said that Grandpa lost the ranch in a poker game. He supposedly signed an I.O.U. for the money he lost, but according to my uncle Vic Wells, thirty days after Grandpa signed the piece of paper in faith, because he couldn't read, the whole family was escorted off the homestead by the Sheriff. So much for faith."

Gloria's father, now deceased, was "the son of dirt-poor parents that were for the most part shunned by the [white] people." Her father was a cowboy, a bronc rider; he and his brothers were known in nearby white communities as the "rowdy Indians." The Wells brothers ran alcohol to whites between Roundup and Lewistown by way of Forest Grove. Gloria reminisces,

> Many times my dad and uncles would take my cousins and myself along the old dirt roads and reveal to us the ranch homes that would put them up for [the] night while they were busy ducking the law. I would sit in the back seat and listen to Dad tell tales of the days gone past and couldn't get the sadness out of my mind. I felt the pain of his past, the rejection, the feeling of being an outcast. I knew what is was like to be that outcast person because I grew up in the same country. I was the kid with the alcoholic for a father and enabler for a mother. I knew the rejection of being different.

Gloria's childhood was tainted by the hideous racism she experienced in Lewistown and other nearby white towns. One of the few Native children in town, she continually faced harassment of the worst kind that would take its psychological toll on her. Gloria says: "Many times, I would come home from school crying because some white kid had called me dirty names. I didn't know why nobody liked me, and a lot of times I'd come home and ask, 'Why do we have to be Indian? Why can't we be like other kids?' I was, in my mind, a squaw slut before I ever knew what a slut was." Gloria's mother would try to calm her by reminding her that Natives were in the United States first, the rightful owners of the land, and that whites had stolen Native land. Yet for Gloria, "Somehow that didn't ease the pain or take away the hurt. A child of six is hardly capable of debating the wrongs dealt Native American people, so instead of being a debater I became a fighter. Nobody was going to call me any dirty names and get away with it. I'd teach them a thing or two. It didn't matter that I could get the tar knocked out of me. I had to stand up for what I thought was right." This notion, that she had to shield herself to safeguard her dignity and integrity, saturated Gloria's life and is especially noticeable in her incarceration experiences as a young girl in reform school and later as an adult in the women's prison.

THE EASY PATH TO REFORM SCHOOL

Gloria's father worked for the railroad, and her family was uprooted several times a year following his employment. Because of her father's alcoholism, her parents continuously battled each other, and Gloria invariably felt responsible for their arguments. In a normal reaction to her parents' marital problems, she sensed she had to choose between them: "Trying to choose between the two was hurtful and often I felt if I loved one the other would be mad at me. If I tried to love them both—well, it just didn't happen."

Gloria's mother, who is white, was concerned for her Native daughter and warned: "You already have two black marks against you: your father's a drunk and you are an Indian." Gloria recalls being overwhelmed with shame: "Trying to hold my head high was unheard of due to the feelings of low self-worth. After all, how dare I think I could ever amount to anything. I had bad blood—a lost cause in my mother's eyes."

This feeling of self-debasement, a result of emotional and physical abuse, produced an overachiever. School became a refuge. Gloria was an excellent student and received high marks, despite the discrimination she faced. She excelled not only at her studies in school but also at cooking and sewing. Trying to please her parents, Gloria notes that "No matter what it was it was never good enough for Mom and Dad. Dad was always preoccupied and, after all, he was an alcoholic." After her father beat her one night when he was drunk, Gloria decided to move out of the house. Searching for a safe place to live, she remarks: "I was fourteen going on twenty-five. Bruised up and beat up physically and emotionally, I moved in with someone I was baby-sitting for. To be truthful, she was known for her loose, immoral ways and not exactly the role-model type. I knew, though, at her house I would not get beat up."

Gloria's father demanded that she return to the family home by Sunday evening or he would report her to the authorities as a runaway. Gloria was unable to return immediately because she had no transportation. She relayed her father's wishes to the woman she was staying with, who simply threw Gloria the car keys and told her to drive with the children to Gloria's family home. In order not to violate her father's orders, Gloria loaded the car with five small children, whose mother had gone out of town, and drove to the family home on the appointed day. En route she was stopped by the city police of Lewistown and cited for driving without a license.

Gloria went to court the following Monday and was sentenced to the weekend in jail for her infraction. She recalls:

> Into jail I went for the weekend. I was so scared, so very scared. And bad—I was so very bad because only bad people go to jail. Nice girls didn't go to jail, so what Mother had said was right. I was bad. God wouldn't let this happen to a nice girl. My heart was hardened. There I was in jail—a mere kid of fourteen. I felt lost and ashamed, abandoned by my mother and father, and in my eyes there was no God—there couldn't be.

While Gloria was in jail a sinful event transpired: she was molested by the jailer. The courageous fourteen-year-old managed to fight off her perpetrator, and the intended rape was not completed. She remembers the molestation: "The jailer decided I was his next victim for sexual abuse. I thought, 'Where is God now? I am bad. I must have walked a certain way to entice him. Maybe he can see the bad in me like Mom can. Why does he keep grabbing me?' My heart was hardened, my self-esteem low. I was a filthy squaw slut."

On Sunday afternoon, when Gloria was to be released, the under-sheriff, sheriff, and her parents were informed of the molestation. According to Gloria, the sheriff demanded the jailer's resignation—an insignificant punishment for a considerable crime. Remarkably, on the following Monday, Gloria was taken back to court on a truancy charge. Her parents were present when the judge read the charges: endangering her life and the lives of others, and truant from school. The charges puzzled Gloria because she had only missed a few days of school. She recalls her feelings: "My insides were screaming, 'What is happening here? Why is Mom crying? What does she mean, "Is it that easy to take my little girl away?" Where am I going?'"

The judge and the county attorney, according to Gloria, escorted her into another room and explained, "We have decided that it would be in your best interests to commit you to Mountain View School for Girls," a reform school. A confused Gloria asked: "What? Reform school? I thought only tough, rough, bad girls go to reform school. Why then am I?" Once everyone returned to the courtroom, Gloria was sentenced to reform school until age twenty-one.

Gloria's parents were visibly upset. Gloria cried and contemplated what had gone wrong—why she was being punished when the only law she had violated was driving without a license. Immediately Gloria assimilated her "crime" and the hefty punishment of reform school into the context of her sexual abuse. She comments, "I had no idea of the results of the molestation and how the big cover-up of getting me out of the picture—sent to reform school—was an easy out for the authorities to stop any further embarrassment for Fergus County." Gloria maintains that the incident was racialized: "Lewistown would not have done that to a white girl. In the first place, they would not have thrown me in jail if my father hadn't been a drunken Indian." Gloria arrived at reform school embittered:

> Arrival at Mountain View found me with feelings of being cheated out of life, loneliness, and loss of freedom. I was incarcerated without fault. I was hurt and then I felt the terrible deep-seated anger, low self-worth. I was bad! Mom said I was bad, and now here I was in reform school. A place for bad girls. There were times when a small cry from within would surface, "Gloria, you are not bad." A small word of praise would give me hope that maybe I was okay, maybe I could amount to something. A ray of hope.

The counselor at reform school was bewildered regarding the truancy charge because school records reported that Gloria had missed only three days of school and had excelled in her studies. When the counselor questioned Gloria as to why she had been sent to reform school despite such a good record, all she could do was rage at him. Gloria believed he, as well as others, knew she had been sent to Mountain View because she was molested by the jailer. She says, "You know by this time the little chip on my shoulder was growing. I thought, 'You know damn well why I'm here.'" The counselor, according to Gloria, saw an angry teenager, perhaps one who rightfully belonged in reform school. Reform school was a bleak and lonely existence for Gloria:

> I recall being so afraid of the girls, of the counselors, of the matrons. I trusted no one, needed no one. After all, I would just get let down again. Why give anybody a chance to mess me around again? I would become self-sufficient; I could rely on just myself to meet all my needs. I had been molested. I had trusted our judicial system and I thought I had trusted God. I had trusted my parents, trusted the jailer, and I had trusted myself—all of whom let me down.

Unwilling to trust anyone, a fearful Gloria decided that being a fighter and manipulator was key to her survival:

> Coping is what different people call the techniques used in surviving the trauma of molestation. Unless one is able to identity these coping methods, it becomes harder for one to be accountable for their actions. My behaviors toward people, life, God, and authority figures became one of manipulation. The Mountain View School became a playground for me.

Gloria discovered that some staff members at reform school were drinking partners with her relatives. Thus, it was easy for her to receive weekend passes from the school to nearby Helena and reacquaint herself with her relatives. Gloria remembers: "I began a life of drinking, drugging, and stealing. I thought it was great that someone cared enough to get me out of that reform school, that someone actually cared." Gloria took full advantage of the easy weekend releases from reform school and began taking mind-altering drugs and playing dangerous games, such as "chicken" with cars.

> I was sitting in the back seat and my cousin said in a slurred voiced, "Now, Gloria, we are going to drive cars at one another." I remember saying, "I can handle it." The next few minutes seemed like hours. I was screaming and totally out of control, which of course

turned these loving relatives and friends into laughing jackals. The more terrified I became, the harder they laughed.

After this event, Gloria began taking drugs on a regular basis. Emotionally needy, it was easy for her to feel as though she finally had a group to which she belonged—people who truly cared for her. Gloria describes her involvement with drugs as "insanity" and a way for her to avoid the reality of her situation.

While Gloria was in reform school, she wrote countless letters to her mother blaming herself for family problems and offering to change to make the family well. Gloria believed her family situation was improving—her parents were in counseling—and she looked forward to her release date. In reality, her family had not changed, and upon her early release she found her parents separated. Gloria's dream of a "normal" family life was shattered, and she discovered that her father was living in a shed by the railroad tracks. Gloria, who continued to blame herself for her parents' marital problems, was devastated and begged her mother to reconcile with her father. She reasoned that if she was a "good" girl, she could bring family harmony to her home. In an effort to appease Gloria, her parents lived together for two short weeks before her father moved into an apartment. Feeling sorry for her father and reasoning that he needed her more than her mother did, Gloria moved out with him. Her father continued to work, and when he returned in the evening, Gloria, then only fifteen years old, would have a hot supper ready for him.

A girlfriend of Gloria's spent the summer with them, the two girls feeling a new-found freedom from strict parental control. One morning they awoke to find a police officer inside the apartment. He told Gloria that she was wanted at the jail. Puzzled, she arrived as instructed and was told that she was being returned to reform school because she had moved out of her mother's house, thereby violating the terms of her early release. That Gloria was living with her father apparently did not matter. She was returned to reform school, where she spent most of the next two years, interspersed with foster homes.

Today, Gloria is very bitter that her parents did not aid her when she was molested by the jailer. She clarifies that she came to mistrust them because they did so little to correct the transgression: "I thought, why the hell should I trust them? They burned me once. I mean, if my kid ever got molested, you better believe I would have gone through hell and high water for them. I don't care if they were molested by the president of the United States, I would have fought for them."

While in reform school, Gloria was temporarily released to visit her family in Lewistown. On one such visit, she stormed into the county attorney's office and raged at him for his role in her sentence:

> I said, "What in the hell is wrong with you? I finally realized what took place here. Why didn't you try to find me a foster home? Why didn't you try to put me in a group home? What about an orphanage? Why did you roll my ass up to the girl's school? I learned to smoke dope there! I drank in skid row! Why didn't you find me a foster home, a group home—anything but the girl's school?" And he said, "Gloria, I was new on the job then and you were my first juvenile case." And I said, "Because you didn't know your job, I had to pay for it? I think you're the lowest, rottenest son-of-a-bitch that ever lived."

After reform school, Gloria graduated from Helena Senior High School, attended Carroll College, and studied psychology at the University of Montana. She married, had a baby, and moved to Portland, Oregon. She later divorced and relocated to Arizona, where she met her second husband and had another child. Again she divorced; this time she moved back to Lewistown, where she met her present husband, Grady Norlin. Together they have a son, Gabriel.

TIME IN THE WOMEN'S CORRECTIONAL CENTER

In 1990 Gloria was sentenced to prison for five years for felony theft. She does not like to discuss her incarceration experience because reflecting on it is depressing. The most painful part of her imprisonment was the separation from her children, especially from her baby.

Reading from her personal diary, Gloria shares the following narrative she recorded while in prison: "It is visiting day here at the Expansion Unit [maximum-security unit] at the women's prison. There's not a dry eye in the place as one of the girls was not allowed to see her little two-year-old boy, whom she hasn't seen in approximately three months. That wouldn't seem like a long time to a person. . . ." At this point, Gloria is in tears and cannot finish. She says, "I just keep it buried and then I have to cry over it." Weeping, she continues her story:

> That wouldn't seem like a long time to a person not doing time; however, to a two-year-old not seeing his mother and vice versa it seems like an eternity. The loneliness an inmate has to put out of her mind in order to cope with the system is truly cruel and unusual punishment. I can recall one of the guards who works here saying to us, "Well, you put yourself here." But to the inmate that may not have committed the crime, what is the answer to that? There is none—there is no answer. Many times the only way we are to cope with the treatment is to recall the prisoners in the Bible and the way that Jesus himself suffered for the word of the Lord. The guards call it being phony—seeking the word of the Lord.

According to Gloria, she was imprisoned for a more important rea-son than punishment by the state of Montana. While imprisoned, she focused on her spiritual growth and helped form the Sisterhood of Seven Breaths, comprised of Native women prisoners. The only support Gloria had inside prison was other Native prisoners, who organized the Sisterhood to promote Native culture and provide unity. Nevertheless, the practicing of Native culture was not encouraged in prison. Gloria imagines that if they had been able to practice their culture, even in some small way such as a drumming and singing group, they would have been empowered. Gloria claims that by practicing Native culture, they would have been living rather than merely surviving.

> They gave us all these programs and all these little loopholes—not loopholes, but rings of *fire*—that we had to jump through. You see, when we began to *live* inside the prison, then they saw that as a power play and an administrative problem. When we had the Sister-hood inside prison, we took care of one another. The Sisterhood was our extended family. If one of us was out of cigarettes then the other one gave, which was a Class II write-up! So we were still doing "illegal" things but there was no one there to rat on us or snitch us off. There was a camaraderie in the Sisterhood that says,

"We're here for one another and each of us can do our part to build this and make it strong." Probably the strongest it ever was, was when we had two medicine women come from Browning.

Gloria's experience with the Sisterhood was short-lived because she spent the majority of her time in maximum security. In this unit she was not allowed, by prison rules, to participate.

One factor that continues to anger Gloria is the apparent prison ban on Native religion. While imprisoned, Gloria contacted the Native American Prisoners Rehabilitation Research Project regarding the denial of religious freedom at the prison. The director of the research project sent a letter to the prison stating: "It appears that the women are not being permitted to adequately practice their traditional spiritual beliefs, such as by being able to participate in sweat lodge ceremonies, which is an integral aspect of their religion." According to Gloria, those women who struggled for the right to practice their religion were subsequently punished by prison staff.

Imprisoned Landless Native women have a particularly difficult time because of their lack of tribal social services. According to Gloria:

I think if Gabe was taken from us, and he wouldn't even be considered for placement in any Indian home because we have no landbase. Who could we call? A tribal chairman whose office isn't even manned? The same with [another Landless prisoner's] children. Who could we have called about that? She was not even aware of the Indian Child Welfare Act until she got to prison, and then it was too late because the state already had their clutches on her children.

Remembering another imprisoned Landless Native, who was raised in abject poverty and treated by prison staff, according to Gloria, as a "dumb Indian," she informs:

She would wax the halls for an extra cigarette because she had no money. There was no one at home helping her, so in order for her to get her cigarettes or any commissary at all, she would do these extra jobs. We weren't allowed to share things—that was a writeup. To do things that were traditional in the Indian way. If you had something, you shared something; that was traditional. There were rules against that. You could get written up; you could get your commissary pulled. You could get your cigarettes pulled. That could be a Class II write-up and could stop you from going to the parole board. Because you *shared* a pack of cigarettes with someone? It doesn't make any sense!

When I first met Gloria, she had been in the maximum-security building for five months. Once in maximum security, she was denied counseling and the practice of her religion. Gloria insists that she was singled out by prison staff primarily because she continually pushed for the freedom to practice Native religion and for the improvement of conditions for other prisoners. From the onset of her imprisonment, she decided that no person or event would break her spirit.

Nevertheless, everything fell apart for Gloria on 29 September 1990—three months from the day she was sentenced to prison. One seemingly uneventful evening, prison staff conducted a random cell shakedown. The cell selected was number 211—the cell Gloria shared with another prisoner. According to one guard's report, on Gloria's side of the cell they found various items considered contraband: a pair of toenail clippers, sewing needles, a seam-ripper, cutoff jeans belonging to another prisoner, and an electrical outlet device not on the inventory list. The report further stated that during the search Gloria cursed the guards and walked away, although she was ordered to stay in the hall.

Another guard's search of the cell produced a pair of scissors "hidden" between the mattress cover and mattress pad, a metal lighter holder, a tube of medication prescribed to another prisoner, a broken light fixture, and a bottle of fingernail polish remover. Additionally, a large hole in the wall was discovered, and inside the hole the guard found a double-sided razor blade. In the closet the guard found a compact mirror, a pair of jeans owned by another prisoner, and a pair of slippers not on Gloria's clothing inventory. The guard wanted to inspect Gloria's sweetgrass, juniper, and sage and asked her to open the boxes they were in. The guard alleged in the report that at that point Gloria "stomped down the hallway yelling in a disrespectful manner, 'let the red road get her,' pertaining to spiritual vengeance." As a result of the shakedown, Gloria was cuffed at the waist and ankles, transferred to the maximum-security unit, and placed in temporary lockup because of the "dangerous contraband" found in her cell. Upon her arrival to maximum security, she was strip-searched.

The electrical outlet device, seam-ripper, scissors, and needles had all been approved by the prison for her crafts. Gloria accounted for these approved items, now listed as contraband, with memos from prison staff. She used the scissors daily; thus, she remarks, she would not hide them. On the day of the shakedown, she had been working with the craft materials on her bed; she speculates that when the guards stripped her bed, the scissors may have become lodged between the mattress and box spring. However, she really believes the guards made up the story regarding the scissors' being hidden. Additionally, why would she conceal the scissors and not the seam-ripper if her intent was to hide dangerous contraband?

Gloria maintains that the light fixture was broken when she moved into the cell and wonders, not wishing any misfortune or placing blame, why her cellmate was not also charged with this violation. She does not know where some of the items came from, was "guilty" of the borrowed jeans, and maintains she had permission from the prison to have the slippers and lighter holder. Gloria bought the fingernail polish remover at the canteen (approved by the prison). The toenail clippers, cutoffs, and acne medication belonged to a prisoner recently released, who had been incarcerated in Gloria's cell and had apparently left the items behind. Gloria admits to no knowledge of the razor but had noticed the hole in the wall when she was transferred to the cell.

When the guards were investigating her cell, they came across a picture of her young son and, according to Gloria, made rude comments about his appearance. Gloria reports that she left the cell at this time because she was afraid she would respond to the guards in a way she might later regret. When she returned, the guard asked her if it was appropriate for her to touch Gloria's sweetgrass, sage, and juniper. According to Gloria, she responded, "You can touch anything in there; it's not like the wrath of the Red Road will come down on you."

Six complaints were lodged by the prison against Gloria: conduct which disrupts, threatening another person with bodily harm, insolence, destruction of state property (the broken light fixture), dangerous contraband, and substance abuse (tube of acne medication). All offenses were the most serious of violations—Class II write-ups.

On 1 October 1990 Gloria, as instructed by one of the guards, sent kites (memos) from lockup to other prisoners requesting that they make statements on her behalf in regard to the shakedown. None of the prisoners, however, received her correspondence. Gloria was told by another member of the prison staff that she had not followed the correct procedure. A memo from the warden states that Gloria's Class II disciplinary hearing, originally set for 3 October, was rescheduled. Although she remained in the maximum-security building, she was released from lockup and classified as a Medium I status pending the outcome of the charges. Gloria is unsure why she was released from lockup but speculates that one particular guard was influential in her release.

At the disciplinary hearing, Gloria was found guilty and sentenced to thirty days in maximum security because her "behavior during the entire shakedown was deplorable, disruptive and disrespectful," and because "concealing a pair of scissors is a threat to security." The scissors were, according to the inmate policy manual, allowable for arts and crafts items. Additionally, a hobby permit issued by the prison to Gloria for the construction of dolls stated that all doll materials, which included scissors, were approved by prison staff. Gloria's appeal of this decision was denied, with the following explanation: "It is not the role of an appeal to re-hear the case. You had an opportunity to state your position to the Hearing Officer. You are also well beyond the 24 hour period for submitting an appeal."

While in lockup, Gloria did not receive soap or a towel and was not permitted to shower for four days. She was without writing materials for three days. She finally received paper and a felt-tip pen; however, prior to this, she wrote all correspondence with the metal part of her bra strap on carbon-papered forms. Gloria determined that this withholding of supplies was a violation of her rights, as was the fact that no witnesses were called on her behalf during her hearings. She also had no access to the policy manual or legal library and consequently was unprepared for her hearings. Gloria received a letter from the Department of Institutions stating that they would not hear her request for an appeal until she exhausted all remedies offered at the prison.

Without a hearing, on 25 October, Gloria's status was dropped from a Medium II to a Medium I and she was reclassified from maximum to Close custody as a result of the five Class II write-ups. The lowering of classification level meant that Gloria would be denied privileges, including an overnight visit with her one-year-old son that she had worked four months to accomplish. A memo to Gloria from the classification committee stated that she would serve thirty days in maximum security as her punishment for the write-ups and that her custody level would not be reviewed for six months. Gloria submitted an appeal of her classification on the grounds that her rights had been violated. Gloria also noted in her appeal that she was told by prison staff that she was now reclassified as Close custody, not a Medium I, and would be in maximum security for six months. A memo from prison staff outlined the rationale for her reclassification as Close: Gloria's disciplinary history justified Close custody, and her rights were not violated because she had "been given full access to both the Disciplinary and Classification process."

Gloria again wrote to the Department of Institutions regarding the grievance about her reclassification. In this letter she clearly stated that she could not have possibly written an appeal within the twenty-four-hour limit because she was in lockup and not given any writing materials with which to write the grievance. Gloria reiterated that her due process rights had been violated and reminded the Corrections administrator that she had received no write-ups prior to this incident.

Seeking help from outside agencies, Gloria sent a letter to the Native American Prisoners Rehabilitation Research Project regarding her lengthy time in lockup and the racialized tactics employed by the prison. In the letter Gloria outlined her issues: She was held in disciplinary lockup for five days without a hearing, and for three or four of those days she was not allowed to shower or change clothes; without a hearing, her classification level was dropped; she was written up for various contraband items that were in her cell when she moved in; she was written up for a broken light fixture that was already broken when she moved into the cell. In addition, she expressed her opinion that she was singled out for punishment because she continually pursued culture-specific programming at the prison. She also pointed out that the offense with which she was charged would now bar her from applying for a supervised release program; that her reclassification had lost her a visit with her one-year-old baby; and that women in lockup were denied access to the legal library.

The director of the Native American Prisoners Rehabilitation Research Project, addressing Gloria's issues as well as those of other imprisoned women, sent a letter to the warden on 31 October 1991:

> I would very much appreciate it if you would personally look into Ms. Wells' allegations/complaints and to remedy the situation appropriately and with all fairness. The punitive sanctions she is receiving (and has already received) for charges which she seems

not to have been accorded procedural due process for, are exceedingly harsh.

While in maximum security, Gloria sent prison staff numerous memos asking permission to engage in various activities. One notice to prison staff requested permission to attend church services and the Native American spirituality group on Sundays, to secure her sweetgrass, and to attend her regularly scheduled assertiveness training. She never received a reply. A week later, Gloria kited prison staff and requested to see the Native American counselor. Receiving no reply, she sent another request the next week. Again, there was no response, so she issued another request—again, it was not answered.

Gloria sent correspondence to prison staff requesting, for the third time, permission to attend the Native American Spirituality group on Sundays and to have her sweetgrass, juniper, and sage returned. The prison's response read simply, "You are not allowed to attend functions in the other building." Gloria issued a fourth request, this one regarding her confiscated beading needles. The response from prison staff read, "It is unfortunate that this is the fourth kite but what is more unfortunate is that the great majority of my time is spent dealing with games. I will get these as soon as possible."

Gloria received another letter from the Department of Institutions stating that she could not appeal the prison's reclassification decision to their office; her only recourse was to appeal to the District Court. On 6 February 1991 Gloria received another memo from the classification committee that affirmed her status as Close custody. The committee justified their decision as follows: Gloria's being found guilty on 11 October 1990 of five Class II write-ups, the seriousness of the write-ups, and numerous reports about her "disruptive behavior." Effective 29 March 1991, she was reclassified from Close to Medium I because she remained "disciplinary free." As part of the reclassification, Gloria was directed by prison staff to attend "anger management" classes.

GETTING OUT

Gloria was released from prison on 15 November 1991. Her husband and youngest son, then two years old, picked her up at the WCC.

To be able to walk from that place was the best feeling in the world. Some inmates had to go to pre-release before they could return home. I guess in a way I had been to pre-release—I had graduated from the Lighthouse program, which is the toughest drug treatment program in the state. I felt very free to be driving down the Interstate with my family. It seemed as though I had been waiting for this day forever and it finally came. I was amazed, scared, insecure— after all, just that morning I was an inmate. It all seemed so unreal to just get into the car and drive away. The first thing we did was stop and have dinner.

When I got home, I had a bunch of hoops they wanted me to jump through: AA meetings twice a week, counseling once a week, and to see my probation officer once a week. I lived thirty-five miles from Bozeman and after not driving for a year and a half, in the winter month of November, the roads were pretty scary.

The first thing I noticed was the price of groceries. They had gone up so much! I recall telling a friend of mine, "Do you know cereal is almost four dollars a box?"

I felt everyone knew I just got out of prison. I felt very much ashamed.

Despite the available programming at the prison, Gloria concludes that what is offered is not adequate preparation for survival on the outside. She notes that she found her "real" counselors, her probation officer and a Native counselor from Montana State University, after her release from prison. Gloria believes the counseling offered at the prison is inadequate, due primarily to the hiring of staff that, in her opinion, is unqualified.

Once a prisoner is released and on probation, her relationship with her probation officer is vital to the transition from prison to the outside world. Gloria highly praises her probation officer because he allowed her to reacquaint herself with her family before pushing her into AA meetings; thus, she survived the initial shock of being out of prison. According to Gloria, Bozeman offers the best probation officers in the state because they treat ex-prisoners "like human beings, with respect."

Ultimately, Gloria felt alone when she was released from prison. She wishes there had been a support system available to facilitate the adjustment. Something Gloria would like to see is a support group to help newly released prisoners reintegrate into their communities. While she views this as possible for tribes with a landbase and social services, she wonders if it is feasible for the Little Shell: "We don't have that to fall back on now. So that's something that I couldn't even perceive asking for. For a welcoming—a tribal welcoming back."

A factor that enables Gloria to survive is recognizing the hypocrisy of the criminal justice system: "They can continue to fill you full of bullshit that you're supposed to believe, and if you believe it, you're going to fail." Gloria intensely dislikes ex-prisoners who proclaim, "Prison straightened me out." One of the conclusions she reached while imprisoned is that prison is not the answer for most female offenders. A strong proponent of alternatives to prison, she reasons that because most of the women imprisoned in Montana are there for nonviolent crimes, they would be better served by such programs as community service work, intensive in- and outpatient treatment programs, in-house arrest, and supervised release. These programs would eliminate overcrowding at prisons and, most important to Gloria, decrease the possibility of children being placed in the foster-care system.

CHARGES OVERTURNED: YET ANOTHER MURKY APPEAL

When Gloria was initially sentenced to prison she began an appeal of her conviction for a crime she did not commit. This process was occurring simultaneously with the appeal of the write-ups she incurred while in prison. One of the stumbling blocks, not only for Gloria but for other imprisoned women, was the minimal access to legal resources. The inadequacy of the law library at the prison, the minimal contact with the Montana Defender Project, and the stance of attorneys who do not encourage appeals, in combination with the lack of access to a copy machine or carbon paper (some prisoners handwrote four letters of appeal), produces an environment that makes it exceedingly difficult to file an appeal. Women wishing to appeal their convictions need to be—like Gloria—absolutely persistent in their efforts.

Gloria's appeal is a classic example of the many barriers imprisoned women face. One major stumbling block is securing an attorney who will argue your case. People without financial resources encounter a multitude of problems, including the necessity of relying on court-appointed attorneys. Another obstacle is the racism operating in the criminal justice system.

Gloria's appeal process is tedious and perhaps difficult to follow; however, it clearly illustrates the typical process that low-income Native American prisoners experience. The easiest way to present Gloria's case, and subsequent appeal, is to outline the events chronologically. She was charged with felony theft (a woman's ring) and misdemeanor theft (blank checks from the complaining witness). On 9 May 1990 Gloria's non-jury trial was held in Fergus County District Court. Shortly thereafter, she received a letter from her court-appointed attorney, A.B., and a copy of the Pre-Sentence Investigation Report that recommended she serve "an appropriate term" in prison. A.B.'s letter to Gloria suggested that no errors were made by the judge or county attorney during the trial; hence, there was no basis for an appeal. On 29 June 1990 Gloria was sentenced to five years in prison. A letter from her attorney dated 19 July informed her that if she continued to pursue an appeal, he would withdraw from the case. He wrote:

> Contrary to what you said in your letter, a Defendant does not have a constitutional right to appeal from a conviction in a criminal case. Generally, the decision as to whether or not to appeal is left to the discretion of the defense attorney, especially if the defense attorney has been court-appointed. As I have told you on the last two occasions, I feel an appeal would be frivolous in that there are absolutely no grounds to support an appeal. No errors of law were made in the Court that might lead the Supreme Court to reverse the decision, and if there were errors of the law that would lead to a reversal, the Supreme Court would do nothing more than send it back for a new trial. The decision that faced the Judge was whether to believe your testimony or the complaining witness. Obviously, he believed [the complaining witness's] testimony, and found your guilt beyond a reasonable doubt. Such a situation does not provide grounds for an appeal. If you do not accept my opinion and still want to appeal I will formally withdraw from the case, stating in my petition for withdrawal the reasons why the case should not be appealed. . . .

Gloria was perplexed; this was her attorney—the one whose job was to defend her, not accuse her of guilt. She received another letter from her attorney, A.B., estimating the cost of the trial transcript at approximately one thousand dollars and the cost of the transcript from her sentence hearing at around two hundred dollars. A.B. added, "Although the county will cover the costs of that transcript [of the sentence hearing], I must caution you in regards to the filing of a notice for hearing for sentence review." Because the Sentence Review Board had the authority to increase her sentence, there was, according to A.B., danger that the Board

> might feel that [Judge R.] was too lenient and feel that something more than 5 years is appropriate. I talked to [Judge R.] after the sentencing and he admitted that he had planned to give you a sentence of ten years. . . . The sentencing was on June 29, 1990, and therefore the 60 days for the time for appeal will expire on August 28, 1990. But again, an appeal will be hopeless as well as frivolous.

Gloria requested from Judge R. a new court-appointed attorney because A.B. would not represent her in an appeal. She had already filed for court trial transcripts, filing *forma pauperis*, and additionally asked to know when she would receive them. In the same month, Gloria submitted a handwritten request for extension to file briefs, outlined a foundation for appeal, and requested a mistrial due to inadequate counsel. Gloria inquired about a change of venue because of her inability to receive a fair trial after an article about her case was printed in a local newspaper. The article published prior to her trial, in which Judge R. was interviewed, reported the expense of Gloria's case for Fergus County and especially emphasized that she used a court-appointed attorney.

On 3 December, an order from Judge R. stated that Gloria's motion for a new court-appointed attorney was granted. A.B. was replaced with C.D. as her appeal attorney. C.D. happened to be the same attorney who was the county attorney when Gloria was sentenced to reform school—the one she raged at regarding the mishandling of her molestation. On 24 January 1991 Gloria sent a letter to C.D. asking what his position was regarding her appeal: "I am asking you to be honest enough to me to either work on the case or remove yourself from it so the Judge can re-appoint another appeal attorney." One week later, C.D. filed a Motion for Substitution of Attorney because he and Gloria were unable to agree on the case. Correspondence from C.D. to Gloria, dated 6 February, revealed that the "judge declined the [30 January]

motion and instructed me to continue at this time. . . . Please do not
make further telephone calls to the office unless there is an emergency."
Gloria received word from Chief Justice Turnage that an Order for Extension of Time to File Brief was established: Gloria was granted until
25 April 1991 to file her appeal.

Gloria sent Chief Justice Turnage a letter on 1 April inquiring about
a change of venue, which she had already requested through her attorney. Although C.D. had been appointed as her attorney, she had had no
contact with him for five months. Gloria desperately wanted to know
from C.D. the date to file her appeal. She heard nothing from him, and
Judge R. had not responded either; therefore, Gloria concluded that she
was denied proper representation.

Gloria then wrote Judge R. asking why her attorney was not allowed
to withdraw. A motion was finally issued by Judge R. to withdraw C.D.
as her attorney, although he said:

> There has been a history of Defendant's dissatisfaction with her
> court-appointed counsel herein and it is not the Court's obligation
> to permit her to shop around for a lawyer who pleases her. But in
> the interest of untangling the web woven in this case the Court is
> going to make this effort to get to the meat, the substantive justice
> of this case.

Although Judge R. had previously refused to allow C.D. to withdraw
as Gloria's attorney, C.D. was removed on 10 April 1991 and replaced
by E.F. The court minutes disclosed that the newly appointed attorney
(E.F.) had been discharged on 23 April and replaced with yet another
attorney, G.H. Not receiving any correspondence from the last court-
appointed attorney, Gloria hung in limbo. On 24 April, Chief Justice
Turnage informed Gloria that E.F. was her new attorney, in conflict
with the court decision recorded on 23 April. The chief justice commented that she needed to communicate with him so he could file a motion for an extension. This would be quite an accomplishment for someone who was not adequately informed.

In sum, Gloria had great difficulty obtaining legal counsel for her appeal. Evidently, the attorneys were not interested in her case. Furthermore, she had to handwrite all correspondence and steal carbon-paper
to make copies. This alone would have been a major write-up if de-

tected by prison officials. In desperation, Gloria wrote additional letters that her husband mailed. In the letters she explained the course of events over her year of incarceration. Gloria issued a form letter addressed to various attorneys and to the Native American Prisoners Rehabilitation Research Project regarding her inability to obtain due process. Continuing to seek assistance for her appeal, Gloria also wrote to the American Civil Liberties Union, but she received a letter stating that their office could not offer assistance.

An Appellant's Brief (*State of Montana v. Wells*), filed by G.H., offered the following reason for why Gloria's case should be appealed: on cross-examination, the complaining witness had admitted that she was fully aware Gloria had the ring, and that her relationship with Gloria had been friendly during this time. The appeal presented this as evidence that Gloria had permission to possess the ring, which she had never denied having. A second point was the clearly improper use of "other crimes" evidence used to destroy Gloria's character. The complaining witness had testified that Gloria was "heavy into drugs." Additionally, the complaining witness had said Gloria was "doing a lot of criminal things I wouldn't do. . . . there was a time when she stuck a gun in my face." According to the brief, Gloria had purposefully been imaged as a "bad" person, and those so imaged are generally viewed to be "guiltier" than other people. The document concluded: "The evidence that Wells wrongfully came into possession of the ring is weak at best; yet, [Judge R.] had no trouble finding Wells guilty *the minute the trial ended* without any time for reflection" (emphasis in original). Moreover, the attorney asserted: "This case cries out for a reversal. The barrage of inadmissible 'other crimes' evidence clearly could not help from being and was prejudicial. This is sufficient grounds for reversal of Wells' conviction."

After serving one and a half years for a crime she did not commit, on 15 November 1991 Gloria was released from prison. Nearly one month later, an appeal was submitted. On 25 February 1992 Gloria's conviction of felony theft and misdemeanor theft was reversed and the case remanded to district court. On 27 May 1992 a Motion to Dismiss With Prejudice was issued by Fergus County District Court.[2]

The time Gloria lost while imprisoned deeply affected her life and her family, bringing her much anger and frustration. She was not afforded the opportunity to bond with her baby, and she faced marital difficulties upon her release. Moreover, she confronted severe problems when she decided to start a business. One difficulty that continues is finding an attorney to represent her as she seeks compensation for false imprisonment and valuable time away from her family, especially her youngest child. In her preparations, Gloria must sift through files, provoking bad memories: "I was going through those papers and I saw where I got sentenced to prison. And I thought, do I have the strength to go through all of this again? And I thought about what it would do to my business and my family. I'm already on the edge. Is this going to shame my folks at home, again?"

Gloria does not want another innocent person to be imprisoned. Compensation, although an important factor, is not the primary issue for her. Rather, it is the principle of jailing an innocent person that is paramount. Gloria believes she was imprisoned because of a racialized justice system: "All the way through the whole thing, I was always a second-class person—through the whole trial. There was a white girl who got up and lied, and there was an Indian girl who got up there and told the truth, and they believed the white girl."

READJUSTMENT ON THE OUTSIDE

Gloria's biggest problem when she was released from prison, aside from reconciling the successful appeal of her case, was reacquainting herself with her husband and sons, particularly her youngest. She expresses: "It was very hard for me to adjust to the fact that Grady and Gabe had been together for so long without me. I felt different, like I didn't belong with them, and sometimes even now I feel like an outsider." Upon release, she frantically wanted to reacquaint herself with her family, and to do so she chose to remain fairly isolated for three months with her family, with no outside distractions such as required rehabilitative programming. Fortunately, Gloria's probation officer complied with her wishes and made few demands on her. Moreover, there were few truly rehabilitative programs offered in her community.

It was during Gloria's stay in Arizona that she became addicted to cocaine. She maintains that her drug and alcohol addiction began at age fourteen when she was incarcerated in reform school. Gloria and her husband, Grady, readily admit they are substance abusers—"cross-addictive" according to Gloria—something they are determined to overcome. She believes that because they have led drug- and alcohol-free lives for several years, they are going to make it many more years.

While she was imprisoned, Gloria was apprehensive about her husband as the primary caretaker of Gabriel; she worried that Grady would fall into old drug and alcohol habits. Gloria has immense respect for her husband, who supported her while she was incarcerated and took care of their baby—something that is unusual for men with incarcerated wives. Four years after her incarceration, Gloria's family is beginning to regain respect for her. A remaining problem, however, is that their youngest son does not recognize Gloria as a primary parent. Gloria, nevertheless, works exceedingly hard to keep her family stable.

One consequence of being imprisoned is that you cannot apply for credit cards in your name. If you are married, your spouse can apply in his or her name; however, Gloria's husband had no credit history. With no way to establish a credit history, she labored extraordinarily hard and started her business with cash. Eventually, she went to a local bank to secure a merchant's card that would enable her to accept credit cards at her store. She had lost some large sales because people typically pay for those with charge cards. The bank official noted that Gloria had no record of paying bills for the time she was incarcerated; there was a time lapse that needed an explanation. Courageously, Gloria informed the bank that she had been in prison; consequently, there was no record for the period in question. After she explained her incarceration, she added that she had won her appeal.

Gloria not only encountered racism in the criminal justice system, she now faces discrimination in the community of Bozeman. Perhaps the most damaging racialized incident occurred in the fall of 1995 when Gloria's youngest son, Gabriel, was called a "dirty fuckin' Indian" by a white neighbor. When Gloria intervened, the neighbor, an adult white woman, called her a "dirty fuckin' squaw." These racialized slurs stirred emotions from Gloria's childhood. When the event transpired, her first thoughts were about what had happened to her as a child: the taunts of "dirty Indian." She remembered that her parents did little in her defense, and it became increasingly important for her to protect her children from the same type of psychological damage she had incurred.

Gloria notified the Bozeman Police Department and was told nothing could be done because the harassing woman did not commit an illegal act. Several telephone calls to local attorneys produced the same information—the racist woman had not broken the law. The offending woman began to follow Gloria's young son, now six years old, to the bus stop on his way to school. She badgered him with statements such as "Nobody likes you" and "The other kids won't play with you today." Of course, these comments reduced the child to tears and anger. On the way home from school, Gabriel retaliated by spitting on several children after they called him vile names—names they had heard racist adults utter. These were the children of the offensive, racist woman. This woman called the local police, who promptly arrived at Gloria's house to admonish Gabriel. Gloria was incredulous: This was the same police department that had refused to come to her home when she called them about the racial slurs hurled at her and Gabriel.

Gloria's next step was to file a restraining order against the attacking woman; she just wanted her child left alone. A local judge refused to sign it. Eventually, an attorney from the local Legal Aid Office wrote a "threatening" letter to the offensive white woman, requesting that she cease her racial insults and not have contact with Gloria or Gabriel.

Certain that racial harassment was against the law in Montana, after hearing of these incidents I called several lawyers in Montana and discovered that they did not know whether racial harassment was against the law. I was stunned—these are attorneys schooled in the law; after all, it is their job. Several lawyers offered to call me back after they searched for someone who might know; however, no one returned my telephone calls. Finally, I reached an attorney who insisted that racial harassment was a legal violation in Montana. He was outraged that Gloria had not been informed of this by the local law enforcement officials and state officials she had contacted. He suggested that Gloria file a civil suit against the offending woman for disorderly conduct and child abuse, given the horrendous treatment she allegedly issued to young Gabriel, and punitive damages for distress. Not one of the attorneys initially contacted in Montana offered this information and advice, nor did the state office. Either they were ignorant of the law, or, as a more sinister interpretation would hold, local and state officials purposefully withheld the information from Gloria. According to Gloria, she was treated by everyone she contacted as a woman overreacting to a minor offense.

As Gloria searched for an attorney to handle the racist harassment, Gabriel's problems continued. As he walked to the bus stop one morning, the offending woman motioned for him to cross the street. He obeyed and ran in front of the school bus, whereupon the driver issued him a "green slip" for a behavioral violation. Gabriel's offense, dropped after Gloria intervened, was "running and playing in the street." The state office suggested that Gloria file a grievance against the managers of the trailer park for not adequately protecting her. Gloria refused because she did not view them as the wrongdoers. She now worries about filing any charges because of how it will affect her business. Meanwhile, Gabriel is in counseling for the racialized events that have plagued his young life.

Although Gloria has battled institutionalized racism, this type of discrimination—precise and direct—is the most difficult psychologically and, evidently, legally to combat. How are we to battle racism if the law against it is not known by the general public? Or worse, not enforced? Again, powerful gatekeepers of the status quo surface. The oppression is relentless; however, Gloria refuses to submit and continues to defend herself and her children.

LIVING, NOT SURVIVING

Gloria says that she originally encountered the justice system, as a youth and later as an adult, because of what she terms her "renegade spirit." It is this same rebel spirit that has enabled Gloria to endure. She has survived a dysfunctional family, substance abuse, racism, sexism, and prisonization because "I guess I finally realized that I was the only one who could send my spirit away, and I was the only one who could call it back. Nobody in any position could ever take that spirit. Nobody ever broke my spirit."

Some people do not survive prisonization, as witnessed in previous chapters. Gloria makes a distinction between the harsh reality of survivance and the luxury of living. She suggests that embracing Native culture will give those recently released from prison a better chance of surviving on the outside. It was Native culture that enabled Gloria to endure prisonization and it is her culture that allows her to live, rather than merely survive, today. Gloria's spiritual journey and healing have started, and today she is a Sun Dancer and Pipe Carrier. She is on a virtuous path and cannot return to a life characteristic of a substance abuser.

COMPLEX SYSTEMS OF DOMINATION

Two notable themes emerge from Gloria's narrative: the reality of closed institutions—prison and Euro-American jurisprudence—and the notion of social control. These themes illuminate the interrelationship of race, gender, and class that form the experiences of Native American women. Gloria's experiences are gendered and racialized. We need to be cognizant of the various ways in which Native women are imprisoned and violated by social institutions. We must acknowledge the inherent prohibitive conditions in Euro-American social institutions, whether prisons, boarding schools, reform schools, Euro-American jurisprudence, financial institutions, or the family. Native women live precariously: Gloria served time in reform school and prison for crimes she did not commit. Oppression, as witnessed by Gloria's narrative and the stories of other imprisoned women, is multifaceted and multilayered. Moreover, not only is it complex, it is unyielding.

Native women, because of interrelated systems of domination, are vulnerable to various types of violence. For instance, sexual abuse is a prominent experience in the lives of many Native women. Acts of violence against Native women are manifestations of a racialized patriarchy and have the power to eliminate the desire for survival. Many Native women do not survive the violence; some go insane and others exist in a depression they cannot, or dare not, name. Native women, therefore, need superior strength to combat colonization and prisonization. One way Native women can resist oppression and facilitate social change is by defining their own realities and telling their stories. Jeopardizing relationships with her family, the success of her business, and her standing in the community, Gloria took an enormous personal risk in disclosing her story.

Today, Gloria is an internationally recognized artist. She has received high honors for the traditional Native clothing she creates and has gained the respect of many people across the United States. Gloria uses her creative anger to engage in acts of resistance and survivance. Although life has not always been kind to Gloria, she learned years ago to fight oppression. To Gloria, silence is dangerous. Gloria speaks out when she witnesses oppression, although she has received few rewards for her resistance. Women such as Gloria remind me of the late Audre Lorde's wise words: "America's measurement of me has lain like a barrier across the realization of my own powers. It was a barrier which I had to examine and dismantle, piece by painful piece, in order to use my energies fully and creatively" (1984, 147).

Gloria has fought insidious discrimination on many different levels and survived. She knows the anger that lies inside her, and she knows that no matter the odds, she was true to herself. Gloria finds strength in her soul, her spirit, her culture. Of great importance is Gloria's Anishi-nabé name, Ka min di tat, which was her grandmother's name. Literally translated, Ka min di tat means "Life's Hard She Said." Gloria has lived the life of her real, true name—Life's Hard She Said.

EPILOGUE

*Native survival was and remains a contest over life,
humanity, land, systems of knowledge, memory, and
representations. Native memories and representations are
persistently pushed aside to make way for constructed
Western myths and their representations of Native people.*

THERESA HARLAN [SANTO DOMINGO,
LAGUNA, JEMEZ PUEBLOS], "CREATING
A VISUAL HISTORY"

History reveals the process of how the "savage" was invented. Racial oppression, then as now, is not a discrete phenomenon, independent of
larger political and economic tendencies. Twentieth-century laws and
their enforcement can readily be seen as instruments for creating and
maintaining social and economic stratification created centuries before.
Indeed, past deeds illuminate present treacheries. The colonization of
Native people informs their current socioeconomic position. History
tells us that Native people were not lawless "savages" but rather were
experiencing a clash of conflicting worlds where Native legal systems
collided with Euro-American law.

As Native people, we cannot divorce ourselves from Euro-American
society. Yet, as Lloyd Delany warned (1970), to define who we are as
people of color, we must not simply imitate the sick model of Euro-
American society. In fact, assimilation to the sick model presented is
not truly available to people of color. It has been proven that there is
no access for certain subgroups to society's opportunity structure. Also,
one must question whether indigenous people, currently involved in decolonizing efforts, want to assimilate.

Early on, Albert Memmi (1965) and Frantz Fanon (1963, 1965) wrote
about the effects of colonialism and the significance of decolonizing.

Understanding the importance of not reproducing a diseased society, Fanon expressed:

> [L]et us not pay tribute to Europe by creating states, institutions, and societies which draw their inspiration from her. Humanity is waiting for something from us other than such an imitation, which would be almost an obscene caricature. If we want to turn Africa into a new Europe, and America into a new Europe, then let us leave the destiny of our countries to Europeans. They will know how to do it better than the most gifted among us. But if we want humanity to advance a step further, if we want to bring it up to a different level than that which Europe has shown it, then we must invent and we must make discoveries. (1963, 315)

It is essential to address the intricate factors, within the context of limited self-government and sovereignty, that contribute to social ills found in Native communities. While nothing is ever monocausal, the equation of Native criminality and deviance with the loss of sovereignty is convincing. Neocolonial racism may well account for the overrepresentation of Native people in jails and prisons, and decolonizing efforts may alleviate some social problems found in contemporary Native communities. In fact, this premise has been effectively put into practice. The Alkali Lake Band of Salish, on a reserve in Alberta, Canada, saw sobriety grow from less than 5 percent to 98 percent today. The Salish tell other Natives how they regained control over their land and their destiny by ousting white traders, setting up Native commerce, reinstating a traditionally designed council, and gathering for communal prayer. They gained control and sovereignty and they became well; criminal/deviant activity decreased (Chelsea 1988).

One way tribes can exercise their sovereign rights, and thereby regain control over their communities and nations, is to design and direct rehabilitative programs. Although the Swift Bird Project, a pilot correctional program started on the Cheyenne River Sioux Reservation in 1979, was unsuccessful for a variety of reasons, indigenous people must seriously consider such projects. It is encouraging that in Canada, the Okimaw Ohci (Thunder Hills) Healing Lodge, specifically designed for Native Canadian female offenders, opened in August of 1995 (Keane 1995). The concept underlying this alternative prison is true rehabilitation and healing through culture-specific programming. The Healing

Lodge encourages an environment conducive to the empowerment of Native women—one that is free of racism, sexism, and classism. All people, regardless of race/ethnicity, would greatly profit from a similar program.

The criminal justice system in the United States needs a new approach. Of all the countries in the world, we are the leader in incarceration rates—higher than South Africa and the former Soviet Union, countries that are perceived as oppressive to their own citizens. Euro-America builds bigger and better prisons and fills them up with "criminals." Society would profit if the criminal justice system employed restorative justice and readily used alternatives to incarceration such as community service, house arrest, electronic surveillance, and treatment programs. The incarceration of nonviolent offenders is self-defeating, and the cases of women who kill their abusers demand the acknowledgment that we live in a patriarchal society. Before we can move forward as a society, we need to recognize that issues of race/ethnicity, gender, and class are inexplicably bound together. Additionally, it is important to recognize the impact of violence, no matter the form, on the seemingly eventual deviant status accorded those defined as Other. Because the contextualizing of the criminalization process is central to the understanding of deviance, the personal lives of those imprisoned must be perceived within the gendered and racialized nature of their lives.

Most prisons in the United States are, by design, what a former prisoner termed "the devil's house." Social environments of this sort can only produce dehumanizing conditions. However, we must be careful not to condemn individuals working within the criminal justice system for these conditions. A management consultant suggested that individual blame implies incompetence, which has the effect of dehumanizing criminal justice system staff in the same way that prisoners are dehumanized. What may readily be seen as ineptitude may be deficient training and instruction. I agree that we should avoid the adoption of a "blame mentality" (Eric Sandberg, pers. comm. 1997). As well, I propose that if our goal is to improve the criminal justice system, it is imperative to examine institutional factors regarding criminalization of individuals *and* the apparent incompetence of individual prison staff members. At the same time, we must remember that male employees of the criminal justice system who commit violence against female prisoners will continue this behavior regardless of the institution. This issue, of course, speaks to the structural issue of patriarchy and has little to do with individual incompetence.

The purpose of this book is not to absolve all Native people and women of their responsibility for criminal behaviors. Some people do commit crimes and should face consequences. Because many people are damaged, and thus criminal, one goal of the criminal justice system is to protect law-abiding citizens by imprisoning offenders. Likewise, it is becoming increasingly more difficult for offenders to obtain parole; again, this is done to protect society. It is imperative, however, that the prison system be redesigned with regeneration as the focus. All societies require social control; what we must rethink is how this notion is implemented.

All people in Euro-America, regardless of race/ethnicity, need healing. The criminal justice system would greatly benefit from the philosophy of traditional Native societies. As expressed by Chief Justice Robert Yazzie:

> Imagine a system of law that permits anyone to say anything they like during the course of a dispute, and no authority figure has to determine what is "true." Think of a system with an end goal of restorative justice, which uses equality and the full participation of disputants in a final decision. If we say of law that "life comes from it," then where there is hurt, there must be healing. (1994, 29)

APPENDIX

VIOLATIONS

AND DESCRIPTIONS

The Women's Correctional Center divides violations into two categories: Class II and Class III. Violations marked with an asterisk (*) are mandatory "temporary lockup" charges. The rules and regulations manual states that the behaviors described are simply examples. The manual further states, "other actions that fit the violation definitions are also misconduct even though they are not mentioned in the right-hand column" (i.e., the column that describes the behavior).

The following Class II infractions are considered the most serious forms of misconduct.

- Homicide*: causing death of another person

- Assault*: attacking another person, or interference with an employee

- Fighting with Another Person*: fights between prisoners

- Threatening Another Person with Bodily Harm*: threats of sexual assault made by one prisoner to another prisoner; writing threatening letters to another person

- Felony: aggravated assault

- Sexual Assault*: rape; touching sexual areas without consent; kissing and embracing another person without consent

- Escape, Attempt to Escape*: leaving prison grounds

- Disobeying a Direct Order*: refusal to submit to a shakedown; refusal to go to lockup when ordered; refusal to give a urine sample when requested

- Insolence: cursing; written or verbal abuse of an employee; abusive gesture directed at an employee

- Counterfeiting, Forgery: falsifying furlough or parole papers

- Rioting*: encouraging or participating in a group demonstration

- Possession of Dangerous Contraband*: gasoline, sulfuric acid, lye, prison-made knives, pipe bombs

- Substance Abuse: possession and/or selling controlled medications or narcotic paraphernalia

- Setting a Fire*: setting books, blankets, or mattress on fire

- Possession of Money: any cash over two dollars

- Destruction of State Property: tampering with any security or locking device; breaking windows; destroying blankets or mattresses

- Unauthorized Area: prisoners in day-room when on restriction or having their cells locked without permission; a prisoner in another prisoner's cell after hours; missing a work assignment without permission

- Fraudulent Claims for Prison Programs: providing false information to receive indigent status

- Theft or Possession of Stolen Property: possession of a staff member's personal items; possession of any item reported stolen; unauthorized possession of state materials valued over five dollars

- Bribery of an Employee: giving or offering to give hobby items to an employee

- Gambling, Possession of Gambling Paraphernalia: possession of dice, betting slips, or lottery materials

- Interference with Due-Process Hearings: intimidating an informant or witness; tampering with evidence; interfering with an employee in the process of writing a conduct report; making a false statement of misconduct against another prisoner or staff

- Sexual Misconduct: excessive kissing/hugging; unauthorized touching of other prisoners or visitors

- Extortion, Blackmail, Protection: insurance schemes; threatening to tell on someone

- Conduct Which Disrupts or Interferes with the Security or Orderly Operation of the Institution: missing count; interfering with a shakedown; disrupting an employee; being late to program assignments; not returning directly from on-the-job training assignments

- Self-Destruction or Self-Mutilation: tattooing or ear-piercing; cutting self, head-banging

- Failure to Abide by Consequences or Conditions of a Class II or III Disciplinary Disposition: failure to comply with a summary action (e.g., being in the dayroom when on restriction or without permission).

The following Class III violations are considered minor infractions.

- Providing a False Statement: giving a false name, number, or cell assignment

- Health, Safety, or Fire Hazard: dirty cell; lack of personal hygiene; smoking in an unauthorized area; excessive accumulation of personal property

- Possession of Cash: any money over one dollar

- Contraband: unauthorized items; anything with someone else's number or name on it

- Destruction or Misuse of State Property: any destruction, removal, alteration, tampering, or other misuse of state property valued at less than five dollars

- Unauthorized Communication: passing property on a visit; communication with a visitor through any channel other than the visiting room; unauthorized use of the telephone

- Unexcused Absence or Late for Scheduled Work or Program Assignments: missing or being late for work or programs without permission

- Horseplay: any physical contact between two or more prisoners done in a "prankish or playful manner"; towel-snapping, or attempted physical wrestling

- Unauthorized Area: being present in an unauthorized area (lesser charge of Class II violation)

- Conduct with a Visitor: failure to follow visiting-room rules

- Violation of Posted Rules or Institutional Policy: violation of posted rules in confinement unit or work area

- Loan-Sharking: loaning of property or anything of value for profit or increased return

- Conduct Which Disrupts or Interferes with the Security or Orderly Operation of the Institution: purposefully engaging in acts that disrupt institutional security or routine (lesser charge of Class II violation)

- Obstructing, Altering, or Darkening of Light Fixtures or Bulbs: covering light bulbs; obstructing view from the windows or doors

- Failure to Comply with Medical Orders: refusal to take prescribed medication or attempting to hide medications.

NOTES

INTRODUCTION

1. *Race* is generally used in the literature to refer to physical, social, political, and cultural characteristics. I use *race/ethnicity* to emphasize worldview and issues of sovereignty (nationhood), and as a reminder that race/ethnicity is important in the experiences of white people as well as for people of color. For an analysis of the importance of race/ethnicity in the lives of white people see *White Women, Race Matters* (1993) by Ruth Frankenberg. For an examination of the increasing significance and complexity of racism see *Living with Racism* (1994) by Joe Feagin and Melvin Sikes, and the video *The Color of Fear* (1995), directed by Lee Mun Wah.

2. For a detailed account of the methodology of this study, see my dissertation (Ross 1992) and my essay "Personalizing Methodology: Narratives of Imprisoned Native Women," to appear in a book edited by Ines Hernandez-Avila, *On Our Own Terms: Critical/Creative Representations by Native American Women* (forthcoming).

3. In Montana, Native Americans generally fall into one of three categories: reservation, off-reservation, and nonreservation. Reservation Natives are enrolled in federally recognized tribes and maintain a residence on an Indian reservation. Off-reservation Natives are enrolled in federally recognized tribes but live off their respective reservations. They are generally entitled to full tribal benefits (such as education, health, social services) and access to the tribal court system. Nonreservation status refers to those who are enrolled in tribes that do not have a landbase and are not federally recognized. Although there may be an official tribal government, these tribes generally do not offer specific services to tribal members. For example, nonreservation tribes in Montana have no social service programs or tribal courts. Nonreservation Natives in Montana are Cree, Little Shell Chippewa (Anishinabé), and Métis. Collectively they are known as "Landless"; this category is discussed in more detail in Chapter 2.

1. WORLDS COLLIDE

1. While it is beyond the scope of this book, the awareness of traditional legal systems provides a context and a fuller understanding of contemporary Native criminality and deviance (see Deloria and Lytle 1983, 1984; Hagan 1966; Hoebel 1954; Kawashima 1986; Llewellyn and Hoebel 1941; Reid 1970; Strickland 1975; Washburn 1971).

2. The term *Indian Country* has a legal meaning outside its familiar usage among Natives. Generally, *Indian Country* defines the geographic area where tribal or federal laws apply and state laws do not (Barsh and Henderson 1980).

3. In a recent essay, Brad Asher suggests that one cannot simply propose that American law was "relentlessly expansionist" or that the Native people "doggedly" resisted "white legal imperialism." Asher argues that in the late 1800s in Washington Territory many Native Americans found American law beneficial in intra-Native disputes. Asher notes, "American law emerges as an often inept, reactive institution forced into action against intra-Indian violence by settlers concerned with social order" (1996, 209).

4. One such judge was Northern Cheyenne, John Wooden Legs. For an emotional story, filled with much good humor, of how Judge Wooden Legs was forced to give up one of his wives, see *Native American Testimony*, edited by Peter Nabokov (1992, 229–231).

5. The original seven major crimes were murder, manslaughter, rape, assault with intent to kill, arson, burglary, and larceny. Added in 1976 were incest, kidnapping, assault with a dangerous weapon, robbery, carnal knowledge of a female under the age of sixteen, assault with the intent to commit rape, and assault resulting in serious bodily injury (Deloria and Lytle 1983).

6. As in the days of the nineteenth century polluted with colonial racism, neocolonial racism thrives in Montana in the twentieth century. One well-known and much publicized court case that clearly illustrates bigotry is that of *Windy Boy v. Big Horn County* (1986). Tainted with sentiments of yesteryear, as expressed in the Montana Enabling Act of 1889 that effectively excluded Natives from voting, the "pattern continued as white politicians prevented reservation dwellers from voting" (Svingen 1987, 275). Unraveling a complex and vicious pattern of bias, Svingen examines the history of the denial of voting rights for Native Americans in Montana. The findings paint a bleak picture: Natives were denied citizenship rights, as expressed by Euro-American law, of any kind throughout their contact with whites. The ruling in *Windy Boy v. Big Horn County* halted the most pernicious legal discrimination; however, neocolonial racism, in its many forms, prevails.

7. A larger challenge would be the comparison of PL 280 and non–PL 280 reservation arrest rates. Such a challenge will have to await the collection of relevant information, however: when I asked for data several years ago from the Bureau of Justice Statistics regarding arrest rates of Natives on both PL 280 and non–PL 280 reservations and the number of tribal police, federal and state authorities, and local police on both PL 280 and non–PL 280 reservations, the employee contacted was puzzled by my usage of "PL 280" and "non–PL 280" and referred me to the Federal Bureau of Investigation (FBI). I had already written the FBI requesting the same material; they had referred me to the BIA.

Of course, I had already asked the BIA, who responded that they could not forward the information because they did not retain it. The BIA sent statistical information on arrests, law enforcement personnel, and so forth, but it was of little use in approaching PL 280 versus non–PL 280 distinctions. For comparisons of PL 280 and non–PL 280 reservations, one must look for other sources, such as statistics kept by individual tribes or possibly by states, or take a narrower field of inquiry.

8. *Race* is the operative word here; ethnicity is generally not recognized by this law. For example, if an unenrollable Native (less than one-fourth Salish or Kootenai) who is a descendant of an enrolled parent commits a crime on a PL 280 reservation, the case may be heard in either state court or tribal court. All parties negotiate, with the authority of the state as primary, to reach an agreement as to which court will assume jurisdiction. Additionally, the U.S. Supreme Court decision in *Duro v. Reina* (1990) opined that tribes have no jurisdiction over nonmember Natives in criminal matters.

9. For information on the traditional legal system of the Cheyenne see *The Cheyenne Way: Conflict and Case Law in Primitive Jurisprudence* (1941) by attorney Karl Llewellyn and anthropologist E. Adamson Hoebel, who describe their system as possessing "juristic beauty."

2. RACIALIZING MONTANA

1. Several recent documentary films, *The Place of the Falling Waters* (1990), *Transitions: Destruction of a Mother Tongue* (1991), and *Warrior Chiefs in a New Age* (1991), provide valuable information on the colonizing of indigenous people in Montana and their subsequent resistance and adaptation efforts. Also see *White Shamans, Plastic Medicine Men* (1995) for an insight into the appropriation of Native culture by non-Natives, and *Without Reservations: Notes on Racism in Montana* (1995) on contemporary Native-white interaction in Montana. *Lighting the Seventh Fire* (1994) is an excellent resource on the Lac du Flambeau Anishinabé of Wisconsin and the racialized hatred they encounter over fishing rights. This film contains disturbing accounts of white children encouraged by their parents to spit on Native children and white adults carrying signs that read, "Spear a pregnant squaw and save a walleye" as they yelled, "Timber nigger!" to nearby Native people.

2. The pass system is curious because although there was no statute that legalized the mandate, the notion was that Natives were not citizens of the United States and therefore could not leave the reservation without permission (Cohen [1942] 1971). Reports from the Indian Commissioners (*Commissioner of Indian Affairs Annual Report, 1877–1878, 1879–1880, 1880–1881*) all discussed

the pass system, which was possibly implemented in Montana in 1877, just after the Battle of the Little Big Horn. The reports noted that passes were not handed out freely but were generally issued by Indian agents for visiting sick relatives, seeking employment, or hunting, fishing, and the gathering of berries. (The above reports specifically mention Montana.) I cannot find any information on the duration of the pass system; however, I speculate that it operated well into the 1920s in Montana.

3. Give-aways are one way members of the community redistribute wealth. Indeed, historically they were clearly a threat to capitalism and the goals of Americanizing Native people (Beck and Walters 1977).

4. For an examination of the rhetoric and reality of assimilation and an insight into policy makers' justifications, see Fred Hoxie's *A Final Promise: The Campaign to Assimilate the Indians, 1880–1920* (1984).

5. Although treaty making did not occur in the United States after 1870, a letter dated 15 October 1892, from Indian agent John Waugh to the Turtle Mountain Agency, specifically mentioned the treaty. Verne Dusenberry, an expert on the history of the Landless in Montana, wrote: "At long last, on April 21, 1904, nearly twelve years after the McCumber Commission presented its report, Congress ratified the so-called treaty" (1958, 37). I believe Dusenberry used the phrase "so-called treaty" because of the deceptive process employed by the government in procuring Native land, not because he did not view it as a treaty in the way treaties were considered prior to 1870. Therefore, the information regarding the ratification of a treaty in 1904, years after the federal government discontinued the treaty-making process, is confusing. Moreover, the invisibility of Landless Natives is illustrated by the fact that Dusenberry is one of few scholars to have published information about them.

6. According to Gloria Wells Norlin, enrolled Little Shell, there are also approximately four thousand unenrolled Landless in Montana.

7. For a thorough analysis of Native people, colonialism, and substance abuse, see *Native American Postcolonial Psychology* (1995) by Ed and Bonnie Duran and *A Poison Stronger Than Love* (1985) by Anastasia Shkilnyk.

8. For an eye-opening analysis of neocolonial racism in Montana as it relates to the Crow Nation, see *Oppressors, Power, and Tears* (1989b) and *White Oppression and Enduring Red Tears* (1990) by attorney Clarence Belue.

9. Vizenor cites Matei Calinescu's *Five Faces of Modernity*, defining kitsch as "a world of aesthetic make-believe and self-description. . . . kitsch may be viewed as a reaction against the 'terror' of change and the meaninglessness of chronological time flowing from an unreal past into an equally unreal future. . . . Kitsch appears as an easy way of 'killing time,' as a pleasurable escape from the banality of both work and leisure. The fun of kitsch is just the other side of terrible and incomprehensible boredom." To Vizenor, then, kitschymen "are the simulations of banal spiritualism, the iterance of boredom, the closure of survivance, and the resistance enterprises of consumer sun dances" (1994, 154).

10. While push-out rates are attributed to system deficiency, including racism, drop-out rates are ascribed to individuals who voluntarily withdraw from school.

11. It is encouraging to note that in 1995 the state of Montana passed a bill, after a long and arduous fight led by Vivian Brooke, that will study the compliance of public schools to the state's commitment to the preservation of Native American culture.

12. According to the *Klanwatch Intelligence Report* (1995) and journalist Dan Nailen (1996), there are a number of hate groups formally organized in Montana. Some are in the guise of "religion" and bear the name of national groups such as the Church of Jesus Christ Christian of Montana (Noxon) and the Church of the Creator (Billings). Other groups are more blatant; for example, Montana has one Ku Klux Klan organization, one neo-Nazi group, and an organization appropriately named the Golden Mean Team at Missoula. There is also an organized Montana Militia and a group called the Freemen, who believe that the constitution applies only to white people.

13. Indian gaming is government gaming and, similar to state gaming, offers economic benefits to communities. Presently, the Confederated Salish and Kootenai Tribes have not reached an agreement with the state regarding Class III gambling, which is illegal within reservation boundaries.

3. PRISONER PROFILE

1. Early prisoner descriptions are from prison records located at the Territorial Prison Museum, Deer Lodge, Montana (State of Montana, Prison Convict Register, 1878–1977), and the Montana Historical Society Archives, Helena (State of Montana, Descriptive List of the Convict).

2. The Native American population in the United States, estimated by some at approximately 10 to 12 million prior to colonization, decreased to perhaps 228,000 in 1890 due to warfare and disease (Snipp 1989). After gleaning numerous documents, including reports from Indian agents, I estimate the Native population in Montana during the early 1900s at roughly 11,000 (2.9 percent of the total state population).

3. When I questioned my uncle about this case, he said that "everyone" knew she was innocent. I assume that by "everyone" he meant Native people.

4. Jaimes and Halsey (1992) estimate that 42 percent of all Native women of childbearing age were sterilized during this time.

4. LIVES DICTATED BY VIOLENCE

1. For an analysis of violence on Indian reservations, see *Death and Violence on the Reservation* (1992) by Ronet Bachman.

2. Jerry McKinney (1995) conducted a study at the WCC one year after I gathered my data. His sample, therefore, contains many women from my study.

3. Montana's court system appears to be permissive regarding violence and sexual deviance when carried out by those in power. For example, on 24 January 1995 the *Billings Gazette* reported that a former Sanders County sheriff was charged with sexual assault, endangering the welfare of children, and two counts of official misconduct. The fifty-one-year-old man was accused of violating three teenage girls. He supplied the girls with alcohol, showed them porno films, and made sexual advances toward them. The misconduct charges for mis-use of community service surfaced when one of the girls was arrested for pos-session of alcohol, a year after the other violations occurred. She was sentenced to thirteen hours of service in the community. As luck would have it, the sheriff was to oversee her work and commanded that she, as "community service," wash his car and mow his lawn. Wisely she arrived at his house with two of her friends, and when the sheriff tried to persuade them to take their clothes off and sunbathe nude, they declined. His punishment? Removal from office and a two-year deferred sentence.

4. Although the word *syndrome* is commonly used to denote disease or disor-der, it is used here as a sane response to a sick situation.

5. In 1996, the California Supreme Court extended the usage of the battered woman's syndrome by those who claim to have killed abusive partners in self-defense (Chiang 1996). With the ruling, juries are now permitted to hear testi-mony that reveals a battered woman acted "reasonably," thus in self-defense, in the killing of an abusive partner. Subsequently, defendants can be acquitted of all charges.

6. This is not to suggest that Montana is the only patriarchal or racist state. For an excellent example of the operation and function of sexism and neocolo-nial racism in the state of California, see the documentary *Shasta Woman: The Story of Norma Jean Croy*, directed by Crystal Mason (1994). Norma Jean Croy is imprisoned for a crime she did not commit. Her brother, Hooty Croy, killed a white police officer and served twelve years in prison (eight on death row); it was eventually ruled that he killed the officer in self-defense. Although Hooty was shot twice by police officers, he received the death penalty, and Norma Jean, who was shot in the back by police officers at the scene but did not shoot any-one, received life in prison. She was denied parole numerous times and, prior to her release in February 1997, served just over eighteen years in prison for a crime neither she nor her brother committed. Unfortunately, the case of Norma Jean Croy is typical of the treatment Native Americans receive in the criminal justice system in Euro-America.

7. Arnold (1994) notes that African American women experience tremen-dous racial oppression in the educational system, thereby adding to the aliena-tion process. Boarding schools for Native children were notoriously oppressive.

Some Native women at the WCC previously attended Indian boarding schools. For an examination of the brutal experiences in Indian boarding school and how these are connected to imprisonment, see "Punishing Institutions: The Story of Catherine" (Ross, forthcoming 1997). For an excellent analysis of Native girls and boarding schools, comparing mixed-blood and full-blood and offering insight into the interrelationship of race/ethnicity, gender, and class, see *Cultivating the Rosebuds* (1993) by Devon Mihesuah.

5. EXPERIENCES OF WOMEN IN PRISON

1. The classification system changed twice during the time I conducted interviews; thus, the system was confusing. Generally, there are five basic classifications at the WCC, complete with levels within those categories. "Close status" prisoners are confined to isolation in the maximum-security unit and not allowed to work, participate in any programs, or receive visitors. "Maximum status" prisoners are confined in the maximum-security unit and not allowed to work for pay, participate in any prison programs, or receive visitors. "Medium I status" prisoners are housed in the general-population building and have access to inside prison programs, in-house employment, and some visitation privileges. These prisoners cannot leave the prison without an escort. "Medium II" prisoners, housed in the general population building, are eligible for all programming available on the prison grounds, in-house employment, and visitation privileges. They cannot leave the prison grounds for recreational or vocational activities and are supervised at all times. "Minimum status" prisoners are housed in general population, have all the privileges of "Medium status" prisoners, and additionally are permitted supervised recreational and vocational activities outside the prison.

2. The historical information on the women's prison is from a report prepared by Susan Byorth (1989), the *Montana Prison News*, various Montana newspapers, and conversations with Elaine Way, archivist at Montana's Territorial Prison Museum, Deer Lodge, Montana.

3. The new women's prison, renamed the Women's Correctional System, opened in the fall of 1994 in Billings. I was appointed to the Prison Selection Site Committee in 1991 by the governor. Billings was chosen specifically because it is not geographically isolated from Indian reservations and is racially/ethnically diverse.

4. Under the leadership of the new warden, Jo Acton, the women's prison spent $9,800 on prisoner uniforms. One reason given for this action was that "it was difficult to tell staff from prisoners" (McLaughlin 1995, B4). Scott Crichton, director of Montana's ACLU, conveyed his opinion that it would have been more beneficial to spend the money on rehabilitative programs.

5. *Kite* is prison slang referring to the memoranda prisoners send to each other or prison staff.

6. *Good-time credit* refers to a reduction in the original sentence. For example, if a woman is given a five-year sentence, she may actually serve only three years due to the good-time credit given for participation in various prison programs. This is another example of indirect discrimination, because Native women tend not to join programs they view as worthless or assimilationist. Furthermore, prisoners with a "designated dangerous" attached to their sentences are not allowed good-time credit. For example, if a prisoner receives a sixty-year sentence and is designated dangerous, she is not eligible for parole until she serves seventeen and a half years. She accumulates no good-time credit until the seventeen and a half years are served. None of the programming she participates in counts toward good-time credit; thus, good-time credit discriminates against prisoners designated dangerous. For an examination of good-time credit, see Weisburd and Chayet (1989).

7. The lawsuit, filed on behalf of all female prisoners at the WCC, cites unsafe buildings; inadequate medical and mental health care; gender discrimination in regard to recreation, education, and vocational opportunities; and racial discrimination in regard to religious services. The state assured the ACLU that conditions would change once the new prison was built. Primarily due to unsafe prison conditions and overcrowding, the legislature approved the building of a new women's prison. A new prison was never built; however, in September 1994 the women's prison relocated from the campus of the state mental institution at Warm Springs to the former site of Rivendell Psychiatric Center at Billings. On 6 March 1995 I telephoned the director of Montana's ACLU regarding the status of the lawsuit. He said that it was in limbo because the prison had recently moved. The rationale is that the prison needs time to adjust to its new location. A team of experts has one year to monitor the prison's progress regarding the conditions specified in the lawsuit. (See also Chapter 6 for more on this lawsuit.)

6. REHABILITATION OR CONTROL

1. A write-up is a formal complaint filed by the prison against the prisoner for a rule violation. Multiple write-ups affect a prisoner's good-time credit; therefore, prisoners with many write-ups serve longer sentences. See the appendix for a list of rule infractions and descriptions.

2. A sweat lodge is similar to a church. In the purification ceremony conducted within the sweat lodge, one is cleansed physically, emotionally, and spiritually. The idea is that one enters the sweat in ignorance, then exits enlightened and purified in all ways. In Native cultures, the sweat lodge is of utmost importance and is seen as reintegrating the person as a whole human being.

3. See Elizabeth Grobsmith's book, *Indians in Prison: Incarcerated Native Americans in Nebraska* (1994), for an examination of imprisoned Native men and the denial of religious freedom.

4. Prison officials at the new prison in Billings now permit respected Crow elder Ben Pease to counsel and pray with the imprisoned Native women.

5. *Count* refers to the process in which prisoners line up outside their cells. The guards then count the prisoners to ensure that no one has escaped. At the WCC, this occurs four times a day: at 6:30 A.M., 10:45 A.M., 4:00 P.M., and 10:30 P.M.

6. *Bulldog* is a term used by prison staff at the WCC to describe a prisoner who intimidates other prisoners, physically and emotionally, to obtain what she wants.

7. In the foreword of her book, Edna Walker Chandler states that she and her husband were invited by a friend, who was the superintendent at the California Institution for Women, to offer a program for inmates. Hence, she began her "research" that was to offer a firsthand look at the experience of imprisoned women. Chandler's idea was to follow the advice of her friend and write a "factual, objective book that would give an outsider some idea of what it's like to be confined in a modern prison" (1973, x). According to Chandler, the book would serve as "a readable eye-opener to young girls who may be in that very dangerous, shadowy area between delinquency and crime" (x).

8. Recent research regarding sexual intercourse in men's prisons reveals that typically sex is consensual rather than coercive (Saum et al. 1995).

9. This image also affects lesbian mothers who are not imprisoned. On 31 August 1996 the *San Francisco Chronicle* reported that a Florida court awarded custody of a twelve-year-old to a father who was convicted of murdering his first wife twenty-two years ago. Apparently, the court feels that he is a better parent than the mother, who is a lesbian. The mother alleges that her daughter was removed solely because she is a lesbian. The judge, however, said that he removed the child because she had poor manners and liked men's cologne.

10. A Class II write-up is a serious violation (see the appendix for clarification). Conduct that disrupts, assault, murder, and escape are examples of Class II write-ups. With this sanction, prisoners are classified as Close or Maximum status and transferred to the maximum-security building.

7. PRISON SUBCULTURE

1. The documentary *Without Reservations: Notes on Racism in Montana* (1995) provides an insight into the way neocolonial racism is fashioned and waged against Native Americans in Montana. Also see Jack Forbes's book *Columbus and Other Cannibals* (1992) for an examination of racism as a sickness that emerges from colonialism. For an analysis of the evolution and varying structures of

racism in the United States, see *Racial Formation in the United States* (1994) by Michael Omi and Howard Winant, the film *The Color of Fear* (1995) directed by Lee Mun Wah, and Joe Feagin and Melvin Sikes's *Living with Racism* (1994). *Unequal Justice: A Question of Color* (1993), written by Coramae Richey Mann, provides an analysis of the criminal justice system and racism in the United States. Additionally, see *Racism and Criminology* (1993), edited by Dee Cook and Barbara Hudson, for an examination of racism and sexism in the criminal justice system.

2. Although molestation by guards may be typical, few incarcerated women strike back at their attackers (Feinman 1986). An exception is the case of JoAnne Little, an African American who, in North Carolina in 1974, killed a white jailer who attempted to rape her. Rural jails in the southern part of the United States are known to be "targets for sexual abuse" of incarcerated women, especially African American women (Sims 1976, 139). Women of color are marked for sexual abuse because of racist attitudes. A Black woman describes a racist stereotypic image with which many women of color must contend: "There's a particular fear of white men that Black girls grow up with. We know they think we're hot, sexual animals, that we're always available. It goes back to slavery. What they think about us sexually is a part of the racism" (Hall 1985, 48).

3. Warden Steve MacAskill was fired in August of 1995 for returning to work after drinking in a local tavern (Field 1995). In the late fall of the same year, Ms. Jo Acton was appointed as the warden.

8. MOTHERHOOD IMPRISONED

1. The categories are generally based on Zelma Weston Henriques's study (1982) on imprisoned mothers.

9. DOUBLE PUNISHMENT

1. In this study, Baunach unfortunately uses only two categories of race/ ethnicity: white and Black. Included in the Black category are mostly African American women but also Native American, Asian American, and other women of color incarcerated in two prisons. Baunach, therefore, ignores the particular social and cultural features of different racial/ethnic groups.

2. However, the Henriques study (1982) suggests that although the imprisoned mothers (African American and Puerto Rican) are generally satisfied with the placements of their children in the extended family, the guardians report that the children greatly miss their mothers and appear sad and angry. Further-

more, some extended families feel they have enough problems of their own (mostly financial), and caring for extra children proves difficult.

3. I informed the state employee that the child must be one-fourth Native, not one-fifth, and enrolled in a federally recognized tribe or demonstrate eligibility for enrollment. I also explained that the act has strict guidelines concerning the definition of Native American and that many Native children fell through the cracks because they were not recognized by the federal government as Native.

10. REHABILITATION AND HEALING OF IMPRISONED MOTHERS

1. *Ethnostress*, as it relates specifically to Canadian and American Natives, is defined by Antone, Miller, and Myers (1986, 7) as feelings of powerlessness and hopelessness that "occur when the cultural beliefs or joyful identity of a people are disrupted. It is the negative experience they feel when interacting with members of different cultural groups and themselves."

11. NARRATIVE OF A NATIVE WOMAN ON THE OUTSIDE

1. While I have found evidence that corroborates much of Gloria Wells Norlin's narrative, the reader is reminded that this is her interpretation.

2. Motion to Dismiss With Prejudice means that the case is dismissed and cannot be brought up again. In other words, she won.

BIBLIOGRAPHY

Ackerman, L. A. 1995. Complementary but Equal: Gender Status in the Plateau. In *Women and Power in Native North America*, ed. L. Klein and L. Ackerman, 75–100. Norman: University of Oklahoma Press.

Adams, D. 1991. The Troubled Tale of Two Prison Moms: They're Trying to Break Cycle of Abuse, Neglect. *Montana Standard*, 4 July, 8–9.

Adoption Assistance and Child Welfare Act of 1980. U.S. Public Law 967-272. 96th Cong., 2nd sess., 17 June 1980.

Allen, P. G. 1985. *The Sacred Hoop: Recovering the Feminine in American Indian Traditions.* Boston: Beacon Press.

American Correctional Association. 1990. *The Female Offender: What Does the Future Hold?* Washington, D.C.: St. Mary's Press.

The American Indian Religious Freedom Act of 1978. U.S. Public Law 95-341. 95th Cong., 2nd sess., 11 August 1978.

Andersen, M. L. 1988. *Thinking about Women: Sociological Perspectives on Sex and Gender.* 2d. ed. New York: Macmillan, 1988.

Anez, B. 1995. Language Bill a Slap to Minorities Say Foes. *Char-Koosta News*, 17 February, 2.

Antone, R. A., D. L. Miller, and B. A. Myers. 1986. *The Power within People: A Community Organizing Perspective.* Deseronto, Ontario, Canada: Peace Tree Technologies.

Arnold, R. 1994. Black Women in Prison: The Price of Resistance. In *Women of Color in U.S. Society*, ed. M. B. Zinn and B. T. Dill, 171–184. Philadelphia: Temple University Press.

Asher, B. 1996. "Their Own Domestic Difficulties": Intra-Indian Crime and White Law in Western Washington Territory, 1873–1889. *Western Historical Quarterly* 27(2):189–209.

Assimilative Crimes Act of 1825. Vol. 4, Chap. 65, p. 115. 18th Cong., 2nd sess., 3 March 1825.

Assimilative Crimes Act of 1889. Vol. 25, Chap. 333, p. 783. 50th Cong., 2nd sess., 1 March 1889.

Azure, B. L. 1995. Bison Range-Management Opponents Try to Buffalo Officials. *Char-Koosta News*, 1 September, 4.

Bachman, R. 1992. *Death and Violence on the Reservation: Homicide, Family Violence, and Suicide in American Indian Populations*. New York: Auburn House.

Barry, E. 1985a. Children of Prisoners: Punishing the Innocent. *Youth Law News* 12:12–17.

———. 1985b. Reunification Difficult for Incarcerated Parents and Their Children. *Youth Law News* 14:13–17.

Barsh, R. 1980. Kennedy's Criminal Code Reform Bill and What it Doesn't Do for the Tribes. *American Indian Journal* 6(3):2–15.

———. 1991. "Indian Law," Indians' Law, and Legalism in American Indian Policy: An Essay on Historical Origins. In *American Indians: Social Justice and Public Policy*, ed. D. E. Green and T. V. Tonnesen, 8–43. Milwaukee: The University of Wisconsin Institute on Race and Ethnicity.

Barsh, R., and J. Y. Henderson. 1980. *The Road: Indian Tribes and Political Liberty*. Berkeley: University of California Press.

Baunach, P. J. 1982. You Can't Be a Mother and Be in Prison . . . Can You? Impacts of the Mother-Child Separation. In *The Criminal Justice System and Women: Women Offenders, Victims, Workers*, ed. B. R. Price and N. J. Sokoloff, 155–169. New York: Clark Boardman.

———. 1985a. Critical Problems of Women in Prison. In *The Changing Roles of Women in the Criminal Justice System: Offenders, Victims, and Professionals*, ed. I. L. Moyer, 95–110. Prospect Heights, Ill.: Waveland Press.

———. 1985b. *Mothers in Prison*. New Brunswick, N.J.: Transaction Books.

Beck, A. J., and D. K. Gilliard. 1995. *Prisoners in 1994*. (Bureau of Justice Statistics Report No. NCJ-151654). Washington, D.C.: U.S. Department of Justice.

Beck, P. V., and A. L. Walters. 1977. *The Sacred: Ways of Knowledge, Sources of Life*. Tsaile, Ariz.: Navajo Community College Press.

Becker, H. 1963. *The Outsiders: Studies in the Sociology of Deviance*. New York: Free Press.

Beckerman, A. 1991. Women in Prison: The Conflict Between Confinement and Parental Rights. *Social Justice* 18(3):171–183.

———. 1994. Mothers in Prison: Meeting the Prerequisite Conditions for Permanency Planning. *Social Work* 39(1):9–14.

Belknap, W. W. 1874. *Letter from the Secretary of War upon the Petition of the Legislature of Montana Territory Asking Protection of Citizens of Deer Lodge and Missoula Counties against Depredations of Roving Bands of Indians*. Senate Executive Doc. No. 46, 43rd Cong., 1st sess., serial 1581.

Belt, R. V. 1889. *Letters Received by the Office of the Adjutant General, 1889*. Letter from R. V. Belt to the Secretary of War, 25 June 1889. National Archives, Roll 696, No. 689.

Belue, C. T. 1989a. For the Good of the Tribe: The Law of the Crow Nation during the Buffalo Days. Unpublished manuscript. Little Big Horn College Library. Duplicated.

————. 1989b. Oppressors, Power, and Tears: A History of White Control of Crow Lands. Unpublished manuscript. Little Big Horn College Library. Duplicated.

————. 1990. White Oppression and Enduring Red Tears: Indian Law and the Real Rules for White Control of Crow Lands. Unpublished manuscript. Little Big Horn College Library. Duplicated.

Berkhofer, R. F., Jr. 1978. *The White Man's Indian: Images of the American Indian from Columbus to the Present*. New York: Vintage.

Bernstein, I., J. Cardascia, and C. Rose. 1979. Defendant's Sex and Criminal Court Decisions. In *Discrimination in Organizations*, ed. R. Alvarez and K. Lutterman, 329–354. San Francisco: Jossey-Bass.

Blauner, R. 1972. *Racial Oppression in America*. New York: Harper and Row.

Bloomer, K. 1993a. Battered Woman Syndrome: A Reason to Kill. *Missoula Independent*, 3 December, 6.

————. 1993b. Woman Kills Husband. *Missoula Independent*, 19 November, 6–9.

Bowker, L. H. 1981. Gender Differences in Prisoner Subculture. In *Women and Crime in America*, ed. L. H. Bowker, 409–419. New York: Macmillan.

Brant, B. (ed.). 1988. *A Gathering of Spirit: A Collection by North American Indian Women*. Ithaca, N.Y.: Firebrand.

Braroe, N. W. 1975. *Indian and White: Self-Image and Interaction in a Canadian Plains Community*. Stanford, Calif.: Stanford University Press.

Bresler, L., and D. Lewis. 1983. Black and White Women Prisoners: Differences in Family Ties and Their Programmatic Implication. *The Prison Journal* 63 : 117–122.

Brown, D. 1970. *Bury My Heart at Wounded Knee*. New York: Washington Square.

Bryan, W. L., Jr. 1985. *Montana's Indians: Yesterday and Today*. Helena, Mont.: Montana Magazine.

Bureau of Justice. 1994. *Domestic Violence: Violence between Intimates* (Selected Findings Report No. NCJ-149259). Washington, D.C.: U.S. Department of Justice.

Burkhart, K. W. 1973. *Women in Prison*. New York: Doubleday.

Butler, A. M. 1988. Still in Chains: Black Women in Western Prisons, 1865–1910. *Western Historical Quarterly* 20(1) : 19–35.

Bynum, T., and R. Paternoster. 1984. Discrimination Revisited: An Exploration of Frontstage and Backstage Criminal Justice Decision Making. *Sociology and Social Research* 69(1) : 90–108.

Byorth, S. 1989a. *History of Women Inmates*. A Report for the Criminal Justice and Corrections Advisory Council (May). Submitted to the Montana Department of Corrections, Helena. Duplicated.

————. 1989b. *Profile of Adult Female Inmates in Montana*. A Report Prepared for the Criminal Justice and Corrections Advisory Council (May). Submitted to the Montana Department of Corrections, Helena. Duplicated.

Camp, C., and G. Camp. 1995. *The Corrections Yearbook*. South Salem, N.Y.: Criminal Justice Institute.

Cardozo-Freeman, I. (ed.). 1993. *Chief: The Life History of Eugene Delorme, Imprisoned Santee Sioux*. Lincoln: University of Nebraska Press.

Carlen, P. 1983. *Women's Imprisonment: A Study in Social Control*. London: Routledge and Kegan Paul.

————. 1985. *Criminal Women: Autobiographical Accounts*. Cambridge, U.K.: Polity Press.

————. 1988. *Women, Crime, and Poverty*. Philadelphia: Open University Press.

Caulfield, M. D. 1974. Imperialism, the Family, and Cultures of Resistance. *Socialist Revolution* 20:67–85.

Chadwick, B., J. Stauss, H. Bahr, and L. Halverson. 1976. Confrontation with the Law: The Case of American Indians in Seattle. *Phylon* 37:163–171.

Chandler, E. W. 1973. *Women in Prison*. New York: Bobbs-Merrill.

Chelsea, I. 1988. Speech given during Cultural Awareness Week. The Center for Native American Studies, Montana State University, 13 May.

Chesney-Lind, M. 1981. Judicial Paternalism and Female Status Offenders: Training Women to Know Their Place. *In Women and Crime in America*, ed. L. H. Bowker, 354–366. New York: Macmillan.

————. 1991. Patriarchy, Prisons, and Jails: A Critical Look at Trends in Women's Incarceration. *The Prison Journal* 71(1):51–67.

Chesney-Lind, M., and N. Rodriguez. 1983. Women under Lock and Key: A View from the Inside. *The Prison Journal* 63(2):47–65.

Chiang, H. 1996. A Win for "Partners Abuse" Defense. *San Francisco Chronicle*, 30 August, sec. A1 and A19.

Churchill, W., and G. T. Morris. 1992 Key Indian Laws and Cases. In *The State of Native America: Genocide, Colonization, and Resistance*, ed. M. A. Jaimes, 13–21. Boston: South End Press.

Clark, J. 1995. The Impact of the Prison Environment on Mothers. *The Prison Journal* 75(3):306–329.

Cobell, T. 1969. *Montana Attorney General's Office Records*. Letter from Tom Cobell to Barney Reagan, 6 March 1969. RS 111, Box 11, Folder 21, Montana Historical Society Archives, Helena.

Cohen, F. [1942] 1971. *Handbook of Federal Indian Law*. Albuquerque: University of New Mexico Press.

Coleman, E. 1979. *Laws of the Colonial and State Governments Relating to Indians and Indian Affairs, from 1633 to 1831*. New York: Earl M. Coleman Enterprises.

Collins, P. H. 1991. *Black Feminist Thought: Knowledge, Consciousness, and the Politics of Empowerment*. New York: Routledge.

The Color of Fear. 1995. Directed by L. M. Wah. 90 mins. Stir-Fry Productions. Videocassette.

Commissioner of Indian Affairs. 1879. *Annual Report, 1877–1878*. Washington, D.C.: U.S. Government Printing Office.

Commissioner of Indian Affairs. 1881. *Annual Report, 1879–1880*. Washington, D.C.: U.S. Government Printing Office.

Commissioner of Indian Affairs. 1882. *Annual Report, 1880–1881*. Washington, D.C.: U.S. Government Printing Office.

Concurrent Resolution of the 83rd Congress. House Concurrent Resolution 108. 83rd Cong., 1st sess., 1 August 1953.

Confederated Salish and Kootenai Tribes of the Flathead Nation. 1991. Briefing Document: Public Law 280 and Retrocession Affecting the Flathead Indian Reservation. Unpublished manuscript. Duplicated.

Conley, F. 1899. *Montana Governors' Papers*. Letter from Frank Conley to Governor White, 10 November 1899. MC 35a, Box 31, Folder 3. Montana Historical Society Archives, Helena.

Cook, D., and B. Hudson (eds.). 1993. *Racism and Criminology*. Thousand Oaks, Calif.: Sage.

Cooley, C. H. 1964. *Human Nature and the Social Order*. New York: Schocken.

Crichton, S. 1993. *ACLU Class Action Suit Filed on Behalf of Female Prisoners*. Press Release 21 April 1993. Duplicated.

Crisp, D. 1995. Warrior Societies Revive Values: Cheyenne Seek to Promote Traditions. *Billings Gazette*, 25 November, sec. A1 and B6.

Cross, J. 1982. The Economics of Indian Crimes. In *Indians and Criminal Justice*, ed. L. French, 53–64. Totowa, N.J.: Allanheld, Osmun and Co.

Cushman, R. E., and R. F. Cushman. 1958. *Cases in Constitutional Law*. New York: Appleton-Century-Crofts.

Datesman, S. K., and F. R. Scarpitti. 1980. Unequal Protection for Males and Females in the Juvenile Court. In *Women, Crime, and Justice*, ed. S. Datesman and F. Scarpitti, 300–319. New York: Oxford University Press.

Davis, K. C. 1995. Ethnic Cleansing Didn't Start in Bosnia. *New York Times*, 3 September, sec. 4, 1 and 6.

DeFleur, L. B. 1975. Biasing Influences on Drug Arrest Records: Implications for Deviance Research. *American Sociological Review* 40:88–103.

Delany, L. T. 1970. The White Psyche: Exploration of Racism. In *White Racism: Its History, Pathology and Practice*, ed. B. N. Schwartz and R. Disch, 55–65. New York: Dell Publishing.

Deloria, V., Jr., and C. Lytle. 1983. *American Indians, American Justice*. Austin: University of Texas Press.

————. 1984. *The Nations Within: The Past and Future of American Indian Sovereignty*. New York: Pantheon Books.

DelVecchio, R. 1996. Neighbors Delay Oakland Prison. *San Francisco Chronicle*, 27 January, sec. A15 and A17.

Department of Corrections and Human Services. 1992. *Corrections Division Report: Fiscal Years 1989-1991*. Montana Department of Corrections and Human Services, Helena.

Descriptive List of the Prisoner. RS 197, Montana Historical Society Archives, Helena.

Dobash, R. P., R. E. Dobash, and S. Gutteridge. 1986. *The Imprisonment of Women*. New York: Blackwell.

Dobyns, H. 1983. *Their Number Become Thinned: Native American Population Dynamics in Eastern North America*. Knoxville: University of Tennessee Press.

Dumars, T. 1968. Indictment under the "Major Crimes Act": An Exercise in Unfairness and Unconstitutionality. *Arizona Law Review* 10:691–705.

Duran, E., and B. Duran. (1995). *Native American Postcolonial Psychology*. Albany: State University of New York Press.

Dusenberry, V. 1958. Waiting for a Day That Never Comes: Story of the Dispossessed Metis of Montana. *Montana: The Magazine of Western History* 8(2): 26–39.

Ehli, N. 1995a. Caller Claims Racism by Police Secretary. *Billings Gazette*, 23 November, sec. A1 and A13.

————. 1995b. Cop Fired over Complaints of Molesting Women. *Billings Gazette*, 5 October, sec. A1 and A9.

————. 1995c. Judge Met Bias in Ranks of Police. *Billings Gazette*, 16 November, sec. A1 and A10.

Ellison, R. 1953. *The Invisible Man*. New York: New American Library.

An Enabling Act. Vol. 25, Chap. 180, p. 676. 50th Cong., 2nd sess., 22 February 1889.

Enlarged Homestead Act of 1909. U.S. Public Law 245. 60th Cong., 2nd sess., 19 February 1909.

Erez, E. 1992. Dangerous Men, Evil Women: Gender and Parole Decision Making. *Justice Quarterly* 9(1):105–127.

Espinosa, S. 1993. Women Prisoners Allege Drugging during Trials. *San Francisco Chronicle*, 26 January, sec. B1 and B6.

Etienne, M., and E. Leacock (eds.). 1980. *Women and Colonization: Anthropological Perspectives*. New York: Praeger.

Faith, K. 1993a. Media, Myths and Masculinization: Images of Women in Prison. In *Conflict with the Law: Women and the Canadian Justice System*, ed. E. Adelbery and C. Currie, 174–211. Vancouver, B.C.: Press Gang Publishers.

————. 1993b. *Unruly Women: The Politics of Confinement and Resistance*. Vancouver, B.C.: Press Gang Publishers.

Fanon, F. 1963. *The Wretched of the Earth*. New York: Grove/Weidenfeld.

———. 1967. *Black Skins, White Masks*. New York: Grove.

Farrington, D., and A. Morris. 1983. Sex, Sentencing and Reconvictions. *British Journal of Criminology* 3:229–235.

Feagin, J. R., and M. P. Sikes. 1994. *Living with Racism: The Black Middle-Class Experience*. Boston: Beacon Press.

Feinman, C. 1986. *Women in the Criminal Justice System* (2nd ed.). New York: Praeger.

Fenner, D. 1994. County Must Pay $22,910 in Race Case. *Billings Gazette*, 15 November, sec. A1 and A10.

Field, S. M. 1995. Candidates for Women's Prison Warden Interviewed. *Billings Gazette*, 19 October, sec. C4.

Flanagan, T. J. 1983. Correlates of Institutional Misconduct among State Prisoners. *Criminology* 21(1):29–39.

Flathead Reservation Information Agency. 1905. How Will You Select Your Own Homestead. *The Western Homeseeker* 1(1):24.

———. 1906. Are You Prepared? We Are. *The Western Homeseeker* 1(6):30.

Foley, L. A., and C. E. Rasche. (1979). The Effect of Race on Sentence, Actual Time Served and Final Disposition of Female Offenders. In *Theory and Research in Criminal Justice: Current Perspectives*, ed. J. A. Conley, 93–108. Academy of Criminal Justice Sciences Series: Anderson.

Forbes, J. 1992. *Columbus and Other Cannibals: The Wetiko Disease of Exploitation, Imperialism, and Terrorism*. Brooklyn, N.Y.: Autonomedia.

Fordham, M. 1993. Within the Iron Houses: The Struggle for Native American Religious Freedom in American Prisons. *Social Justice* 20(1–2):165–171.

Foucault, M. 1979. *Discipline and Punishment: The Birth of a Prison*. New York: Vintage.

Frankenberg, R. 1993. *White Women, Race Matters: The Social Construction of Whiteness*. Minneapolis: University of Minnesota Press.

Freire, P. 1970. *Pedagogy of the Oppressed*. New York: Herder and Herder.

French, L. 1977. An Assessment of the Black Female Prisoner in the South. *Signs* 3(2):483–488.

Friedman, L. M. 1993. *Crime and Punishment in American History*. New York: Basic Books.

General Allotment Act of 1887 (Dawes Severalty Act). Vol. 24, Chap. 119, p. 388. 49th Cong., 2nd sess., 8 February 1887.

General Crimes Act (Indian Country Crimes Act) of 1817. Vol. 3, Chap. 92, p. 383, 14th Cong., 2nd sess., 3 March 1817.

General Crimes Act of 1854. Chap. 341. 48th Cong., 2nd sess., 27 March 1854.

Getting Out. 1993. Directed by A. Pick. 60 mins. Why Not Productions. Videocassette.

Giago, T. (Nawica Kjici) 1984. *Notes from Indian Country, Volume I*. Pierre, S. Dak.: State Publishing Company.

————. 1995. Navajo's Albert Hale Big Enough to Forgive. *Char-Koosta News*, 26 May, 2.

Giallombardo, R. 1966. *Society of Women: A Study of a Women's Prison*. New York: Wiley.

Gilfus, M. E. 1988. Seasoned by Violence/Tempered by Law: A Qualitative Study of Women and Crime. Ph.D. diss., Brandeis University. Cited in M. Chesney-Lind, 1991. Patriarchy, Prisons, and Jails: A Critical Look at Trends in Women's Incarceration. *The Prison Journal* 71(1):51–67.

Glick, R. M., and V. V. Neto. 1977. *A National Study of Women's Correctional Programs* (National Institute of Law Enforcement and Criminal Justice No. 74-N1-99-0052). Washington, D.C.: U.S. Government Printing Office.

Goetting, A. 1985. Racism, Sexism, and Ageism in the Prison Community. *Federal Probation* 49:10–22.

Goetting, A., and R. M. Howsen. 1983. Blacks and Prison: A Profile. *Criminal Justice Review* 8(2):21–31.

Goffman, E. 1959. *The Presentation of Self in Everyday Life*. Garden City, N.Y.: Doubleday.

————. 1961. *Asylums: Essays on the Social Situation of Mental Patients and Other Inmates*. Garden City, N.Y.: Doubleday.

————. 1963. *Stigma: Notes on the Management of Spoiled Identity*. Englewood Cliffs, N.J.: Prentice-Hall.

Gordon, M. 1964. *Assimilation in American Life*. New York: Oxford University Press.

The Great Spirit within the Hole. 1983. Produced and directed by C. Spotted Eagle. 50 mins. Spotted Eagle Productions. Videocassette.

Green, R. 1976. The Pocahontas Perplex: The Image of Indian Women in American Culture. *Massachusetts Review* 16(4):698–714.

Greenfeld, L. A., and S. Minor-Harper. 1991. *Women in Prison* (Bureau of Justice Statistics Special Report No. NCJ-127991). Washington, D.C.: U.S. Department of Justice.

Grobsmith, E. 1994. *Indians in Prison: Incarcerated Native Americans in Nebraska*. Lincoln: University of Nebraska Press.

Grossman, J. 1984 (September). Bedford Hills Mothers Follow-up: A Report Prepared for the State of New York Department of Correctional Services. Unpublished manuscript.

Grossmann, M. G. 1992. Two Perspectives on Aboriginal Female Suicides in Custody. *Canadian Journal of Criminology* 34(3–4):403–416.

Haft, M. 1980. Women in Prison: Discriminatory Practices and Some Legal Solutions. In *Women, Crime, and Justice*, ed. S. K. Datesman and F. R. Scarpitti, 330–38. New York: Oxford University Press.

Hagan, J. 1994. *Crime and Disrepute*. Thousand Oaks, Calif.: Pine Forge Press.

Hagan, W. 1966. *Indian Police and Judges: Experiments in Acculturation and Control*. New Haven: Yale University Press.

Haley, K. 1977. Mothers Behind Bars: A Look at the Parental Rights of Incarcerated Women. *New England Journal on Prison Law* 4:141–155.

Hall, E., and A. Simkus. 1975. Inequality in the Types of Sentences Received by Native Americans and Whites. *Criminology* 13(2):199–222.

Hall, R. E. 1985. *Ask Any Woman: A London Enquiry into Rape and Sexual Assault. Report of the Woman's Safety Survey Conducted by Women Against Rape*. Bristol, Eng.: Falling Wall Press.

Harlan, T. 1995. Creating a Visual History: A Question of Ownership. In *Strong Hearts: Native American Visions and Voices*, 20–32. New York: Aperture Foundation.

Harring, S. L. 1994. *Crow Dog's Case: American Indian Sovereignty, Tribal Law, and United States Law in the Nineteenth Century*. Melbourne, Australia: Cambridge University Press.

Hartjen, C. A. 1978. *Crime and Criminalization* (2nd ed.). New York: Praeger.

To Heal the Spirit. 1990. Directed by B. Barde. 40 mins. Why Not Productions. Videocassette.

Heidensohn, F. M. 1985. *Women and Crime: The Life of the Female Offender*. New York: New York University Press.

Heinz, R. P. 1973. *Montana Attorney General's Office Records*. Letter from Richard Heinz and Bill Phillips to Governor Thomas Judge, 1 March 1973. RS 111, Box 11, Folder 22, Montana Historical Society Archives, Helena.

Heizer, R. F. (ed.). 1974. *The Destruction of California Indians*. Lincoln: University of Nebraska Press.

Heney, J. 1990. Report on Self-Injurious Behaviour in the Kingston Prison for Women. Ottawa: Submitted to Correctional Service Canada. Quoted in M. G. Grossmann, 1992. Two Perspectives on Aboriginal Female Suicides in Custody. *Canadian Journal of Criminology* 34(3–4):403–416.

Henriques, Z. W. 1982. *Imprisoned Mothers and Their Children: A Descriptive and Analytical Study*. New York: University Press of America.

Hepburn, J. 1978. Race and the Decision to Arrest: An Analysis of Warrants Issued. *Journal of Research in Crime and Delinquency* 15:54–73.

Herrnstein, R., and C. Murray. 1994. *The Bell Curve: Intelligence and Class Structure in American Life*. New York: Simon and Schuster.

Hoebel, E. A. 1954. *The Law of Primitive Man*. Cambridge: Harvard University Press.

Holm, T. 1992. Patriots and Pawns: State Use of American Indians in the Military and the Process of Nativization in the United States. In *The State of Native America: Genocide, Colonization, and Resistance*, ed. M. A. Jaimes, 345–370. Boston: South End Press.

hooks, b. 1989. *Talking Back: Thinking Feminist, Thinking Black*. Boston: South End Press.

———. 1992. *Black Looks: Race and Representation*. Boston: South End Press.

Hoxie, F. 1984. *A Final Promise: The Campaign to Assimilate the Indians, 1880–1920*. Lincoln: University of Nebraska Press.

Hurtado, A. 1988. *Indian Survival on the California Frontier*. New Haven: Yale University Press.

Indian Child Welfare Act of 1978. U.S. Public Law 95-608. 95th Cong., 2nd sess., 8 November 1978.

Indian Civil Rights Act of 1968. U.S. Public Law 90-284. 90th Cong., 2nd sess., 11 April 1968.

Indian Reorganization Act of 1934. Vol. 48, Chap 576, p. 984. 73rd Cong., 2nd sess., 18 June 1934.

Jackson, M. 1989. Locking Up Natives in Canada. *University of British Columbia Law Review* 23(2):215–300.

Jaimes, M. A., with T. Halsey. 1992. American Indian Women: At the Center of Indigenous Resistance in North America. In *The State of Native America: Genocide, Colonization, and Resistance*, ed. M. A. Jaimes, 311–344. Boston: South End Press.

Jensen, G., and D. Jones. 1976. Perspectives on Inmate Culture: A Study of Women in Prison. *Social Forces* 54:590–603.

Johansen, B., and R. Maestas. 1979. *Wasi'chu: The Continuing Indian Wars*. New York: Monthly Review Press.

Johnston, E. W. 1976. *Montana Attorney General's Office Records*. Letter from Earl Johnston to Attorney General Robert Woodahl, 4 May 1976. RS 111, Box 11, Folder 23, Montana Historical Society Archives, Helena.

Jose-Kampfner, C. 1990. Coming to Terms with Existential Death: An Analysis of Women's Adaptation to Life in Prison. *Social Justice* 17(2):110–125.

Josephy, A. 1984. *Now That the Buffalo's Gone: A Study of Today's American Indians*. Norman: University of Oklahoma Press.

Kawashima, Y. 1986. *Puritan Justice and the Indian: White Man's Law in Massachusetts, 1630–1763*. Middletown, Conn.: Wesleyan University Press.

Keane, K. 1995 (October). Women Prisoners Find a Place to Heal. *Windspeaker*, 2.

Kipp, W. 1995. The Last of the Last Bison. *Char-Koosta News*, 6 October, 2.

Klanwatch Intelligence Report. 1995 (March). Hate Group Listings, 12–16.

Kruttschnitt, C. 1981. Prison Codes, Inmate Solidarity, and Women. In *Comparing Female and Male Offenders*, ed. M. Q. Warren, 123–141. Beverly Hills: Sage.

———. 1982. Women, Crime, and Dependency. *Criminology* 4:495–513.

———. 1983. Race Relations and the Female Inmate. *Crime and Delinquency* 29:577–591.

LaDuke, W., and W. Churchill. 1985. Native America: The Political Economy of Radioactive Colonialism. *The Journal of Ethnic Studies* 13(3): 107–133.

LaFree, G. 1995. Race and Crime Trends in the United States, 1946–1990. In *Ethnicity, Race, and Crime: Perspectives across Time and Place*, ed. D. F. Hawkins, 169–193.

LaFromboise, T. D., and D. S. Bigfoot. 1988. Cultural and Cognitive Considerations in the Prevention of American Indian Adolescent Suicide. *Journal of Adolescence* 11(2): 139–153. Quoted in R. Bachman, 1992. *Death and Violence on the Reservation: Homicide, Family Violence, and Suicide in American Indian Populations*. New York: Auburn House.

Langan, P. 1995. Interview on the Justice Files. Discovery Channel Television. 11 November 1995.

LaPoint, V. 1977. Mothers Inside, Children Outside: Some Issues Surrounding Imprisoned Mothers and Their Children. In American Correctional Association Congress of Corrections, *Proceedings of the 107th Annual Congress of Corrections of the American Correctional Association*, 7–10. College Park, Md.: American Correctional Association.

———. 1980. The Impact of Incarceration on Families: Research and Policy Issues. Paper presented to the Research Forum on Family Issues, National Advisory Committee of the White House Conference on Families, Washington, D.C.

LaPrairie, C. P. 1984. Selected Criminal Justice and Socio-Demographic Data on Native Women. *Canadian Journal of Criminology* 26: 161–169.

———. 1992. Aboriginal Crime and Justice: Explaining the Present, Exploring the Future. *Canadian Journal of Criminology* 34(3–4): 281–298.

Leishman, W. 1969. *Montana Attorney General's Office Records*. Letter from Wesley Leishman to Attorney General Robert Woodahl, 16 July 1969. RS 111, Box 11, Folder 21, Montana Historical Society Archives, Helena.

Lewis, D. 1981. Black Women Offenders and Criminal Justice: Some Theoretical Considerations. In *Comparing Female and Male Offenders*, ed. M. Q. Warren, 89–105. Beverly Hills: Sage.

Lighting the Seventh Fire. 1994. Directed and produced by S. J. Osawa. 58 mins. Upstream Productions. Videocassette.

Limerick, P. N. 1987. *The Legacy of Conquest: The Unbroken Past of the American West*. New York: W. W. Norton.

Llewellyn K., and E. A. Hoebel. 1941. *The Cheyenne Way: Conflict and Case Law in Primitive Jurisprudence*. Norman: University of Oklahoma Press.

Lopez, A. n.d. *Pagans in Our Midst*. Rooseveltown, N.Y.: Akwesasne Notes Publication.

Lorde, A. 1984. *Sister Outsider: Essays and Speeches by Audre Lorde*. Trumansburg, N.Y.: The Crossing Press.

Lundman, R. 1974. Routine Police Arrest Practices: A Commonwealth Perspective. *Social Problems* 22:127–141.

Mahan, S. 1982. *Unfit Mothers*. Palo Alto, Calif.: R and E Research Associates.

Major Crimes Act of 1885. Chap. 341. 48th Cong., 2nd sess., 3 March 1854.

Mann, C. R. 1984. *Female Crime and Delinquency*. Tuscaloosa: University of Alabama Press.

———. 1993. *Unequal Justice: A Question of Color*. Bloomington: Indiana University Press.

———. 1995. The Contribution of Institutionalized Racism to Minority Crime. In *Ethnicity, Race, and Crime: Perspectives across Time and Place*, ed. D. F. Hawkins, 259–280. Albany: State University of New York Press.

Martin, E. P., and J. M. Martin. 1978. *The Black Extended Family*. Chicago: University of Chicago Press.

Masson, K. 1992. Familial Ideology in the Courts: The Sentencing of Women. Master's thesis, Simon Fraser University. Cited in K. Faith, 1993. *Unruly Women: The Politics of Confinement and Resistance*. Vancouver, B.C.: Press Gang Publishers.

Matthiessen, P. 1983. *In the Spirit of Crazy Horse*. New York: Viking Press.

May, P. 1977. Explanations of Native American Drinking: A Literature Review. *Plains Anthropologist* 22:223–232.

McCaughan, E. J. 1993. Race, Ethnicity, Nation, and Class within Theories of Structure and Agency. *Social Justice* 20(1–2):82–103.

McConkey, R. W. 1974. *Montana Attorney General's Office Records*. Letter from Robert McConkey to Attorney General Robert Woodahl, 27 March 1974. RS 111, Box 11, Folder 22, Montana Historical Society Archives, Helena.

McConnel, P. 1989. *Sing Soft, Sing Loud: Scenes from Two Lives*. New York: Athenaeum.

McCracken, G. 1995. Racist Material Left in Hardin. *Billings Gazette*, 21 March, sec. B1.

McGowan, B. G., and K. L. Blumenthal. 1976. Children of Women Prisoners: A Forgotten Minority. In *The Female Offender*, ed. L. Crites, 121–136. Lexington, Mass.: Heath.

———. 1978. *Why Punish the Children? A Study of Children of Women Prisoners*. Hackensack, N.J.: National Council on Crime and Delinquency.

McKinney, J. D. 1995. A Descriptive Case Study of the Impact of Social Learning Experiences on Adult Female Inmates. Ed.D. diss., Montana State University.

McLaughlin, K. 1995. Decision to Buy Uniforms Criticized. *Billings Gazette*, 7 December, sec. B4.

McLeod, L., comp. 1990. *Female Offender: The Child Within*. Compiled and presented by L. McLeod at the Montana Correctional Association, 19 September, Butte. Duplicated.

Memmi, A. 1965. *The Colonizer and the Colonized*. New York: Orion Press.

Merlo, A. V. 1995. Female Criminality in the 1990s. In *Women, Law, and Social Control*, ed. A. V. Merlo and J. M. Pollock, 119–134. Needham Heights, Mass.: Allyn and Bacon.

Michel, M. 1995. Frustrated by Lake County Discrimination. *Char-Koosta News*, 20 January, 2.

Mihesuah, D. A. 1993. *Cultivating the Rosebuds: The Education of Women at the Cherokee Female Seminary, 1851–1909*. Urbana and Chicago: University of Illinois Press.

Miller, L. M. 1974. *Montana Attorney General's Office Records*. Letter from L. M. Miller to Attorney General Robert Woodahl, 5 March, 1974. RS 111, Box 11, Folder 22, Montana Historical Society Archives, Helena.

Minnis, M. 1963. The Relationship of the Social Structure of an Indian Community to Adult and Juvenile Delinquency. *Social Forces* 41(4): 395–403.

Montana Office of the State Coordinator of Indian Affairs. 1963. RS 25, Box 5, Folder 11, Montana Historical Society Archives, Helena.

Montana Prison News. 1970. Montana's Women Prisoners. No Author, 12(2): n.p. Montana State University Library, Bozeman.

Moore, J. P. 1973. *Montana Attorney General's Office Records*. Letter from John Moore to the U.S. District Attorney and the Federal Bureau of Investigation, 3 July 1973. RS 111, Box 11, Folder 22, Montana Historical Society Archives, Helena.

Morris, G. T. 1992. International Law and Politics: Toward a Right to Self-Determination for Indigenous Peoples. In *The State of Native America: Genocide, Colonization, and Resistance*, ed. M. A. Jaimes, 55–86. Boston: South End Press.

Nabokov, P. (ed.). 1992. *Native American Testimony: A Chronicle of Indian-White Relations from Prophecy to the Present, 1492–1992*. New York: Penguin Books.

Naffine, N. 1987. *Female Crime: The Construction of Women in Criminology*. Sydney, Australia: Allen and Unwin.

Nailen, D. 1996. White Hate: Neo-Nazi Church Hopes Superior Conference Is the Spark for "Racial Holy War." *Missoula Independent*, 1–8 August, 9 and 10.

Native American Women Prisoners. 1993. *Position Paper* (29 January). Women's Correctional Center, Warm Springs, Montana. Duplicated.

Newsom, M. 1994. Domestic Abuse: Good Guys Can't Just Watch. *Missoulian*, 27 June, sec. C2.

Norton, J. 1964. *Genocide in Northern California*. San Francisco: The Indian Historian Press.

O'Brien, S. 1989. *American Indian Tribal Governments*. Norman: University of Oklahoma Press.

O'Dwyer, J., J. Wilson, and P. Carlen. 1987. Women's Imprisonment in England, Wales and Scotland: Recurring Issues. In *Gender, Crime, and Justice*, ed. P. Carlen and A. Worrall, 135–148. Milton Keynes, Eng.: Open University Press.

Office of the Coordinator of Indian Affairs. 1987. *The 1980 Profile of the Montana Native American*. Helena, Montana.

O'Neal, J. S. 1968. Flathead Law: Past and Present. Master's thesis, University of Montana.

Omi, M., and H. Winant. 1994. *Racial Formation in the United States: From the 1960s to the 1980s* (2nd edition). New York: Routledge.

Ortiz, R. D. 1977. *The Great Sioux Nation*. New York: The American Indian Treaty Council.

———. 1980. Wounded Knee 1890 to Wounded Knee 1973: A Study in United States Colonialism. *The Journal of Ethnic Studies* 8(2):1–16.

Overholser, J. F. 1932. Livestock Growers Threatened by Indians. *The Frontier* 13(1):68–70.

Palmer, L. W. 1969. *Montana Attorney General's Office Records*. Letter from Lewis Palmer to Attorney General Robert Woodahl, 4 August 1969. RS 111, Box 11, Folder 21, Montana Historical Society Archives, Helena.

Petaja, R. 1990. WCC Educational Status Survey (April). Submitted to the Montana Department of Corrections, Helena. Duplicated.

Petrik, P. 1985. Beyond the Bounds of Misery: Montana's Female Prisoners in the 1930s. *Plainswoman* 9(1):6–8.

Phillips, N. K. 1990. Women in the Slammer: Prison Crowded and Conditions Called Shocking. *Bozeman Daily Chronicle*, 18 March, sec. A1 and A8.

The Place of the Falling Waters. 1990. Directed by R. Big Crane and T. Smith. Produced by D. Hart. 90 mins. Native Voices Production. Videocassette.

Pollak, O. 1950. *The Criminality of Women*. Philadelphia: University of Pennsylvania Press.

Pollock, J. M. 1995. Gender, Justice, and Social Control: A Historical Perspective. In *Women, Law, and Social Control*, ed. A. V. Merlo and J. M. Pollock, 3–35. Needham Heights, Mass.: Allyn and Bacon.

Pollock-Byrne, J. 1990. *Women, Prison and Crime*. Pacific Grove, Calif.: Brooks/Cole.

Pollock-Byrne, J., and A. Merlo. 1991. Against Compulsory Treatment: No "Quick Fix" for Pregnant Substance Abusers. *Criminal Justice Policy Review* 5(2):79–99.

Powers, M. N. 1986. *Oglala Women: Myth, Ritual, and Reality*. Chicago: University of Chicago Press.

Price, M. 1973. *Law and the American Indians: Readings, Notes and Cases*. New York: Bobbs-Merrill.

Prucha, F. (ed.). 1973. *Americanizing the American Indians: Writings by the "Friends of the Indian," 1880–1900*. Cambridge: Harvard University Press.

———. 1984. *The Great Father: The United States Government and the American Indians.* Lincoln: University of Nebraska Press.

Public Law 83-280. 83rd Cong., 1st sess., 15 August 1953.

Quinney, R. 1970. *The Social Reality of Crime.* Boston: Little, Brown.

Rafter, N. H. 1990. *Partial Justice: Women, Prisons, and Social Control* (2nd ed.). New Brunswick, N.J.: Transaction Publishers.

Ramirez, J. 1983. Race and Apprehension of Inmate Misconduct. *Journal of Criminal Justice* 2:413–427.

Randall, A., and B. Randall. 1978. Criminal Justice and the American Indian. *Indian Historian* 11(2):42–48.

Reagan, B. 1969. *Montana Attorney General's Office Records.* Letter from Barney Reagan to Don Marble, 24 February 1969. RS 111, Box 11, Folder 21, Montana Historical Society Archives, Helena.

Reed, L. R. 1989. The American Indian in the White Man's Prisons: A Story of Genocide. *Humanity and Society* 13:403–420.

———. 1990. Rehabilitation: Contrasting Cultural Perspectives and the Imposition of Church and State. *Journal of Prisoners on Prison* 2(2):3–28.

———. 1993a. An Interview with Lenny Foster, Spiritual Advisor and Director of the Navajo Corrections Project. In *The American Indian in the White Man's Prisons: A Story of Genocide,* ed. L. R. Reed, 59–72. Taos, N.M.: Uncompromising Books.

———. 1993b. The Fear of Reprisal. In *The American Indian in the White Man's Prisons: A Story of Genocide,* ed. L. R. Reed, 253–274. Taos, N.M.: Uncompromising Books.

Reid, J. 1970. *A Law of Blood: The Primitive Law of the Cherokee Nations.* New York: New York University Press.

Resnik, J., and N. Shaw. 1980. Prisoners of Their Sex: Health Problems of Incarcerated Women. In *Prisoners' Rights Sourcebook,* ed. I. P. Robbins, 328–330. New York: Clark Boardman.

Rice, M. 1990. Challenging Orthodoxies in Feminist Theory: A Black Feminist Critique. In *Feminist Perspectives in Criminology,* ed. L. Gelsthorpe and A. Morris, 57–69. Philadelphia: Open University Press.

Rickard, J. 1995. Sovereignty: A Line in the Sand. In *Strong Hearts: Native American Visions and Voices,* 51–59. New York: Aperture Foundation.

Riley, G. 1988. American Daughters: Black Women in the West. *Montana: The Magazine of Western History* 38(2):14–27.

Robbins, R. L. 1992. Self-Determination and Subordination: The Past, Present, and Future of American Indian Governance. In *The State of Native America: Genocide, Colonization, and Resistance,* ed. M. A. Jaimes, 87–122. Boston: South End Press.

Roberts, A. R. 1994. Crime in America: Trends, Costs, and Remedies. In *Critical*

Issues in Crime and Justice, ed. A. R. Roberts, 3–18. Thousand Oaks, Calif.: Sage.

Roberts, I. 1995. Untitled. In *The Other Side: Writings from the Women's Correctional Center*, ed. G. Mapes, 35–36. Funding provided by Open Meadows Foundation. Duplicated booklet.

Ross, L. 1992. Mothers Behind Bars: A Comparative Study of the Experiences of Imprisoned American Indian and White Women. Ph.D. diss., University of Oregon.

———. Forthcoming, 1997. Punishing Institutions: The Story of Catherine (Cedar Woman). In *Native American Voices*, ed. Steve Talbot and Susan Lobo. New York: Addison Wesley Longman.

———. Forthcoming. Personalizing Methodology: Narratives of Imprisoned Native Women. In *On Our Own Terms: Critical/Creative Representations by Native American Women*, ed. I. Hernandez-Avila. Boston: Beacon Press.

Ross, R. R., and E. A. Fabiano. 1986. *Female Offenders: Correctional Afterthoughts*. Jefferson, N.C.: McFarland.

Sandefur, G. D. 1991. Economic Development and Employment Opportunities for American Indians. In *American Indians: Social Justice and Public Policy*, ed. D. E. Green and T. V. Tonnesen, 8–43. Milwaukee: The University of Wisconsin Institute on Race and Ethnicity.

Saum, C. A., H. L. Surratt, J. A. Inciardi, and R. E. Bennett. 1995. Sex in Prison: Exploring the Myths and Realities. *The Prison Journal* 75(4):413–430.

Schafran, L. 1990. Overwhelming Evidence: Reports on Gender Bias in the Courts. *Trial* 26:28–35.

Schur, E. M. 1984. *Labeling Women Deviant: Gender, Stigma, and Social Control*. New York: Random House.

Schwartz, B. N., and R. Disch (eds.). 1970. Introduction to *White Racism: Its History, Pathology and Practice*, ed. B. N. Schwartz and R. Disch, 1–66. New York: Dell Publishing.

Shasta Woman: The Story of Norma Jean Croy. 1994. Directed by C. Mason. 30 mins. Produced by the Norma Jean Croy Defense Committee. Videocassette.

Shaw, N. 1982. Female Patients and the Medical Profession in Jails and Prisons. In *Judge, Lawyer, Victim, Thief*, ed. N. H. Rafter and E. A. Stanko, 29–62. Boston: Northeastern University Press.

Shaw, M. 1992. Issues of Power and Control: Women in Prison and Their Defenders. *British Journal of Criminology* 32(4):438–452.

Shaw, M., with K. Rodgers, J. Blanchette, T. Hattem, L. S. Thomas, and L. Tamarack. 1989. *Survey of Federally Sentenced Women*. Report No. 1991-4. Ottawa: Solicitor General Canada. Cited in K. Faith, 1993. *Unruly Women: The Politics of Confinement and Resistance*. Vancouver, B.C.: Press Gang Publishers.

Shay, B. 1996. Breaking the Cycle. In *Justice in Indian Country*, 8–10. A Special Report by the School of Journalism, University of Montana, Missoula.

Shirley, S. 1991. Guards Explain Dangers of Women's Prison. *Great Falls Tribune*, 23 January, sec. B1.

Shkilnyk, A. M. 1985. *A Poison Stronger Than Love: The Destruction of an Ojibwa Community*. New Haven: Yale University Press.

Shore, J. H., and S. M. Manson. 1985. Crosscultural Studies of Depression among American Indians and Alaska Natives. *White Cloud Journal* 2(2):5–11.

Sim, J. 1991. "We Are Not Animals, We Are Human Beings": Prisons, Protest, and Politics in England and Wales, 1969 to 1990. *Social Justice* 18(3): 107–129.

Sims, P. 1976. Women in Southern Jails. In *The Female Offender*, ed. L. Crites, 137–48. Lexington, Mass.: Heath.

Sloan, J. L. 1889. *Letters Received by the Office of the Adjutant General's Office, 1889*. Telegram from J. L. Sloan to General Ruger of the Commanding Department of Dakota in St. Paul, Minnesota, 24 June 1889. National Archives, Roll 696, No. 689.

Smart, C. 1976. *Women, Crime, and Criminology: A Feminist Critique*. London: Routledge and Kegan Paul.

Smead, W. H. 1905. *Land of the Flatheads*. St. Paul: Pioneer Press.

Smith, R. B. 1899. *Montana Governors' Papers*. Letter from Governor Smith to Frank Conley 13 November 1899. MC 35a, Box 31, Folder 3. Montana Historical Society Archives, Helena.

Smith, S. L. 1990. *The View from Officers' Row: Army Perceptions of Western Indians*. Tucson: University of Arizona Press.

Snell, T. L., and D. C. Morton. 1994. *Women in Prison* (Bureau of Justice Statistics Special Report). Washington, D.C.: U.S. Department of Justice.

Snipp, C. M. 1989. *American Indians: The First of This Land*. New York: Russell Sage Foundation.

Snyder-Joy, Z. K. 1995. Self-Determination and American Indian Justice: Tribal Versus Federal Jurisdiction on Indian Lands. In *Ethnicity, Race, and Crime: Perspectives across Time and Place*, ed. D. F. Hawkins, 310–322. Albany: State University of New York Press.

Stanton, A. 1980. *When Mothers Go to Jail*. Lexington, Mass.: Heath.

State of Montana. Descriptive List of the Convict. RS 197, Boxes 43–55, Montana Historical Society Archives, Helena.

State of Montana. Prison Convict Register, 1878–1977, Description of Prisoners, Old Montana Prison, Deer Lodge, Montana.

State of Montana Department of Indian Affairs. 1968. March Bulletin. *Montana Attorney General's Office Records*. RS 111, Box 11, Folder 20, Montana Historical Society Archives, Helena.

Stout, K. 1991. Women Who Kill: Offenders or Defenders? *Affilia* 6(4):8–22.

Strickland, R. 1975. *Fire and the Spirits: Cherokee Law from Clan to Court*. Norman: University of Oklahoma Press.

Sugar, F., and L. Fox. 1989–1990. Nistum Peyako Seht'wawin Iskwewak (First Nations Women): Breaking Chains. *Canadian Journal of Women and Law* 3(2):465–482.

Superintendent's Annual Narrative and Statistical Reports from Field Jurisdiction of the Bureau of Indian Affairs, 1910–1923 (Flathead). National Archives, Reel 42, No. 1011.

Superintendent's Annual Narrative and Statistical Reports from Field Jurisdiction of the Bureau of Indian Affairs, 1907–1938. National Archives, Reel 43, No. 1011.

Superintendent's Annual Narrative and Statistical Reports from Field Jurisdiction of the Bureau of Indian Affairs, 1924–1935. National Archives, Reel 43, No. 1011.

Svingen, O. J. 1987. Jim Crow, Indian Style. *American Indian Quarterly* 11: 275–286.

Sword, S. 1995. How Criminal Justice System Treats Spousal Murders. *San Francisco Chronicle*, 24 November, sec. A1 and A22.

Takaki, R. 1979. *Iron Cages: Race and Culture in Nineteenth-Century America*. New York: Oxford University Press.

Talbot, S. 1981. *Roots of Oppression: The American Indian Question*. New York: International Publishers.

Tittle, C. R. 1969. Inmate Organization: Sex Differentiation and the Influence of Criminal Subcultures. *American Sociological Review* 34:492–504.

Toole, K. R. 1959. *Montana: An Uncommon Land*. Norman: University of Oklahoma Press.

———. 1972. *Twentieth-Century Montana: A State of Extremes*. Norman: University of Oklahoma Press.

Transitions: Destruction of a Mother Tongue. 1991. Directed by D. Kipp and J. Fisher. 27 mins. Produced by D. Hart. Native Voices Productions. Videocassette.

Turk, A. T. 1969. *Criminality and Legal Order*. Chicago: Rand McNally.

———. 1976. Law as a Social Weapon in Social Conflict. *Social Problems* 23: 277–291.

U.S. Commission on Civil Rights. 1981. *Indian Tribes: A Continuing Quest for Survival*. Washington, D.C.: U.S. Government Printing Office.

U.S. Department of Justice. 1987. *Prisoners in State and Federal Institutions on December 31, 1984: A Report Prepared by the Bureau of Justice Statistics* (Report No. NCJ-103768). Washington, D.C.: U.S. Government Printing Office.

Visher, C. A. 1983. Gender, Police Arrest Decisions, and Notions of Chivalry. *Criminology* 21:5–28.

Vizenor, G. 1994. *Manifest Manners: Postindian Warriors of Survivance*. Hanover, N.H.: University Press of New England.

Walker, L. 1984. *The Battered Woman Syndrome*. New York: Springer.

Wall, M. 1995. Quote on title page. In *The Other Side: Writings from the Wom-*

en's Correctional Center, ed. G. Mapes. Funding provided by Open Meadows Foundation. Duplicated booklet.

Wall, R., and M. Cranston. 1977. *Montana Attorney General's Office Records*. Letter from Ron Wall and Monty Cranston to Senator John Melcher, 5 December 1977. RS 111, Box 11, Folder 24, Montana Historical Society Archives, Helena.

Ward, D. A., and G. C. Kassebaum. 1965. *Women's Prison: Sex and Social Structure*. Chicago: Aldine.

Warrior Chiefs in a New Age. 1991. Directed by D. Bear Claw. Produced by D. Hart. 27 mins. Native Voices Production. Videocassette.

Washburn, W. 1971. *Red Man's Land/White Man's Law: A Study of the Past and Present Status of the American Indian*. New York: Scribner.

Wachtel, D. 1980. An Historical Look at BIA Police on the Reservations. *American Indian Journal* 6(3): 13–19.

Weisburd, D., and E. S. Chayet. 1989. Good Time: An Agenda for Research. *Criminal Justice and Behavior* 16(2): 183–195.

Weyler, R. 1982. *Blood of the Land: The Government and Corporate War against the American Indian Movement*. New York: Vintage Books.

White Harvest Jail/Prison Ministry and Transition Center and Program. 1989. *Lynda's Success Story and Testimony: Lynda's Escape from the Serpent's Spells, Snares, and Shambles*. White Harvest Ministry Publication: Billings, Montana.

White, J. 1973. *Montana Attorney General's Office Records*. Letter from Josephine White to Attorney General Robert Woodahl, 16 July 1973. RS 111, Box 11, Folder 22, Montana Historical Society Archives, Helena.

White Shamans, Plastic Medicine Men. 1995. Directed by T. Macy and D. Hart. Produced by D. Hart. 30 mins. Native Voices Productions. Videocassette.

Without Reservations: Notes on Racism in Montana. 1995. Directed by S. Ross, D. Hart, S. Olbeksen, C. Burnside, L. Dreamer, D. Wheelock, P. Mosen, and S. Whittier. Produced by D. Hart. 30 mins. Native Voices Productions. Videocassette.

Women's Correctional Center. 1990. *Corrective Action Plan* (24 May, n.p.). Warm Springs, Montana. Duplicated.

Woodahl, R. L. 1976. *Montana Attorney General's Office Records*. Letter from Attorney General Robert Woodahl to Earl Johnston, 11 May 1976. RS 111, Box 11, Folder 23, Montana Historical Society Archives, Helena.

Wright, E. O. 1973. *The Politics of Punishment*. New York: Harper and Row.

Yazzie, R. 1994. Life Comes From It: Navajo Justice. In *Context: A Quarterly of Humane Sustainable Culture* 38(spring): 29–31.

Zalba, S. R. 1964. *Women Prisoners and Their Families: A Monograph on a Study of the Relationships of a Correctional Institution and Social Agencies Working with Incarcerated Women and Their Children*. Sacramento: State of California Department of Social Welfare and Department of Corrections.

INDEX